Almost Shakespeare

Almost Shakespeare

Reinventing His Works for Cinema and Television

Edited by James R. Keller
and Leslie Stratyner

McFarland & Company, Inc., Publishers
Jefferson, North Carolina, and London

Library of Congress Cataloguing-in-Publication Data

Almost Shakespeare : reinventing his works for cinema
and television / edited by James R. Keller and Leslie Stratyner.
p.   cm.
Includes bibliographical references and index.

ISBN 0-7864-1909-1 (softcover : 50# alkaline paper)

1. Shakespeare, William, 1564–1616 — Film and video
adaptations.   2. English drama — Film and video adaptations.
3. Film adaptations.   I. Keller, James R., 1960–
II. Stratyner, Leslie.
PR3093.A46   2004
791.43'6 — dc22   2004017517

British Library cataloguing data are available

Cover image: ©2004 Clipart.com and Photodisc

Manufactured in the United States of America

*McFarland & Company, Inc., Publishers
Box 611, Jefferson, North Carolina 28640
www.mcfarlandpub.com*

Contents

Introduction

James R. Keller and Leslie Stratyner

Shakespeare seems to be suffering from a multiple personality disorder, and while this diagnosis may not be conclusive, there is some very compelling symptomatic evidence that points toward this condition. Thus far, he has manifested a legion of alternate identities: Shakespeare the Western imperialist, Shakespeare the sage, Shakespeare the racist, Shakespeare the misogynist, Shakespeare the conservative, Shakespeare the progressive liberal, Shakespeare the icon of high culture, Shakespeare the pop idol, Shakespeare the symbol of British culture, Shakespeare the embodiment of his many dramatis personae. He has been equally addled and perplexed by combative analysts over the past four hundred years, who, unable to question him directly, can offer their diagnoses exclusively on the basis of textual, anecdotal, historical, cultural, speculative, and even manufactured evidence. There can be little wonder that the playwright has become progressively confused and perhaps no longer knows himself.

Shakespeare has many faces, and although his shape seems easy enough to recognize, we can never be certain whether it is him we are seeing or someone who looks very much like him (or perhaps we are only seeing ourselves). Many of the recent sightings have been in the cinema, and while the inclusion of the playwright in film and television is nothing new, these apparitions, particularly in teen films, vex those who wonder that he would appear in such degraded settings. However, this concern for Shakespeare's artistic legacy is quite unfounded.

We must remember that Shakespeare's concerns and activities were not always dignified. He was very comfortable with the vulgar and the popular. Working in the theater, he had elected a profession that, in the early modern period, was not (as it is now) considered the harmless pastime of the cultured elite, but was socially marginal and sometimes even dangerously subversive. The playhouses were occasionally sites of civil unrest and the acting companies quasi-criminal. Moreover, Shakespeare was not motivated exclusively by his love of eloquence and the dramatic arts. He was materialistic and was well-rewarded for his endeavors, investing his capital in several properties around Stratford to make his wealth grow.

However, for the present age, Shakespeare's most troublesome practice was his annexation of antecedent literary works, a practice that offends our contemporary veneration of originality. These literary appropriations further confound the effort to trace Shakespeare's legacy and influence. When we see a manifestation of Shakespeare's work in film, are we seeing the Bard, or are we seeing who he saw? A *Thousand Acres* seems to be an adaptation of Shakespeare's *King Lear*, but perhaps the film is also influenced by the second book of Spenser's *Faerie Queene* or Geoffrey of Monmouth's *Historia regum Britanniae* (1136) or the anonymous *True Chronicle History of King Leir* (1594). Is it Shakespeare who is revealed in *My Own Private Idaho*, or is it Raphael Holinshed's *Chronicles*? The obscure film *Royal Deceit* (1994) contains characters and events strikingly similar to those of *Hamlet*, yet one would be mistaken to assume a Shakespearean source, but correct to assume Shakespeare's source for *Hamlet*— François de Belleforest's *Histoire tragiques* (1576). These dilemmas are, of course, merely academic exercises intended to reveal that Shakespeare's own work includes a confusion of creative authority; the search for sources is the same phenomenon with which this very collection is allied.

In spite of his humble beginnings and his socially problematic occupation, Shakespeare's reputation has grown so lofty in the past 400 years that his name is synonymous with high art and elite culture. Thus the embedding of his work in less dignified art forms such as teen films (*10 Things I Hate About You, O, Never Been Kissed, Get Over It, Happy Campers*, etc.) has proven quite troubling to many. Nevertheless, such adaptations are actually congruous with Shakespeare's own professional activities: he borrowed from others in the same way that contemporary screen writers borrow from him; he was not engaged in a specifically elitist enterprise in creating and performing his plays; he was interested in art, money, and position; he was capable of condescending to the lowest segment of his audience; and he was responsive to the popular demand for sequels and recurrent characters.

The playwright's debt to the aesthetic practices of his age is mirrored in contemporary Shakespearean cinema's commitment to a familiar exercise of seventeenth century poets: the creation of extended conceits. Consciously or unconsciously, scriptwriters and filmmakers are engaged in an effort to showcase their cunning and ingenuity by cramming Shakespeare into new and improbable contexts. In the past two decades, King Lear has moved to an Iowa farm; Hamlet has become heir to a corporation; Prince Hal has taken up residence in a homeless shelter; Othello has tried out for the basketball team; Macbeth has taken over a fast food restaurant; Katherina and Rosalind have enrolled in high school; and Hermia and Lysander have spent the summer at camp. In most of these, the joy of viewing the film grows out of an appreciation for the writer's and/or director's inventiveness and wit; the film grabs the audience's attention through its startling improbability and retains its interest by suspending the resolution of the comparison. The audience is intrigued by the effort to match the Shakespearean pieces with the fragments of contemporary culture. The result of these labors is a "discordia concors," a seventeenth century conceit, two incongruous ideas hammered into a poetic harmony.

The same denizens of the film industry are engaged in an additional practice that is distinctively Shakespearean, reinventing highly-regarded materials of the past for contemporary entertainment. Shakespeare's work has become the twenty-first century's mythology, a cultural shorthand for dispositions, predicaments, preoccupations, aesthetics, poetics, and ideologies; while we are not suggesting that the Shakespearean myths have a trans-historical and culturally universal meaning, we are arguing that the Bard and his work are highly suggestive and allusive and that there is an observable overlap in the reader or audience's perceptions of his work. When one alludes to *Hamlet*, the culturally literate are reminded of melancholy, introspection, madness, incest, indecision, and inhibition. *Othello* evokes jealousy and insecurity; *Macbeth*, fear and ambition; *King Lear*, foolishness, senility, and regret. As with classical mythology, these stories have been legitimized by time and are frequently received by contemporary audiences as wisdom worthy of consideration and even emulation. Shakespeare's person has been subject to the same process, his life ratified, sanitized, embellished, and canonized.

This collection does not offer any grand equation that will render accessible the rationale for the current fascination with casting Shakespeare in film and television. However, some limited descriptive analyses are offered. The essays within this volume expose a variety of mechanisms of Shakespearean myth-making within contemporary film, television, and culture. The essays in the collection address what we will term "Shake/spawn" or "Shake/spinoffs," those works that are derivative of Shakespeare, but are not actually Shakespearean productions. The subject matter concentrates on films and television productions that merely appropriate or adapt Shakespeare. Many contributors to this volume reveal an ambivalence toward the Bard: admiration mixed with a mistrust of his prodigious

aesthetic leverage. Despite his own identity problems, his slippery significations, Shakespeare is compelled to lend his cultural capital to the negotiation of American and British social issues such as school violence,
racism, imperialism, and international politics, to name only a few. Many
of the essays examine the negotiation between the textual and contextual
elements of the cinematic appropriations and the politics of this volatile
union of high and low cultures. The films examined within the collection
range from large-budget, studio releases to independent films, from very
recent releases and classic cinema to contemporary television program-
ming.

Two of the chapters within this volume trace the influence of Shakespeare's history plays. In "The Politics of Culture: The Play's the Thing,"
Patrick Finn addresses the impact of Shakespeare's history plays on the
"Posse Comitatus" episode of *The West Wing*. Citing the "muscular liberalism" of Michael Ignatieff, Finn argues that *The West Wing* promotes an
aggressive foreign policy that does not shy from military intervention in
championing human rights abroad. On an evening when the characters of
the drama are scheduled to attend a musical rendition of Shakespeare's
Henriads, entitled *The Wars of the Roses*, President Bartlet is faced with a
foreign policy dilemma that is negotiated by events on stage. On a broader
level, Finn seeks to examine the mutually impactful relationship between
politics and culture. A second chapter addressing Shakespeare's Henry
plays is Andrew Barnaby's "Imitation as Originality in Gus Van Sant's *My
Own Private Idaho*," which traces the transformation of the Prince
Hal/Henry V persona through several cinematic representations including Kenneth Branagh's *Henry V*, Orson Welles' *Falstaff (Chimes at Midnight)*, and Gus Van Sant's *My Own Private Idaho*. Barnaby focuses
particularly on the repetition of the phrase "chimes at midnight," regis-
tering its subtle changes in placement and signification throughout these
three cinematic representations of the familiar story. In his most interesting turn, Barnaby relates the predicament of the homeless male prostitutes in *My Own Private Idaho* to the deteriorating socioeconomic context
of the post–Reaganite '80s.

The play that receives the most attention within the collection is *Othello*. In "Shakespeare Transposed: The British Stage on the Post-Colonial
Screen," Parmita Kapadia is concerned with the way that Merchant-Ivory's
Shakespeare Wallah appropriates and questions both the Shakespearean
canon and the Bard himself, as a consideration of British cultural influence
at that point in time when the Raj begins to intersect with a newly independent India. Performances by a group of Shakespearean actors in India

are repeatedly interrupted by the commotion of their audience, and the dialogue from plays such as *Antony and Cleopatra* and *Othello* comments on British cultural imperialism and the political climate of post-colonial India. In "*Suture*, Shakespeare, and Race: Or, What Is Our Cultural Debt to the Bard?" Ayanna Thompson employs *Othello* as an analogue for the allegory of racial invisibility in the independent film *Suture*. The directors' use of color-blind casting in *Suture* attempts to eradicate racial difference by transforming cultural distinction into a simplistic matter of skin color and then by simultaneously emphasizing and eliding the color difference, thus rendering invisible and invalid the distinct cultural inheritance of African Americans. In "Cinema in the Round: Self-Reflexivity in Tim Blake Nelson's *O*," Eric C. Brown observes the proliferation of visual and auditory references to the letter "O" in the contemporary high school film based on *Othello*. The author argues that the film's "near obsession" with open vowels and circularity reveals an ambivalent relationship with Shakespeare, both reinforcing and subverting the centrality of the parent text. "Sex, Lies, Videotape — and Othello" is R.S. White's examination of the relationship between *Othello* and modern jealousy films, films that are offshoots of Shakespeare's model either deliberately or unconsciously. After discussing several examples from classical cinema, such as *Jubal*, *A Double Life*, *Les enfants du paradis* and *All Night Long*, White turns to Soderbergh's *sex, lies, and videotape* as "an accurate and contemporary derivative of Shakespeare's play."

Hamlet is the subject of two chapters within the volume. Aaron Kelly and David Salter, in "The Time Is Out of Joint," assess the ways in which allusions to *Hamlet* create a mood of melancholy in the cult film *Withnail and I*. The authors argue that the utilization of *Hamlet* aids not only in stripping our perceptions of the 1960s as radical but also in repositioning that decade as the precursor for the conservative 1980s. It is through *Hamlet* that the tragedy of the film is revealed: "the specter of imperial decline and the end of an organic England." In "Horatio: The First CSI," Jody Malcolm explores the relationship between the popular television series *CSI: Miami* and Shakespeare's *Hamlet*, identifying a variety of links that embellish upon the events and characters of the series and even the profession of crime scene investigation.

As one might expect, there is ample space devoted to the union of Shakespeare's comedies and the contemporary teen cinema. Ariane M. Balizet's "Teen Scenes: Recognizing Shakespeare in Teen Film" views the use of Shakespeare in adolescent cinema (including *Romeo + Juliet*, *10 Things I Hate About You*, *Get Over It*, and *O*) via the integration of genre and popular culture. Balizet considers how these films form a discussion of adolescent life, demonstrating that the films "re-cognize" Shakespeare, using him to support their contemporary social message. Similarly, in "An Aweful Rule: Safe Schools, Hard Canons, and Shakespeare's Loose Heirs," Melissa Jones relates the teen film *10 Things I Hate About You* to the social phenomenon that she terms a "conservative retrenchment." Debates on the literary canon and recent court decisions are related to the silencing of Kat/Kate in the film's contemporary adaptation of Shakespeare's comedy *The Taming of the Shrew*. Jones suggests that the appropriation of Shakespeare's work in the organization of the film parallels that restoration of patriarchal authority within the action of the comedy. Kat's "taming" constitutes a silencing of leftist discourses.

Dan DeWeese examines the slippery significations of Prospero in both Shakespeare's *Tempest* and Peter Greenaway's *Prospero's Books*. In "Prospero's Pharmacy: Peter Greenaway and the Critics Play Shakespeare's Mimetic Game," DeWeese interrogates the common assumption that Prospero's abjuring of magic parallels Shakespeare's own farewell to the stage, and he argues that both playwright and filmmaker are teasing their audiences with multiple referents for a previously overdetermined sign. Shakespeare and Greenaway adopt Prospero's magic — appearing and disappearing, acknowledging and denying, making and unmaking meaning — to the frustration of audience and critics.

In "Shakespeare Film and Television Derivatives: A Bibliography," the final chapter of the collection, José Ramón Díaz Fernández offers an extensive list of Shakespearean appropriations in film and television as well as citations of books, articles, chapters, and notes addressing each derivative production. The list is organized into several categories including bibliographies and filmographies, general studies of Shakespeare in film, works addressing individual plays, and miscellaneous studies. The author asserts that the film list is not exhaustive. Citations have been limited by several factors, including language (English references only) and publication space.

Notes about the contributors and an index complete the book.

1

The Politics of Culture: The Play's the Thing

Patrick Finn

Once more unto the breach, dear friends, once more,
Or close the wall upon our English dead!
In peace there's nothing so becomes a man
As modest stillness and humility
But when the blast of war blows in our ears,
Then imitate the action of the tiger:
Stiffen the sinews, conjure up the blood,
Disguise fair nature with hard-favoured rage.

[*Henry V*, III.i.1–8]

Politics today happens outside of mainstream institutional structures; it has taken to the airwaves, the Internet, and a whole host of other informational venues. Scholars have noted the political implications of these cultural phenomena for decades. In this paper I am interested in going further, to argue for a political core at the center of culture.

Noam Chomsky's early work on corporate media posited an organized public deception based on a form of news media controlled by the elite, a position complemented by Bordieu's assertion of the inescapably oppressive nature of televisual expression.[1] Yet, following Foucault, contemporary politics must take account of the notion that power is both restrictive and productive; and this includes the power of the media, of film, and of television.[2] Our present state of information technology and media shows that while politics and culture may have intrinsic ties to existing power structures, there are currently functioning strategies and tactics by which these forms of expression can call their own means of production into question in useful and even exciting ways.

I will raise three questions that will allow us to reflect on these issues as they relate to the current use of Shakespeare's history plays, particularly the two tetralogies, on the American political drama *The West Wing*. Here Shakespeare is used not only as a form of allusion that lends itself to the aesthetics of the show's construction and presentation, but also in a way that connects the show to a long tradition of similar uses of these eight plays. The questions that frame this discussion are:

1. Can televisual media be a double-edged sword, which allows for productive expression from within?
2. Does the recent explosion of television dramas using contemporary politics as their primary subject matter, signal a need for a new consideration of dramatized politics or politics as a dramatic form?
3. Can cultural politics still be thought of as something secondary to institutional politics? What would be the use or effect of viewing political culture and cultural politics in a far more participatory light? Conversely, could this move merely offer critical thinkers a means of exploiting ineffectual armchair politics?

With these three points in mind, it is possible to examine the overt melding of politics and culture, one that not only functions as a deliberately politicized form of culture, but does so by bringing to bear two virulent forms of rhetorical argument. These forms attempt to bookend Western culture in a move to establish a foundational dialogue that is as much a part of a theme of cultural expression as it is a justification of certain modes of Western modernity. In each case, the rhetorical tropes at play extend beyond what can usefully be analysed as cultural or literary allusion and instead fall within the realm of a markedly rhetorical — and progressive — political form of culture.

The two rhetorical lines involve the historical appropriation of British military and political history as recast by Shakespeare and the more recent political art form of the so-called ripped-from-the-headlines television drama format. Both of these elements meet in the popular television show *The West Wing*. In particular, this paper focuses on the episode entitled "Posse Comitatus" (season 3, episode 22, aired March 22, 2002) and its use of Shakespeare's history tetralogies, whose tales chart the rise and fall of the house of Lancaster and include the plays that tell the story of the Wars of the Roses. Shakespeare's two tetralogies move chronologically from the monarchy of *Richard II*, to *Henry IV* of the house of Lancaster, through *Henry V* and *Henry VI*, and culminate with *Richard III*.

These plays, and in particular those of the first chronological period (from *Richard II* to *Henry IV*) were, at the time of their conception, used for political means, as devices of public entertainment that also served to ingratiate the author with the power on the throne (Elizabeth I being descended from the Lancastrian Henries). Indeed, the only time there was even a hint of political trouble for Shakespeare at court was over his seemingly too-sympathetic rendering of *Richard II*. Since the sixteenth century, these same plays have been used repeatedly to undergird other political regimes, most famously in the case of *Henry V*, which was filmed by Sir Laurence Olivier in order to support Allied forces in World War II.[3] During this same period, copies of *Henry V* were distributed to active soldiers as part of the American Service Editions series. These books were provided free of charge by major publishers in the second world war and were designed to fit in a cargo pocket for ease of transportation. This same program was revived for the war in Iraq with a substantially altered list of titles. As Malcolm Jones reported in *Newsweek* on June 3, 2002,

> Between 1943 and 1947, more than 123 million books, called Armed Services Editions, were distributed to American troops. The 1,300 titles in the series included detective stories and poetry anthologies. It was the largest book giveaway in history. Now Andrew Carroll, with help from the Library of Congress and the Veterans of Foreign Wars, has got the program running again. He's currently crossing the country, stopping at military bases to drop off 10,000 copies of "War Letters," his anthology of Americans' correspondence during wartime from the Civil War to Bosnia. The VFW is also shipping out 2.5 million copies of the book to its membership.

As the process evolved, many protested the absence of novels in the new list, which were popular with soldiers, and the exclusion of many books by American authors that had featured prominently in the first series. According to a U.S. Department of Defense news release, the current list of approved books is:

1. *Medal of Honor: Profiles of America's Military Heroes from the Civil War to the Present*. Allen Mikaelian, with commentary by Mike Wallace. New York: Hyperion, 2002.
2. *Henry V*. William Shakespeare. New York: Dover, 2002.
3. *The Art of War*. Sun Tzu. New York: Dover, 2002.
4. *War Letters: Extraordinary Correspondence from American Wars*. Andrew Carroll, ed. Washington Square Press/Simon & Schuster, 2002.

These books were distributed by the Pentagon in hopes that they would serve the same purpose they had during early conflict, namely as "weapons in the war of ideas" (U.S. Department of Defense 2002). In any of these manifestations, the political culture that is at play is a form of muscular ideology that finds its feet in a dance between the cultural and the political. While the use of culture for explicitly political ends is nothing new, the current development of political dramas on television is bringing new considerations to the fore.

In order to pursue the traces of this ideological influence in Shakespeare's history plays and in their current use on NBC's *West Wing*, it is necessary to give a quick history of each. Shakespeare's history plays share a fundamental theme related to the burden of political responsibility, which is in one part individual, but in another more important way is about the social responsibility that comes with leadership. The fall of Richard II came about because of Richard's failure to live up to the obligations of leadership. Richard's attention to cultural life, the life of books, music, celebration, and learning, left him distracted from the duties of state. As a result, Henry Bolingbroke was able to step in and assume power, becoming Henry IV.

Once on the throne, Henry was a victim of fate, even though this fate is seemingly set in motion by his own pretension to the throne. This fate, which in Shakespeare is so often tied to political economy, saw the ruler become responsible for a climate of violence over which he had no direct control. Supporters, who killed the imprisoned Richard in the belief that it would please the new ruler, left Henry IV saddled with the guilt from a crime that was in many ways an extreme outcome of his own machinations of responsibility. Whether or not Richard II was unfit to rule, he was still a king — God's anointed — and as such, his life was marked with a special charm.

What both history and its cultural representation demonstrate is that this guilt is a difficult legacy to overcome. In the most famous speech of *2 Henry IV*, the ailing Bolingbroke speaks to his son Hal (the rowdy, young, pub-crawling prince) about the weight of the crown. In this conciliatory scene, Hal, soon to be Henry V, curses the burden of the crown, which has caused his family so much suffering. This serves as a developmental moment during which the senior leader is able to inform his successor of the necessities of good governance. The central tenet of this is balance: the elder Bolingbroke maintains that people want the stability that comes from the rule of a rightful king. This notion of stability is caught up with the responsibility of leadership and the observance of established power structures, and it surfaces in the interaction between the two Henries:

> God knows, my son,
> By what bypaths, and indirect crook'd ways
> I met this crown, and I my self know well

How troublesome it sat upon my head.
To thee it shall descend with better quiet,
Better opinion, better confirmation,
For all the soil of the achievement goes
With me into the earth. It seemed in me
But as an honour snatched with boisterous hand,
And I had many living to upbraid
My gain of it by their assistances,
Which daily grew to quarrel and to bloodshed,
Wounding supposèd peace. All these bold fears
Thou seest with peril I have answered,
For all my reign hath been but as a scene
Acting that argument. And now my death
Changes the mood, for what in me was purchased
Falls upon thee in a more fairer sort;
So thou the garland wear'st successively.
[*2 Henry IV,* IV.v.183–201]

The first lines remind the audience of the weight of the crown. Within the plays, we are led to believe that part of the reason for the senior Henry's illness is his worry over unrest in the kingdom and the unruly lifestyle of his son. In this scene, once Hal has convinced his father that he is worthy to wear the crown—chiefly by giving voice to his anger that the crown was too heavy on his father's head— Henry IV turns to give his son advice. He is happy because he believes that his death will wash the crown clean of his legacy of guilt. With this concern put aside, the father next turns to a discussion of government. He warns his son of the vacuum of power that he will leave and the danger of this instability (a danger that Shakespeare's audience would have felt through their own anxieties over the transition of power from their aging and heirless queen to her yet unnamed successor) and provides a remedy that will allow the new, untested king to rally his people around the crown. The greatest of the pragmatic directions that the father imparts to the son is the need to attack foreign enemies— in this case the French — in order to distract the British populace from their internal woes and to act as a demonstration of the regent's ability to rule.

In *Henry V,* we find the young king a ready pupil to his father's lessons. Leading the troops against a temporarily ignoble French populace, the new king spends time walking among his troops to learn about the common man, a practice that allows him to deliver the compelling speeches that have since become motivational tools for Western leaders who seek to use this cultural product for political ends. It would be easy here to make assumptions about the currency of media manipulation, but we must revisit the idea that the origins of Western literature lie in the culture of politics and the politics of culture, nowhere more evident than in Shakespeare's history plays. So effective were Shakespeare's creative nonfictions that history texts continue to fight the notions espoused in his plays, the most memorable example being that of Richard III's crooked back and matching character. While Richard may have stooped to rule, we have no proof (in fact all we have are counterfactuals) that Shakespeare's character was physically accurate. Yet, the power of this language was, and is, so complete that Shakespeare's cultural product continues to serve as functional equipment for political expression.

In our current context, Aaron Sorkin's political drama, *The West Wing*, makes use of the same elements of political culture and cultural politics. *The West Wing*, having completed its fourth season, is a show that examines the comings and goings of people and policy within the west wing of the White House. In terms of the current argument, it is relatively easy to see how this drama relates to the culture of politics. The interpretation is literal, but is by no means restricted to a simple inscription in linguistic terms. There are a multitude of political streams beginning in this show, not the least of which is a direct resurrection of classic liberalism, which is then transformed into a new-left-inflected muscular liberalism. In an earlier paper entitled "*The West Wing*'s Textual President: American Constitutional Stability and the New Public Intellectual in the Age of Information," I described this form of internationally aggressive center-leftism as something exemplified in the policies of the political theorist Michael Ignatieff. Since that paper was published, Professor Ignatieff has done us the favor of living up to those earlier assertions.[4] In his speaking and writing, Ignatieff upholds the standard tenets of European liberalism, that is the progressive reform of society with an emphasis on the rights and freedoms of the individual, but he adds to this the notion that liberal values in general and human rights in particular should be pursued across national borders. As such, he advocates the development of a large standing army. Further, Ignatieff's form of liberalism meshes well with the views held on *The West Wing*, since both emphasize the importance of a classical education.[5]

Ignatieff blends old-style European liberal political philosophy with direct engagement (as a war reporter), and he is the child of the individual who helped to formulate *The Universal Declaration of Human Rights*. He has come to be loved both by the soft center of Western globalism (through his support for negotiative policy) and by the neo-Reaganites (as a supporter of the war in Iraq). As head of the Carr Center for Human Rights at Harvard's John F. Kennedy School of Government, he wields a big cultural stick. Lest we doubt his credentials regarding the intersection of politics and culture, readers should be reminded that Ignatieff is also the author of fictional histories that focus exclusively on the politics of the Western world.[6] So why is Ignatieff useful for this discussion? There are two reasons, each of which reflects the interplay between culture and politics and both of which link him to Shakespeare and *The West Wing*'s Aaron Sorkin. First, Ignatieff understands the potency of language in politics. He uses his skills as writer and theorist to effect political change. Second, he is interested in the culture of political life. His theories of exchange, negotiation, and interaction form the foundation of his creative expression. Ignatieff, like Shakespeare and Sorkin, has, for better or worse, used the intersection of culture and politics to cause visceral change.

At the outset, this paper mentioned three areas of general interest that would help to focus its argument. Now that these have established the ground for a response, it will be useful to recall them:

1. Can media be seen as a double-edged sword, which allows for productive expression from within?
2. Does the recent explosion of television dramas that use politics as their primary subject matter show that we need a new consideration of rhetoric?
3. Can cultural politics still be thought of as something secondary to institutional politics?

Given the effects of Shakespeare's Henry plays, there is little doubt that media can be overtly, even radically, effective. The answer to the third question, at least in terms of *The West Wing*, seems to be that cultural representations of politics must be considered relevant to the day-to-day functioning of politics. Surely cultural politics is equal if not superior to institutional politics in its representation of its message. As for the second query, the consideration of current representations of politics and culture relates to the central concern of this essay. It is a contemplation that necessitates a discussion of the form of political economy that each of these views shares in terms of *The West Wing*.

On May 22, 2002, *The West Wing* ended its third season with an episode entitled "Posse Comitatus." The show capped a season that began with an installment called "Isaac and Ishmael," which the creators described as "a very special episode" produced in response to the September 11 attacks on the World Trade Center. That episode, the first cultural response to the events of that day, served as an introduction to my current discussion. Within several days of September 11, I was asked to do dozens of interviews. Wrenched from a banal existence within the book-lined walls of an academic office, I flew around answering questions, all of which had to do with the relevance of creations such as that just aired by Sorkin.

By the end of that same year, industry analysts as well as the general public were worrying about the fate of *The West Wing*, a show that had responded to American apathy surrounding the country's relationship to its foundational political processes. The show tried to find a way to reinvent political involvement while offering itself as a forum for an entirely different kind of debate.[7] The change in the American political climate after September 11 fundamentally altered what *The West Wing*'s writers could reasonably rip from the headlines in order to address such complicated issues as foreign policy and the clash of cultures. As the show attempted to find new ways to address current political issues, many viewers felt that it had lost its way. Critics remain dissatisfied. Gone were the Dickensian recastings of domestic workaday politics, and in were the troubled considerations of an America under international threat. Gone was the worship of such members of the cultural and social elite as Bill Gates, and in was a new expression of love and appreciation for the working class first-responders: the firemen, police and front-line health-care workers upon whom society relies.

As the age-old debate between proactive and reactive government played itself out in the real west wing, Aaron Sorkin offered a response that was and is a deepening of his original liberal position. While many looked to Samuel Huntington in order to justify fears about a series of future threats that would not have negotiable solutions because of fundamental cultural differences, *The West Wing* offered a soothing balm.[8] *The West Wing* looked to Shakespeare and to the muscular liberalism of Michael Ignatieff in order to argue for a deeper form of responsibility, one based on a commitment to a series of political negotiations, the abandonment of which many felt was responsible for the form of isolationist foreign policy put forward by the second Bush White House.[9] While the Bush government found new ways to be left alone — and to extricate itself from external conflicts— the muscular liberals continued to call for intervention and the exportation of human rights.

Shakespeare's *Henriad*, Ignatieff, and Sorkin all argue for war in the name of peace. They argue for the imposition of calm through the establishment of a just world order. In the latter two cases, this position necessitates a return to the authority of the United Nations' *Universal Declaration of Human Rights*. This document of negotiation, of acquiescence, of politics, has become a marker of transgression. In particular, Ignatieff and Sorkin argue that while this document is marked by as many betrayals as commitments, its problems are no excuse to abandon its principles, not as long as people continue to call for good leadership.

In "Posse Comitatus," President Jed Bartlet, played by Martin Sheen, learns that an Arab leader, from the fictional state of Qumar, has plotted a terrorist attack on San Francisco's Golden Gate Bridge. Moreover, he learns that this same individual is a double agent who is responsible for the deaths of many innocent people, particularly Americans. It becomes apparent that the death of this individual could save other lives. However, restrained by his conviction that murder is wrong, the president is reluctant to accept this solution. Bartlet's dilemma is framed, defined, and explored by the litigational certitude of the posse comitatus component of a nineteenth century U.S. appropriations bill that carried the eponymous amendment preventing the use of the military for civilian policing. The argument is complemented by an executive order that the exportation of these same concerns— particularly vis-à-vis the execution of foreign leaders— should be illegal under American law.

After a season of struggling with international issues, which strayed from the show's original focus on the internal machinations of American political life, *The West Wing* finished its third year by consolidating an image that it had used (and still does) in order to ground its political arguments. Central to *The West Wing*'s arguments are the main characters of the show. These are Chief of Staff Leo McGarry (John Spencer), White House Press Secretary C.J. Cregg (Allison Janney), Communications Director Toby Zeigler (Richard Schiff), Deputy Chief of Staff Josh Lyman (Bradley Whitford), and Assistant Communications Director Sam Seaborn (Rob Lowe), the clean-cut Princeton man with a name and persona straight out of a Fitzgerald novel. The staff of *The West Wing* surround President Josiah (Jed) Bartlet, a public intellectual who embodies the conflicts that are central to current American politics, particularly current American politics from a Rawlsian liberal democratic view.[10] As a public intellectual, Bartlet is outside of the standard constructs of power, maintaining a split position on key issues such as abortion and the death penalty. (He is against both in principle, but upholds their application and supports debate and choice.) As such, he is more an embodiment of the complexity of issues than an ideologically driven proponent of one political approach. He is an expert on world history who speaks a number of languages, holds a doctorate in economics, and is, according to episode two, a Nobel laureate ("Post Hoc, Ergo Propter Hoc," season 1, episode 2). We often see Bartlett playing at classical scholarship by quizzing his family and friends about the meaning of various political and philosophical issues. There is a special legitimacy afforded his assumption of the presidency that stems from his noble American ancestry. The audience is informed that Bartlet's great-great-great-grandfather was an original signatory of the Declaration of

The original cast of NBC's *The West Wing*: (from left to right) Dulé Hill as Charlie Young, Rob Lowe as Sam Seaborn, Allison Janney as C.J. Cregg, Martin Sheen as President Josiah Bartlet, Richard Schiff as Toby Ziegler, Stockard Channing as Abigail Bartlet, John Spencer as Leo McGarry, Janel Moloney as Donna Moss, and Bradley Whitford as Josh Lyman.

Independence ("What Kind of Day It Has Been," season 1, episode 22). His link with America's democratic ruling elite runs throughout his family history. The show's back-story informs the audience that the Bartlet family founded New Hampshire, now the site of the country's earliest— and trend-setting— presidential primary.

A central element of the "Posse Comitatus" plot is a trip to see *The Wars of the Roses*, a musical retelling of Shakespeare's Richard and Henry plays. Most of the president's staff will attend. The episode begins with a closeup of a television headline that reads "I [heart] New York: Bartlet and the Bard." Throughout the program, the principal characters face various threats, each of which is addressed through classic liberal means. These means have to do with a vibrant meritocracy based on higher education and cultural awareness. The two primary plot lines concern one threat each, the first being the planned assassination of the Qumari defense minister and the second being the stylized murder of a secret service agent. Qumar, a fictional Arab country created for the show in order to address current political issues while avoiding the overt vilification of a real nation, has as a defense minister a man who is guilty of killing numerous American and Qumari civilians. During the course of the story, the administration decides that the American government, with the participation of British forces, should have this individual killed while he is in international air space. The president, who is morally troubled by the suggestion, elects to make the decision at the last moment. That moment will occur while he and the staff are watching *The Wars of the Roses*.

Just before the opening of this play-within-a-play, we witness the culmination of a subplot that has seen Press Secretary C.J. Cregg under threat from an unidentified terrorist. The secret service agent assigned to protect her has, during the course of several episodes, come to be a romantic interest for C.J.'s character. Before entering the theater, the two are freed to openly fraternize when the terrorist in question is apprehended. In the final scenes of the show, both plot lines are resolved using musical montages. Secret Service Agent Donovan, on his way home to change for a date with C.J., is gunned down while breaking up a robbery at a Korean grocery. As Donovan falls, the audience hears an updated version of Leonard Cohen's "Hallelujah." The slow motion scenes are punctuated by shots of two vases falling from the grocery counter. One vase contains white roses, the other red— the symbols of the houses of York and Lancaster respectively.

During a second montage, President Bartlet must give the go-ahead to kill the Qumari defense minister. The audience listens to Stephen Oliver's "Patriotic Chorus," a song originally composed to accompany another long historical drama, this time involving Shakespeare's *Romeo and*

Juliet. This song, which features the chorus, "and victorious in war shall be made glorious in peace," responds to onstage scenes from *1 Henry VI* and *3 Henry VI*, highlighting the "weight of the crown" and the "burden of leadership" themes. Earlier in the show, Bartlet describes the song as a favorite of his.

These final montages tap into a form of historical expression that connects the political messages of Shakespeare to those more recently articulated by thinkers like Michael Ignatieff. In these cases, rulers face the terrible burden of maintaining or establishing peace through violent means. The connections are not direct: rather, they seek to borrow the cultural force of Shakespeare's plays without incurring the limitations of direct allusion. Agent Donovan does not lose his life nobly as do the soldiers on the field at Agincourt; he is gunned down in a botched robbery on his way home from the battle. The Shakespearean references are only used overtly when they are offered as a demonstration of President Bartlet's education. While the allusion is more cultural than aesthetic, it reveals an awareness of the power that literary allusion can bring. In an early interview on the PBS show *The News Hour with Jim Lehrer*, interviewer Terrence Smith asked Sorkin what gave him the idea to create *The West Wing*. Sorkin replied, "There's a great tradition in storytelling that's thousands of years old, telling stories about kings and their palaces, and that's really what I wanted to do." Here, Sorkin shows his awareness of the cultural capital that can be brought to bear by connecting his subject with the great rulers of history. That he is also able to capitalize on the name of Shakespeare only serves to heighten the effect.

As the curtain rises on *The Wars of the Roses*, the actor playing The Duke of Bedford, Regent of France, joins his counterpart the Duke of Gloucester, Lord Protector, in remembering the recently deceased King Henry V. They utter the opening lines of *1 Henry VI*:

> BEDFORD: Hung be the heavens with black, yield day to night; Comets importing change of times and states, Brandish your crystal tresses in the sky, And with them scourge the bad revolting stars, That have consented unto Henry's death: King Henry the Fifth, too famous to live long, England ne're lost a King of so much worth.

> GLOUCESTER: England ne're had a King until his time: Virtue he had, deserving to command, His brandished sword did blind men with his beams, His arms spread wider then a dragon's wings: His sparkling eyes, replete with wrathful fire, More dazzled and drove back his enemies, Then mid-day sun, fierce bent against their faces. What should I say? His deeds exceed all speech: He ne're lift up his hand, but conquered.

> [*1 Henry VI*, I.i.1–24]

Henry's death was not dramatic. He died, as his father had, from illness. Sorkin may have selected the above passages for their cultural resonance since they emphasize the myth of Henry V as a motivator for soldiers going to war and foreshadow the troubles to come during the reign of Henry VI, a time that would see England torn apart by the Wars of the Roses as competing factions sought to replace the ineffectual king. Henry V, whose reputation as a commander and soldier stretched across the known world, was able to provide stability by following the advice of his father. In contrast, Henry VI, who sought to reconcile differences through negotiation, lost England's position in France and divided the English people against themselves. Thus Shakespeare would seem to agree with Ignatieff's muscular liberalism: good government requires international intervention and cooperation between rival factions at home. Moreover, because the message is included within a stylized Shakespearean musical, Sorkin continues to emphasize that the cultural elite make the best possible rulers. Lest we miss this point, Sorkin has Bartlet meet his Republican rival at the theater. In a brief exchange, the audience is reminded that the central contrast between Bartlet and Ritchie (Robert Ritchie, the fictional governor of Florida who is the Republican nominee seeking to unseat Bartlet) is mental acuity. In earlier episodes, Bartlet has openly called Ritchie stupid, an accusation that is continued in "Posse Comitatus," while Bartlet's campaign workers openly wondered about selling a candidate who might be resented as "the smartest kid in the class."

The melding of the Shakespearean *Wars of the Roses* and Rawlsian (and later Ignatieffian) liberalism creates an overt political message designed to support a position that comments directly on contemporary politics. Sorkin is able to leverage the cultural capital that clings to Shakespeare at the same time that he introduces a system of foundational history connected to British civil strife. In a conclusion, we should pose a question: Can we really consider this use of early modern political expressions a form of literary allusion? The term lacks the ability to capture the political and historical resonance that accompanies Shakespeare's plays. The use of the Shakespeare's Henriad as a tool of political expression would seem to necessitate a reexamination of the culture of politics and the politics of culture. What remains is the question of whose conscience will be captured by the play that is presented.

Works Cited

Bourdieu, Pierre. *On Television.* Translated by Priscilla Parkhurst Ferguson. New York: New Press, 1999.

Finn, Patrick. "*The West Wing*'s Textual President: American Constitutional Stability and the New Public Intellectual in the Age of Information." *The American President on Film.* Syracuse: Syracuse University Press, 2003.

Foucault, Michel. Power/Knowledge: Selected Interviews and Other Writing, 1972–1977. Ed. and trans. Colin Gordon. New York: Pantheon, 1980.

Herman, Edward S. and Noam Chomsky. *Manufacturing Consent: the Political Economy of the Mass Media.* New York: Pantheon Books, 1988.

Huntington, Samuel P. *The Clash of Civilizations and the Remaking of World Order.* New York: Simon and Schuster, 1996, 1997.

Ignatieff, Michael. "American Empire: The Burden" (cover story), *The New York Times Magazine,* 5 January 2003.

_____. *Empire Lite: Nation-Building in Bosnia, Kosovo and Afghanistan.* New York: Penguin, 2003.

_____. *Human Rights as Politics and Idolatry.* Princeton, NJ: Princeton University Press, 2001.

_____. *Isiah Berlin: A Life.* New York: Penguin, 2000.

Jones, Malcolm. "Uniform Editions." *Newsweek*, Vol. 139, Issue 122, 1c.

Macintyre, Ben. "The great novelists not fit for duty in this war of words." *The Times of London.* <http://www.timesonline.co.uk/article/0,,1068-525322,00.html>. Accessed, April 15.

"News Release, No. 627-02" December 10, 2002. *Defense Link: United States Department of Defense.* <http://www.defenselink.mil/news/Dec2002/b12102002_bt627-02.html.> Accessed April 15, 2003.

Olivier, Laurence. *The Chronicle History of King Henry the Fift with his Battell at Agincourt in France.* Laurence Olivier, director. Written by Dallas Bower, Allan Dent, Laurence Olivier and William Shakespeare. United Kingdom: 1944.

Rawls, John. *Justice as Fairness.* New York: Irvington Publishers, 1991.

Shakespeare, William. *The Complete Works of Shakespeare.* Edited by David Bevington. 4th ed. New York: Longman, 1997.

Sorkin, Aaron. *Interview: The News Hour with Jim Lehrer.* Interviewed by Terrence Smith. Sept. 27, 2000. A transcript of the interview can be found online at <http://www.pbs.org/newshour/media/west_wing/sorkin.html>.

_____.*The West Wing.* NBC Television. Distributed by Warner Brothers Inc. <http://www.nbc.com/The_West_Wing/index.html>. Accessed April 15, 2003.

United Nations. *The Universal Declaration of Human Rights.* United Nations. <http://www.un.org/Overview/rights.html>. Accessed April 15, 2003.

Notes

1. See Herman and Chomsky, and Pierre Bourdieu. Both articles present a vision of televised media as a fully coopted form of expression that allows for little or no progressive political expression.

2. See Foucault, p. 119.

3. Olivier's famous version of the film borrows from the other Shakespeare history plays, while drawing most attention to an elaborately portrayed British victory at the Battle of Agincourt.

4. See for example his "American Empire: The Burden."

5. Ignatieff's particular views on classical liberalism show up in the writings of one of his mentors, Isiah Berlin, whose authorized biography Ignatieff published in 2000.

6. The multidimensional facet of Ignatief's position is summed up by an unnamed reporter from the *Edmonton Journal* on the cover of his forthcoming book, *Empire Lite*: "[Ignatieff] combines … the immediacy of journalism, the perspective of history and the implication of philosophy at work in the real world."

7. See my "*The West Wing*'s Textual President: American Constitutional Stability and the New Public Intellectual in the Age of Information."

8. Professor Huntington's book has become a bestseller since the attacks on the World Trade Center. The book's basic premise is that the cultural differences between the world's major religions are the most significant element in the current state of global political conflict.

9. Ignatieff has developed his liberal political theory over a number of years and in a series of books. For his most recent writings on the subject of liberal politics and the need for a large standing army to enforce and export its ideas, see *Human Rights as Politics and Idolatry*, in particular pages 18–19, 42–43, and 37–38.

10. Rawls' famous book outlines three principle of justice: 1) Social cooperation and organization should be determined by publicly recognized rules and procedures that are approved and maintained by those they directly concern; 2) All societal cooperation should be based on fairness, so that each citizen should accept reasonable restrictions at the same times that others accept them in the name of social order. This in turn guarantees that all who participate have a right to fair treatment; and 3) Each participant engages in society in a manner which allows them to pursue their own rational advantage. These principles form the background of twentieth century liberal political philosophy and are continually referred to on *The West Wing*, as recently as the episode entitled "The California 47th" (season 4, episode 28, aired April, 18, 2003) where newly appointed deputy communications officer Will Bailey (Joshua Malina) quotes Rawls while trying to train speech-writing interns.

2

Imitation as Originality in Gus Van Sant's *My Own Private Idaho*

Andrew Barnaby

> Take care that what you have gathered does not long remain in its original form inside of you: the bees would not be glorious if they did not convert what they found into something different and something better.
>
> — Petrarch

The opening scene of Gus Van Sant's *My Own Private Idaho* (1993) shows Mike Waters—a homeless, narcoleptic drifter-prostitute—abandoned on a deserted stretch of highway somewhere between Portland and "Idaho" (at once a state and a state of mind). The sense of déjà vu that Mike claims to be experiencing will, over the course of the film, call our attention to his inability to escape from the dreary, dispiriting repetitiveness of his days and nights: struggling to feed himself, to find a place to sleep, to achieve the normalcy he longs for. The film's opening words are spoken by Mike to himself, or to no one in particular, as he stands in the middle of nowhere on that seemingly endless road:

> I always know where I am by the way the road looks. Like I just know that I've been here before. I just know that I've been stuck here, like this one fucking time before, you know that? Yeah. There's not another road anywhere that looks like this road, I mean exactly like this road. It's one kind of place, one of a kind, like someone's face, like a fucked-up face. [Yelling at a rabbit that bolts from the brush.] Where do you think you're running, man? We're stuck here together, you shit![1]

At the figurative level, this announcement of repetition might also be said to be a marker of the film's narrative memory; that is, Mike's déjà vu stands

22

as a kind of allegory of the trope of "having been here before": allusion or metalepsis. Mike's déjà vu thus marks Van Sant's own self-consciousness that he is returning us to where we have already been: to Shakespeare's stories of Prince Hal and Falstaff and to Orson Welles' own repetition of those stories in his 1966 *Chimes at Midnight*.

Commenting on this creative borrowing (from Shakespeare if not from Welles), Van Sant himself remarked, "The Shakespearean passages make the point that what happens to these two people has been happening for centuries. I find it comforting that the same stories repeat themselves over and over, and I wanted to underscore the timelessness of the story Scott and Mike are enmeshed in."[2] Van Sant suggests here both that the essence of his story — "what happens to these two people" (Mike and Scott) — is merely being repeated from Shakespeare's original telling and that the very repeatability of this essence is comforting because it underscores the timelessness of something. But Van Sant does not say if this is the timelessness of the stories themselves or of certain human experiences; nor does he tell us if the comfort he feels is artistic or moral or something else entirely.

It is hard to know what Van Sant really means when he says that he feels comforted by what he perceives as the timelessness inhering in his

Mike Waters (River Phoenix) and Scott Favor (Keanu Reeves) in Gus Van Sant's *My Own Private Idaho* (New Line Cinema, 1991).

repetitions, but he is not the only one to make this point. The former edi-
tor of *Film Comment*, Richard Jameson, similarly remarked in a blurb for
the film's 1993 laser disc release that "the Shakespearean framework foregrounds the timelessness of the recurring themes of fathers and sons,
masked motives, and the sociopolitical callousness of intimate betrayal.
Van Sant also pays passionate homage to Welles' *Chimes at Midnight*." It
is difficult to assess what advantage any filmmaker might get from his or
her audience being specifically aware that the situations depicted in the film
have happened before, and, even more, that these forms of human conduct or interaction are so typical that they could have been powerfully
represented in literary form as much as four centuries earlier. In the case
of *My Own Private Idaho*, Van Sant's story does not need the echo of Shakespeare to remind us because his own story — the very film we are watching — clearly includes "masked motives ... and the sociopolitical callousness
of intimate betrayal." And yet Jameson apparently believes that it is aes-
thetically noteworthy that Van Sant "*foregrounds* the timelessness" of these
themes, a phrase I emphasize because it seems so strangely paradoxical (can
timelessness be "foregrounded"?). Surely to place in the foreground not
only what has happened before, but also what has been previously represented in literary form, calls attention not to the timelessness of the work's
themes but to the very belatedness of the derivative artist. And if Shakespeare already made all this known, why should we pay attention to Van
Sant's film, which merely says again what Shakespeare already said so
majestically? Moreover, we have the added problem that Van Sant is being
doubly derivative. For, as Jameson is certainly correct to remind us, *My
Own Private Idaho* "also pays passionate homage to Welles' *Chimes at Midnight*." How, then, are we to make sense of Van Sant's work here as anything other than a work of startling unoriginality?[3]

Of course Van Sant's bringing to the fore of his film's relation to the
work of earlier artists allows us to examine another angle altogether, an angle
that brings us closer to the real creative premise of revisionary art: when
done well, it does not repeat the earlier story but rather brings to the surface precisely what in the original story was not fully developed. Making one's
debt clear may force the audience or reader to understand the derivative text
precisely as a revision or re-reading (or, as Harold Bloom might call it, a
misprision or creative misreading). Repeatability is necessary in this context as a way of marking the site of inspiration, where the muse we should
call reading begins to do its work. At times, it becomes necessary to bring
the original text to the foreground in order to mark how creativity can operate by canceling an inspiring earlier work as a misunderstanding or misrep-
resentation of the material. In these cases, the revisionary process comes into

view most clearly when the fundamentals of the story are presented from a different perspective or from a new historical vantage or context that becomes meaningful through the interpretive shell of an earlier work, even where the meaning of that earlier work is not repeated but radically altered.

In a brief accounting of Van Sant's process of adaptation (revising Welles as much as Shakespeare), this essay will attempt to demonstrate that, like other artists who borrow, Van Sant is probably less comforted by his ability to repeat the work of an earlier artist than he is inspired to create something new precisely because of what, to him, is not fully or properly expressed in the source text(s). Just as important, what the derivative artist typically attempts to express is related to very topical concerns, to precisely what is not timeless and what would have special relevance and resonance only in his or her own culture. Creative adaptation works, in short, by repeating not for the sake of universality but as a means of giving voice to what is historically specific, either in cultural or personal terms or both.

In what follows, I will focus less on the theory of adaptation and more on what we might learn from close textual comparisons of individual instances of adaptation. Given space limitations, I will be more suggestive than exhaustive. I will make these comparisons by first commenting on how Welles adapts Shakespeare's plays and then conclude by describing how Van Sant adapts Welles' adaptation (visually and thematically) to produce his most compelling insight — which is itself a revision of the meaning Welles ascribes to the beautiful Shakespearean phrase "chimes at midnight." This interpretive trajectory will allow us to see all the more clearly why and how borrowing is original, why repetition — when it is truly artistic — is never repetitive, and why timelessness is moot where derivative artists succeed in revealing what their predecessors could not have grasped in the later work's formulations. I shall try to demonstrate this idea — repetition as creative reworking — by detailing how the meaning Van Sant creates by borrowing has everything to do with a quintessentially late-twentieth-century American cultural experience: the lost children of our inner cities.

I

Precisely what prompts subsequent reworkings and re-contextualizations of the phrase "chimes at midnight" can best be understood by considering the implications of the original Shakespearean material. The full line in which the phrase appears, "We have heard the chimes at midnight, Master Shallow," is delivered by Falstaff in *2 Henry IV* as part of the following exchange:

SHALLOW: O Sir John, do you remember since we lay all night in the Windmill in Saint George's Field?

FALSTAFF: No more of that, Master Shallow, no more of that.

SHALLOW: Ha, 'twas a merry night. And is Jane Nightwork alive.

FALSTAFF : She lives, Master Shallow.

SHALLOW: She never could away with me.

FALSTAFF : Never, never, she would always say she could not abide Master Shallow.

SHALLOW: By the mass, I could anger her to th' heart. She was then a bona roba. Doth she hold her own well?

FALSTAFF : Old, old, Master Shallow.

SHALLOW: Nay, she must be old, she cannot choose but be old, certain she's old, and had Robin Nightwork by old Nightwork before I came to Clement's Inn.

FALSTAFF : That's fifty-five year ago.

SHALLOW: Ha, cousin Silence, that thou hadst seen what this knight and I have seen! Ha, Sir John, said I well?

FALSTAFF : We have heard the chimes at midnight, Master Shallow.

SHALLOW: That we have, that we have, that we have, in faith, Sir John, we have…. Jesus, the days that we have seen!

[2 Henry IV, III.ii.194–219][4]

The most immediate meaning of the line is that Falstaff and Shallow (and perhaps more broadly Falstaff's companions, Bardolph, Peto, etc.) have lived life fully, that they have been awake, literally and figuratively, when others were asleep. But the lyricism of the line conveys richer, more haunting possibilities as well, possibilities imaginatively at work because the line works within the context of the passage as a whole. For example, the past tense of "we have heard" is linked to the past tense of Shallow's "the days that we have seen" and both are linked to the preceding time reference, "fifty-five year ago," which suggests that the celebration of this life of madness and wonder is at the same time a lamentation for just how much it belongs to the past. The brief mention of Jane Nightwork's antiquity, moreover, seems not only to mark Falstaff himself as "old, old," but also to suggest that, like her, Falstaff may be overdue for death (the midnight chimes now sounding more like Donne's bells tolling their intimation of mortality).

Whatever special glory is reserved for those who have heard the chimes is now replaced by nostalgia for what can never be restored (love as well as youth) and anxiety over losses still to come. Indeed, Falstaff's lament in III.ii is linked to his subsequent rejection at the hands of Prince Hal (now King Harry) in V.v. The link is so strong that it is virtually impossible to separate the elegiac tone of III.ii from events of that final scene (V.v. 41–73; and it is worth noting that Falstaff here is again in Master Shallow's company). Although this version of the "chimes at midnight" line is more muted than what subsequent adaptors will do with it, Shakespeare himself seems to have registered its deeper, if sadder implications: it is a death knell of sorts for one of his greatest dramatic creations. The line, in short, manages to evoke a sense of Falstaff's impending loss even though, at the moment he delivers it, he still holds out the deluded hope that he will share in the new king's inheritance. Moreover, the line stimulates our awareness of how that loss is paired with Hal's coming to the throne, to power certainly, and perhaps to royal maturity.

V.v of *2 Henry IV* seems also to reveal Shakespeare — himself no stranger to the art of revision — adapting material from, or at least building on, his own earlier work. Specifically, the final rejection of Falstaff in *2 Henry IV* harkens back to II.iv of *1 Henry IV*, the scene in which Hal mysteriously reveals his intention to banish Falstaff at some point in the future (II.iv.460–81). The image of what people actually experience when they hear the "chimes at midnight" is provided in I.ii of *1 Henry IV* as part of the very first conversation between Hal and Falstaff. But there the image of "Diana's foresters, gentlemen of the shade, minions of the moon" (I.ii.25–26) expresses Falstaff's continuing vitality, his excess and exuberance. Even in that earlier scene, however, Falstaff's and Hal's midnight carousings are already threatened by Hal's announcement to the audience that he will betray his current companions. Hal's soliloquy at the end of that scene (I.ii.195–217) foreshadows the playacted betrayal of II.iv which, in turn, at once symbolizes and predicts the final rejection of Falstaff in V.v of *2 Henry IV*.

II

Welles' *Chimes at Midnight* conflates the story lines of both parts of Shakespeare's *Henry IV*. Just as in Shakespeare's plays, the main story line here reaches its climax in Prince Hal/King Harry's rejection of Falstaff (material taken from V.v of *2 Henry IV*). The film then adds final material from II.i and II.iii of *Henry V* to reveal the consequences of that rejection: spiritually broken, Falstaff dies shortly thereafter. Falstaff does not actually appear in Shakespeare's *Henry V*; rather, he dies offstage and his death is recounted by Hostess Quickly (II.iii.10–26). Welles is faithful to

Falstaff (Orson Welles) lives the high life at the Boar's Head Tavern in Welles'
Chimes at Midnight (International Films Espanola, 1966).

this fact, choosing to represent the death simply by having an immense
coffin carried off on a wagon to some unknown burial plot.

Although Welles follows the main action of Shakespeare's play, the
film's point of view is shifted so that it is Falstaff's experience of events
that dominates the viewer's perspective. Welles pointedly chooses not to
employ voice-over narration where that might suggest a firsthand account;
he limits the use of voice-overs to narrative segments of historical background, which he takes from Holinshed's *Chronicles*, Shakespeare's primary source for the plays. But Welles' opening scene reworks several lines
from III.ii of *2 Henry IV* to frame the subsequent story line as the retrospective ruminations of an old man, one whose life was indelibly marked
by his earlier dealings with the prince:

> SHALLOW: Jesus, the days that we have seen! [Falstaff laughs; Shallow
> laughs.] Do you remember since we lay all night in the Windmill in Saint
> George's Field?
>
> FALSTAFF: No more of that, Master Shallow.
>
> SHALLOW: [Laughs.] 'Twas a merry night. Is Jane Nightwork alive.

FALSTAFF : She lives, Master Shallow.

SHALLOW: Doth she hold her own well?

FALSTAFF : Old, old, Master Shallow.

SHALLOW: Nay, she must be old, she cannot choose but be old, certain she's old, and had Robin Nightwork by old Nightwork before I came to Clement's Inn. Jesus, the days that we have seen. Ha, Sir John, said I well?

FALSTAFF : We have heard the chimes at midnight, Master Robert Shallow.

SHALLOW: That we have, that we have, that we have, in faith, Sir John, we have. Jesus, the days that we have seen.

(Welles' revised dialogue for the opening scene of *Chimes at Midnight*)

The most obvious change here is that Welles transforms the line "the days that we have seen" into a lyrical refrain for the passage as a whole. And that refrain focuses attention on Welles' deletions so that we see only two old men reflecting on the passage of their best days, even if, for Shallow, there seems to be some satisfaction in recognizing just how full their lives have been. This is less obviously so for Falstaff, however, who, even as the film begins, seems to have suffered emotionally from Hal's rejection, an act that at once empties Falstaff's life of meaning and tinges the audience's own perspective with an awareness of lost vitality. Indeed, in *Chimes at Midnight*, Welles reimagines Shakespeare's Henry-plays as an elegy to Falstaff.

The film's opening expression of loss—lost youth and the awareness of mortality—becomes an important thematic motif for the film as a whole. This fact is borne out in Welles' use of the Shakespearean phrase "chimes at midnight" as the film's subtitle: the film is actually entitled *Falstaff*, although almost everyone remembers the film as *Chimes at Midnight* precisely because of the phrase's deeply elegiac qualities. The narrative framework of Welles' film is that of an old man remembering, and the shadow of his loss is the heart of the new story. Welles sees the story from the perspective of the old man who is rejected rather than from that of a young man who discovers just what he must reject in order to grow up. And if Shakespeare's sequence of Henry-plays, from *1 Henry IV* to *Henry V*, is centrally concerned with Hal's growing up, Welles' film is clearly about growing old.

III

Intriguingly, changes in perspective can be effected even when the adapting artist is being faithful to the source material. To see another example of this process, we might briefly consider a more traditional kind of film adaptation, but one that still reveals the borrowing of source material as an act of creative reworking.

While recognizing that Kenneth Branagh claimed that his 1989 film version of *Henry V* was an antiwar film, it is important to acknowledge that the film is a powerful testament to just how much Shakespeare's story belongs to Prince Hal/King Harry and represents him in a heroic light.[5] And we should note again that Falstaff does not even appear in Shakespeare's *Henry V*. At the same time, Branagh's film periodically invokes Falstaff's presence — visually and verbally — because he wants to pay homage to what Shakespeare's character has meant to Hal's story. At a minimum, Branagh wants to sustain an awareness of what Hal must sacrifice in order to become a worthy ruler.

To help generate this awareness, Branagh incorporates material from both parts of *Henry IV* by splicing a flashback scene into II.i of *Henry V.* The major portion of this inserted material comes from the tavern scene of *1 Henry IV* (II.iv), a scene in which, as we have already noted, Hal play-acts his future rejection of Falstaff. Branagh (re)presents this material as a memory trace in the minds of the aging soldiers, Bardolph, Nym, and Pistol, as they await word of Falstaff's death.[6] The film thus memorializes Falstaff by putting on display scenes from the earlier plays. Falstaff is remembered by filmic re-membering, which is also, in key aspects, a misremembering. That misremembering is marked particularly in Branagh's embedding of the line "we have heard the chimes at midnight" (from III.ii of *2 Henry IV)* in the flashback to *1 Henry IV's* tavern scenes (II.iv).

Neither version of *Henry V's* II.i — Shakespeare's original or Branagh's adaptation — is centrally concerned with Falstaff. Each in its way is more interested in the other aging characters (Nym, Bardolph, and Pistol). More specifically, the two versions of the scene explore the sense of loss these characters feel over Falstaff's death in the context of their impending departure for war in France. Both Shakespeare and Branagh, in short, link lost youth to the threat of death and, through other aspects of the scene, to the loss of love as well: Nym experiences this loss because Mistress Quickly (Nell) has married his rival, Pistol, and Pistol's own parting from Nell at the ending of II.iii poignantly reminds us of just what is put at risk by King Harry's war.

The real possibility of loss with which King Harry's war now threatens these old men is powerfully reinforced in Branagh's version of the scene by his recontextualization of the key line. In Branagh's flashback scene, the line is said by Falstaff to Hal: " We have heard the chimes at midnight, Master Harry." This substitution of Hal for Shallow and the new placement of the line in what should be the tavern scene — a scene that both anticipates and symbolically embodies the newly crowned King Harry's final betrayal of Falstaff in V.v of *2 Henry IV*— transforms Falstaff's comment into a simultaneous lament and accusation: even as Branagh includes Hal in Falstaff's "we" (indeed, all the other companions melt away), he shows Falstaff's recognition that Hal will betray him, a betrayal that Falstaff seems to register already as a fatal blow. One of the effects of this change is to make explicit what is only implicit in Shakespeare's treatment, and even Welles', by establishing a direct causal link between Hal's conduct (his earlier playacted betrayal foreshadowing the later real one) and the sense of loss that Falstaff so acutely feels and that is so delicately balanced in the phrase "chimes at midnight." Indeed, the conflation of material from these different scenes reveals that moment at which the phrase "chimes at midnight" shifts from marking a positive experience (a shared, privileged experience of a way of life most people will never know) to a negative one, an awareness that even in the midst of life we are never far from irreversible loss. And the sense of the inevitability of such loss is made even worse by the recognition that it is hastened by a friend's betrayal. Hal is not responsible for Falstaff's age, of course, but his betrayal saps Falstaff's vitality; indeed, as presented by Branagh, Hal's act transforms a zest for life into a surrender to the destructive forces (age and time) that Falstaff can no longer resist. The flashback material helps clarify Mistress Quickly's claim that "the king hath kill'd [Falstaff's] heart" (*Henry V*, II.i.88) and Nym's that "the king hath run bad humors on the knight" (II.i.121–22). But it does this while revising the end of *2 Henry IV* in its suggestion that Falstaff must have anticipated Hal's betrayal: at a minimum, Branagh seems to hint that Falstaff could not have been so naive as to place his full trust in his "when thou art king" fantasy. Falstaff must have known he was being used, a notion that is more in keeping with what we know and love about him: his ability to pierce the pretensions and deceits of the nobility (most famously on display in his critique of honor in V.i.127–41 of *1 Henry IV*).

Moreover, Branagh's resuscitating of Falstaff within Nym, Bardolph and Pistol's flashback allows the audience to imagine that Falstaff's capacity to see through Prince Hal's designs might have rubbed off on his less intelligent companions. Certainly for the viewer, Branagh's conflations hint at an otherwise unstated proposition that King Harry's war is itself just another act of deceit against old men, men whom the king regards as useless despite the intimacy he once shared with them. But we are also encouraged to hope that Bardolph, Nym, and Pistol can grasp Hal/Harry's real motives and the real threat they now face. In Branagh's revision, Bardolph, Nym, and Pistol come to recognize that Falstaff's chimes are tolling for them as well precisely because the king has no qualms about lying to them or to anyone else when it serves his purpose. Through the continuing presence of Falstaff, they see that the king has no moral conscience and that even his friends are merely pawns in his grand scheme of self-aggrandizement. The flashback material also suggests, in very broad terms, the wastefulness of war and the callousness of rulers: doom might be inevitable, but that is all the more reason to savor the sweetness of life and to despise those who see the fates of others as an opportunity for personal advantage.

In sum, even as the film follows the basic logic of Shakespeare's *Henry V*, Branagh's attentiveness to the implications of the phrase "chimes at midnight" allows him to deflect the story away from King Harry, thus giving Falstaff one last moment. In so doing, he emphasizes Falstaff's perspective on Harry's maturation, career, and triumphs as well as their effects on Falstaff's life. Branagh seems not only to be following Welles' lead here, but also to be doing homage to Welles' film by making a space for it within

Politicized courtship: Henry V (Kenneth Branagh) woos Katherine, the princess of France (Emma Thompson), in Branagh's *Henry V* (the Samuel Goldwyn Company and Renaissance Films, 1990).

his own narrative. For in both Welles' and Branagh's films, the losses Falstaff must endure and our sense of his wasted life shadow — perhaps even critique — the story of King Harry, Shakespeare's hero and, paradoxically, Branagh's as well.

IV

Turning finally to Van Sant's adaptation, we might start by noting that he positions his version of the "chimes at midnight" in a different place entirely, even before his revision of *1 Henry IV's* tavern-scene. The phrase is now spoken by Bob (Van Sant's Falstaff) to Budd (a crazed Master Shallow) as the two return to Portland from their debauched journeys:

> BUDD: Jesus, the things we've seen. Do you remember a thing since we moved from graffiti bridge?
>
> BOB: No more of that, Bud....
>
> BUDD: Is Jane Nightwork alive, Bob?
>
> BOB: She's alive, Budd.
>
> BUDD: Is she holding on?
>
> BOB: Old, old.
>
> BUDD: She must be old. She has no choice.... Jesus, the things we've seen. Aren't I right, Bob, aren't I right?
>
> BOB: We have heard the chimes at midnight.
>
> BUDD: That we have, that we have. In fact, Bob, we have. Jesus, the things we've seen.[7]

Despite the new position of the Falstaff-Master Shallow exchange within the story line, Van Sant's adaptation shares some features with Welles' and Branagh's versions. Like Welles, for example, Van Sant uses the exchange to introduce his Falstaff, although unlike Welles, Van Sant does not position this material at the start of the film because, in the main, *My Own Private Idaho* is not Bob's story (it is really Mike's story).[8] Moreover, much as in Branagh's film, the exchange allows Van Sant to put his Falstaff center stage for a moment before the scene shifts back to younger characters. And each of the three films uses the Shakespearean material in its own distinct way to portray its particular view of Falstaff's strange combination of worldliness and world-weariness (a life at once rich and depleted).

Just at the level of plot, however, Van Sant's repositioning of the Falstaff–Master Shallow exchange is closer to Shakespeare's original in that he places it where his Falstaff, Bob, still hopes to cash in on his friendship with the new Hal, Scott. Indeed, that is precisely the reason Bob has returned to Portland: because Scott is about to turn 21 and come into his inheritance. In Van Sant's version, as in Shakespeare's, then, the line loses at least some of the elegiac luster it acquires in Welles' and Branagh's versions. Nevertheless, even as Van Sant weakens the association between the "chimes at midnight" line and Falstaff-Bob's sense of lost prospects, a feeling of lost youth and of a life wasted—everything that belongs to the phrase "chimes at midnight"—still pervades this version of the story. The elegiac quality of the phrase is retained by Van Sant, however, even as the feeling of loss it symbolizes takes on a decidedly new connotation in relation to a series of social ills on display in the film: stealing, prostitution, drugs, and homelessness. The phrase stands in for all the experiences of the film's young people who have nowhere to go at night and so only reluctantly hear the "chimes at midnight"; they would prefer just about anything else. For them as for Shakespeare's Falstaff, hearing the "chimes" is a kind of death knell.

In short, while Van Sant's story is still very much about lost youth and lost love (both Bob and Mike lose their love, Scott), the sense of loss—both actual and potential—shifts toward a much broader sociological concern, that of the lost youth of America's "lost youths," a concept that, symbolically relocated within Van Sant's story, now only partly suggests a progressive awareness of one's limits or one's mortality as one ages (a point Branagh effectively makes in the portrayal of his aging soldiers). For Van Sant, the lament for what is lost is expanded to create a symbolic equation between Bob's sense that life's possibilities are slipping away and the young people's (especially Mike's) awareness that the chance for the "good life," or even simply a normal life, is disappearing all too quickly.[9] Youth is lost, however, not because time is the enemy (as it is for Falstaff and Bob and for Branagh's Nym, Bardolph, and Pistol), but because society is the enemy. And not possessing what society understands as normal (as Mike says, "like a mom and a dad and a dog and shit like that") leaves one exposed to being left behind, buried in a wasted life if not actually dead. In Van Sant's creative misreading, Falstaff's sense of loss—being rejected or abandoned by someone more powerful than he—represents the marginalization that comes when one has no cultural status at all: impoverished, abused, homosexual, homeless, and hopeless. In this version, in other words, youth is lost or wasted when a young person has no future and nowhere to go, doomed to hear the chimes at midnight when most people are at home with their families, asleep in their beds.

V

Van Sant's adaptation is a very deliberate effort to do something new with the source material — something culturally specific — and not just repeat the work of his predecessors. To get a clearer understanding of this revisionary process, we might consider one of Van Sant's visual echoings of Welles' film, echoings that — paradoxically, from the perspective of originality — bear out Jameson's observation that *My Own Private Idaho* is influenced as much by *Chimes at Midnight* as by Shakespeare's plays.

Material that both Welles and Van Sant take from II.iv.482–523 of *1 Henry IV* offers a simple visualization of this influence. Welles and Van Sant both present the tavern scene after the announcement that there are law-enforcement agents at the door looking for suspects in the previous night's robbery (the sheriff in Welles, looking for Falstaff; Portland police officers in Van Sant, looking for Bob). Van Sant clearly borrows from Welles a series of details, including the increased number of extras in the scene and the mad scramble for hiding places after the announcement that the sheriff and his men have come to search the premises. However, Van Sant's most important borrowing follows an addition that Welles first makes to the original material: during his search of Hostess Quickly's inn, Welles' sheriff discovers Hal in bed with an unnamed woman (who may or may not be a prostitute). This detail is echoed by Van Sant who has his Portland police officers discover Scott in bed with Mike (who is definitely a prostitute).[10] This particular adaptation is crucial for understanding the germinal idea of Van Sant's creative misreading of Shakespeare: Van Sant takes Welles' unnamed woman/prostitute, transforms her into a "him" (Mike), makes it clear that he is in love with this soon-to-be rich, powerful person, and then gives him the opportunity to tell his side of the story.

Van Sant said in an interview that, although *Chimes at Midnight* had "given [him] the idea," he "tried to forget" it in the making of *My Own Private Idaho* because he "didn't want to be plagiaristic or stylistically influenced by it" (Fuller xxxvii). But here is precisely where we might view influence or even plagiarism as a form of creativity. To understand this creative process, we might connect that image of the (male) prostitute in bed with the rich young man he loves (at once a borrowing from and a revision of Welles tavern scene) to an experience Van Sant claims to have actually had (one can almost imagine Van Sant's first viewing of Welles' film as the point of origin for his retelling).[11] Van Sant observes that he "started working on this story in 1978. It's based on kids I used to see on Hollywood Boulevard."[12] Van Sant no doubt connected his image of street hustlers (adolescent girls and boys selling their bodies in order to feed themselves) with other social realities: some of these kids had run away from home; some were drug dealers or drug abusers; all were terrified; none had a home except whatever shelter they could find for that night; many had no family except for their fellow street dwellers; and none had a steady job or health insurance.

Van Sant, like Shakespeare and Welles, still tells the story of "masked motives and the sociopolitical callousness of intimate betrayal," although now it is Scott's betrayal of Mike rather than of Bob that is emphasized. And that betrayal becomes more important in this version because, in a wonderful revision, Van Sant transforms Shakespeare's character Poins, Prince Hal's fellow conspirator in the mockery of Falstaff and his confidante elsewhere in the Henry IV plays, into Welles' prostitute.[13] Van Sant reimagines Poins as a special character, his unexplained intimacy with Hal now taking on the homoerotic overtones of Mike's love for Scott. And it is Scott's cruel or callous betrayal of this intimacy (not for social gain precisely but in that context) that is the heart of the story. At the same time, Van Sant reminds us that in Shakespeare's original, Falstaff is the one who is betrayed, not Poins. Van Sant keeps this memory alive not only by including Bob's death scene, but also by linking Bob and Mike in the film:

Intimacy betrayed: Mike (River Phoenix) as Van Sant's new Poins and Scott (Keanu Reeves) as the new Hal.

when the film opens, Mike is wearing an old gas-station attendant shirt with the name "Bob" above the pocket.[14]

In his filmic blending of borrowed story lines, visual images, and dialogue along with that real lived experience from Hollywood Boulevard, Van Sant reimagines the story so that it is not simply a repetition of something timeless in Shakespeare's art. Rather, it is an artistic vision meaningful in a modern historical and social context. The jacket cover of the 1993 laser disc observes that this is "a fable of love and belonging," "a story of innocence and desire," and "a parable of friendship and betrayal." But it is really a story of loss. Indeed, Van Sant recognizes that it might make sense, dramatically and conceptually, to re-present Falstaff as the main character of Shakespeare's plays (something Welles had also seen) but that to make him the main character would require the reinvention of the story. In a complicated way, Van Sant creates this new version by combining Falstaff and Poins in Mike even as he doubles Falstaff with Mike and Bob. By means of this transformation, Van Sant increases Hal's culpability in the betrayal of his friends because in the Henry IV plays, Poins is actually closer to Hal than Falstaff is.

But, in the end, why does it matter to the story that Van Sant revises Shakespeare in this way? And why is that other "ton of man," Welles, so important in the revisionary history, or creativity by (mis)interpretation? Van Sant follows Welles on these points:

1. Although Hal (now Scott) is no longer the main character in this story, his actions are the condition of the story by providing the context.
2. The main story concerns the learning process undergone by Falstaff or his surrogate (more Mike than Bob), whose life is shaped by his experiences with Hal (Scott). Of course, to the extent that Van Sant keeps it a story about growing up whereas Welles tells a story of growing old, Van Sant is actually closer to the Shakespearean original.
3. Both films position the "chimes at midnight" line early on (Welles at the very beginning) so as to frame the story with the Falstaff character looking back on things, reflecting precisely on what Hal/Scott has meant to him. (One wonders if Van Sant ever considered giving this line to Mike in his opening soliloquy.)
4. Van Sant wants to stress Welles' essential correctness in presenting the protagonist's perspective as his gained understanding of how his life has been shaped by loss: of intimacy, love, friendship, youth.

Van Sant could have told a modern day Falstaff-story, but perhaps he felt that this would be too close to Welles' story. Thus he reinvents Shakespeare's Poins (Mike) as a character who suffers a similar fate (rejected or betrayed by Hal/Scott) but now in a more intimate context: Mike is in love with Scott. At the same time, Van Sant also reworks the basic material by transforming Falstaff's lovable excess (thieving, eating, drinking, whoring) into something much more sinister or disheartening. This is important, as it is at once difficult and necessary to distinguish the excesses of the marginalized from the excesses of the privileged. Van Sant resituates his new understanding of his predecessors' work within a distinctively modern American context: urban youth culture and a series of broader cultural contexts— the disenfranchised within the capitalist system; institutional abuse, the corruptive power of money (which can buy pleasure and privilege), and even the exploitation of sexuality (used by Scott as a way of constructing his identity for public consumption). In essence, Van Sant misreads Shakespeare's and Welles' stories as a dark fable of the American dream.

Confirmation of the preceding argument is provided by Van Sant's re-contextualization of the Gadshill robbery (II.iii of *1 Henry IV*), a revision that clarifies a motive left somewhat obscure in the Shakespearean original. Why exactly does Shakespeare's Falstaff need to steal? In the most obvious sense, he is simply too lazy to work, but good historicists would have much to tell us about the late–Elizabethan crisis of the aristocracy and what this might have meant in Shakespeare's Henry plays, which in the main are concerned with responsible rule (especially in the context of militarist expansion). *My Own Private Idaho* suggests that there is an American aristocracy, but historically speaking, of course, that is not the same thing as the Elizabethan aristocracy. Made at the end of the Reagan-Bush era (when the downturn in the economy was starting to become a sociopolitical issue, one that would influence the 1992 presidential campaign), *My Own Private Idaho* is clearly a story about those people left behind, left out, or simply forgotten even during the years of economic expansion. In this sense, its tone is closer to the scene from Branagh's *Henry V* where the old men at the tavern see that the world is leaving them behind. But clearly, in Van Sant's version, this feeling of impending loss (along with the "masked motives ... and the sociopolitical callousness of intimate betrayal" to which Jameson refers—both of which are also part of Welles' story) gets developed in terms specific to the cultural situation of America in the late 1980s and early 1990s.

In *My Own Private Idaho*, the division between Scott and the homeless drifters marks the gap in American class structure itself. In other words, as presented by Van Sant at least, the power-differential between Scott and his companions is caused by the discrepancy between those who are culturally advantaged and those who are disenfranchised or marginalized. Here, some privileged few lord it over those who cannot defend themselves, a situation symbolized by the plight of the young prostitutes in the film (especially those with abusive clients): they get fucked. And those with power expect service without any obligation to reciprocate. Van Sant provides a final image of the redeemed Scott, riding in a limousine, looking out at a homeless person, and feeling no sense of shared experience; the image leaves little hope that, now that he is close to power, he will do anything for these people, his former companions on the street. Of course, this may be Shakespeare's point as well. As king, will Harry do anything useful for the lower classes of England other than lead them into a war they do not want, one that serves only his interests? Does Van Sant see Shakespeare's hero as something less than heroic, something closer to the callousness of Scott, and would his "misreading" be a good interpretation of Shakespeare's Hal?

If Hal and Falstaff compete for the moral center of Shakespeare's plays, Mike is unquestionably the moral center of Van Sant's film. He is looking for a life, for what has been denied him because he is not "normal." And Van Sant's retelling provides a motivation for Mike's attraction to Scott, whereas Falstaff's desire for what Hal can give him has a different motive, or at least a different historical context. This element in Van Sant's version certainly complicates Falstaff's character psychologically. The key difference is in the representation of need: as material necessity or as hedonistic desire. In effect, Van Sant changes Falstaff's playful hedonism into a form of cultural desperation and Hal's slumming into a political hedonism, the site of which Van Sant also shifts more definitively to the privileged class (though Branagh's version suggests something of this as well): the political self-interest pursued by the powerful, the monied, the well-connected, the corrupt. Van Sant's Bob is certainly no role model (Mike is only marginally better), but, as the film presents it, material need organizes the world, and this desire subjugates others. Reading Van Sant's film as an act of misreading, we also see that creative adaptation typically works by repeating not to reveal a story's timelessness, but rather to give voice to what might otherwise go unsaid.

Works Cited

Donaldson, Peter S. "Taking on Shakespeare: Kenneth Branagh's *Henry V.*" *Shakespeare Quarterly* 42 (1991): 60–71.
Falstaff (Chimes at Midnight). Dir. Orson Welles. Internacional Films Española, 1966.
Fuller, Graham. "Gus Van Sant: Swimming Against the Current" (an interview). In Van Sant, pp. vii–liii.

Hedrick, Donald K. "War is Mud: Branagh's Dirty Harry V and the Types of Political Ambiguity." In *Shakespeare the Movie: Popularizing the Plays on Film, TV, and Video.* Edited by Lynda E. Boose and Richard Burt. London: Routledge, 1997. 45–64.

Henry V. Dir. Kenneth Branagh. Samuel Goldwyn Company and Renaissance Films in association with the BBC, 1990.

Lyons, Donald. "Gus Van Sant." *Film Comment* 27 (1991): 6–12.

My Own Private Idaho. Dir. Gus Van Sant. New Line Cinema 1991; laser disc: Image Entertainment, 1993.

Shakespeare, William. *The Riverside Shakespeare.* 2nd edition. Edited by G. Blakemore Evans et al. Boston: Houghton Mifflin, 1997.

Van Sant, Gus. *Even Cowgirls Get the Blues & My Own Private Idaho.* Boston: Faber and Faber, 1993.

Wiseman, Susan. "The Family Tree Motel: Subliming Shakespeare in *My Own Private Idaho.*" In *Shakespeare the Movie: Popularizing the Plays on Film, TV, and Video.* Edited by Lynda E. Boose and Richard Burt. London: Routledge, 1997. 225–39.

Notes

1. Except where noted, throughout the essay I will quote directly from the film rather than from the published screenplay.

2. I quote here from the jacket of the 1993 laser disc. In an interview with Graham Fuller, Van Sant puts it this way: "The reason Scott's like he is is because of the Shakespeare, and the reason the Shakespeare is in the film is to transcend time, to show that those things have always happened, everywhere" (Fuller xlii–xliii).

3. Fuller asks in the interview, "When you wrote the *Henry IV* scenes for *Idaho*, did you actually go back to the text of the plays or was your reference point *Chimes at Midnight*?" Van Sant responds: "I tried to forget the Welles film because I didn't want to be plagiaristic or stylistically influenced by it, even though it had given me the idea. So I referred to the original Shakespeare." He claims, moreover, that even as the film "toned the Shakespeare down" (especially in terms of language) "it was literally, from beginning to end, a restructuring of the *Henry IV* plays"; later he goes so far as to call the Shakespeare scenes in the film "an editing job," one that "didn't involve too much creation" (Fuller xxxvii, xxv, xlvi). The central issue of this essay is that even an editing job may require real creativity, though the nature of that creativity is complex.

4. Citations from Shakespeare's plays are by act, scene, and line number.

5. For differing views on whether or how Branagh's film demystifies warfare and military ideology more generally, see Donaldson and Hedrick.

6. From Branagh's revision of Shakespeare's *Henry V*, II.i.117–28:

> HOSTESS: If ever you come of women, come in quickly to Sir John. He is so shaked of a burning contagion fever, that it is most lamentable to behold. Sweet men, come to him.
>
> PISTOL: Poor Sir John. A good portly man, i' faith.
>
> [Flashback, which concludes with:]
>
> FALSTAFF: If sack and sugar be a fault, God help the wicked. If to be old and merry is a sin, if to be fat is to be hated. But no, my good lord, when thou art king, banish Pistol, banish, Bardolph, banish Nym, but sweet Jack Falstaff, valiant Jack Falstaff, and therefore more valiant being, as he is, old Jack Falstaff, banish not him thy Harry's company. Banish plump Jack and banish all the world.
>
> PRINCE: I do, I will.[from *1 Henry IV*, II.iv.470–81]
>
> FALSTAFF : But we have heard the chimes at midnight, Master Harry. Jesu, (the) days that we have seen.[from *2 Henry IV*, III.ii.214–15, 219]

PRINCE: I know thee not, old man.[from *2 Henry IV*, V.v.47]

[End of flashback]

NYM: The King hath run bad humors on the knight.

PISTOL: Nym, thou hast spoke the right.

His heart is fracted and corroborate.

NYM: The King is a good king, but it must be as it may. He passes some humors and careers.

PISTOL: Let us condole the knight, for, lambkins, we will live.

7. It is noteworthy that the line "we have heard the chimes at midnight" does not even appear in the published screenplay; the line there reads: "We have seen the light at the end of the tunnel" (Van Sant 133).

8. For elaboration of this point, see Lyons 8–12 and Wiseman 234–35, 237.

9. Mike's longing for normalcy is most explicitly articulated in the film's most poignant scene, where he dares to speak love's name to Scott as part of a longer revelation of his wish to have a normal life: "normal, you know, like a mom and a dad and a dog and shit like that ... normal"; to which Scott responds, in his typically skeptical-cool-non-committal manner, "You didn't have a normal dog?"

10. Van Sant's revision of Welles is more graphic: the police come upon Scott humping Mike (or at least pretending to hump him). Mike would actually prefer the real thing.

11. It is worth noting that, in the context of recounting his work on the original script, Van Sant claims that he "didn't fully know who [Scott] was until" he had seen "Orson Welles's *Chimes at Midnight*" (Fuller xxiii).

12. I quote this line from the jacket of the 1993 laser disc. In the interview with Fuller, Van Sant puts it a bit differently: "[I]n *My Own Private Idaho*, I was fashioning those characters after people that I had met in Portland who are street hustlers.... The original script was written in the seventies when I was living in Hollywood. It was actually set on Hollywood Boulevard.... Meanwhile I had shot *Mala Noche* and eight years went by. Then I started writing again about these same street characters" (Fuller xxiii).

13. Van Sant himself recognizes at least part of this adaptation: "I realized that Shakespeare's *Henry IV* plays had this gritty quality about them. They had the young Henry, Prince Hal, who is about to become king, slumming on the streets with his sidekick. The young Henry seemed to be Scott and the sidekick seemed to be Mike, so I adapted the Shakespeare story to modern Portland" (Fuller xxv).

14. This marks yet another intriguing change from the published screenplay, which contains the following direction: "Mike enters the frame ... He has a Texaco gas station attendant's shirt on with a name tag that reads: BILL (not Mike, his name)" (Van Sant 109).

3

Shakespeare Transposed:
The British Stage on the
Post-Colonial Screen

Parmita Kapadia

Released in 1965, *Shakespeare Wallah* was the second offering from the then fledgling Merchant-Ivory Productions. The film was shot in black and white and entirely on location in India because of Merchant-Ivory's financial limitations. Widely praised for its elegiac tone and attention to setting, the film depicts the end of the British Raj. As Robert Emmet Long observed, "Much of the interest of *Shakespeare Wallah,* indeed, is its immersion in mood and atmosphere, the dreamlike setting that frames the declining fortunes of the old order" (48). Visual and narrative examples of the film's evocation of mood are many. My concern here is not to reiterate these, but to examine how *Shakespeare Wallah* constructs a cinematic text that consciously appropriates the Shakespearean canon and, through this appropriation, questions the cultural purpose and position of the Bard and more broadly British culture within India. *Shakespeare Wallah* signifies the uneasy — and unequal — relationship between opposing cultures — Indian and English — whose differences are marked by race, class, religion, and power. Investigating the position Shakespeare occupied within India, the film takes a critical look at the nexus of the British Raj and independent India. With its narrative set in the aftermath of independence, *Shakespeare Wallah* creates a multivalent text that brings to the foreground the cultural anxieties between a colonial power and its onetime colonial possession. *Shakespeare Wallah* employs Shakespeare's texts to critique the unique historical moment that bridges the colonial period and the emerging post-colonial nation.

The film re-contextualizes well-known and oft-quoted lines as well as longer speeches and scenes from all of Shakespeare's dramatic genres except the romances. Russell Jackson writes, "Films made from Shakespeare's plays exist at a meeting-point between conflicting cultural assumptions, rival theories and practices of performance, and — at the most basic level — the uneasy and overlapping systems of theater and cinema" (8). *Shakespeare Wallah* deliberately emphasizes these competing cultural assumptions, alternative performance techniques, and overlapping theatrical and cinematic structures both narratively and visually: the cultural struggle between former colonizers and the colonized is played out as a struggle between British high theater and Indian film. Functioning as tropes for the dissolution of the British Raj and the emerging post-colonial nation-state, theater and film are put into conflict. By using the particular cultural icons of Shakespeare and the Hindi massala movie, *Shakespeare Wallah* allows us to explore issues surrounding colonialism and the emergence of a post-colonial identity. Hindi cinema and Indian culture emerge as forces that counteract the influence of British imperialism. A rereading of *Shakespeare Wallah* prompts us to locate the film against the historical developments of Indian independence and the end of British colonial rule. I argue that by putting the film's predominant tropes of Shakespearean theater and Hindi cinema into a dialectical relationship with one another, we can resituate *Shakespeare Wallah* within the broader cultural and historical contexts that press upon post-colonial Indian culture. Through such a rereading, the film provides a nuanced narrative illustrating the post-colonial struggle to balance modernity with traditional identity.

In "Other Shakespeares: Translation and Expropriation," Kenneth Rothwell discusses *Shakespeare Wallah,* beginning with the idea that

> Movie makers from non–Anglophone countries all over the world have resituated Shakespeare's plays in the idiom of their own language and film culture. Not needing to record in English on the soundtrack, they enjoyed the luxury of reinventing the plays in purely cinematic terms, as if they were silent movies.... [I]n all instances these non–Anglophone films show the universal appeal of Shakespeare as a cultural trophy [168].

He argues that once the plays have been "removed from the original Anglophone context," they are "converted" into what Dennis Kennedy in his introduction to *Foreign Shakespeares* labeled "other Shakespeares, Shakespeares not dependent on English and often at odds with it." According to Rothwell, once the plays are freed from their dependence on English, the "shadow of cultural imperialism gradually diminishes." Rothwell sees *Shakespeare Wallah* as "captur[ing] the flavor of Anglo/Indian culture," and for him, the film "evoke[s] a compelling, almost Chekhovian, nostalgia for a lost Anglo/Indian culture that might rightly be entitled 'A Passage From India'" (168). However, the film does not construct Shakespeare as a "cultural trophy"; rather, Shakespeare's position is threatened throughout the narrative.

Shakespeare Wallah explores the complicated Anglo/Indian relationship by conflating historical reality with fictionalized storytelling. Loosely based on a diary kept by Geoffrey Kendal during his troupe's Shakespeareana tour across India, the film uses real events to give credence to its fictional narrative. Although the Kendal troupe successfully performed in India for nearly 20 years, *Shakespeare Wallah*'s traveling thespians have come upon hard times due to changes in audience taste following independence. Cinematic representation further blurs historical accuracy via the film's casting, which relies heavily on actors from the Shakespeareana troupe. *Shakespeare Wallah* casts Geoffrey and Laura Kendal to play their fictional filmic counterparts, the Buckinghams. Their real daughter, Felicity, plays fictional daughter Lizzie. Jennifer Kendal also has a small role as the owner of the Glen Eagles hotel. Indian actors Utpal Dutt and Shashi Kapoor, both Shakespeareana alums, take part in the film as well.[1] According to director James Ivory, Ruth Prewar Jhabvala's screenplay adapted the Kendals' experiences so that the film could be seen as "a metaphor for the end of the British Raj" (87). Set in post–1947 India, *Shakespeare Wallah* tells the story of a mostly British theater troupe that travels the country staging Shakespeare's plays for schools and private audiences.

Shakespeare Wallah employs narrative and cinematic techniques to contrast the waning of British influence with the emergence of Indian independence. For example, the theater troupe's car breaks down, stranding them for hours on the side of the road. Their accommodations range from tents to derelict hotels. By contrast, the film shows the two modern Indian characters as having money, fast cars, and luxurious homes. However, the film does more than simply contrast the two cultures; it inverts the traditional colonizer/colonized or us/them paradigm. The film turns post-colonial Indian audiences into the "other" through its representation of the contemporary public as unappreciative of Shakespearean theater. Aware that their life's work is no longer valued by post-colonial Indian society, the elder members of the troupe lament the changes and reconstruct their judgment of Indians. At one time, the Buckinghams believed Indians to be "the most wonderful audience in the world" because they "laughed at all the jokes, cried in all the right places."[2] However, attitudes have "all changed, slowly, over these past years" (Ivory121). Having suffered the obviously negative influences of political independence, the people have been damaged. Indians are no longer capable of understanding good theater. Tony tells Carla, "We should have gone home in '47 when the others did." Mrs. Bowen, the Anglo-Indian landlady who owns the depressing Glen Eagles hotel, tells the Buckinghams, "It's not like the old days. What do these people know about our theater? Shakespeare and all that?" After independence, "the best audience in the world" has been effectively divided from us and "our" theater (Ivory 120–122).

The film exacerbates the division between Indian audiences and the mostly British performers by using various cinematic strategies such as camera perspective, split screens, scene juxtaposition, focus, lighting, music, and sound effects. The film also employs textual juxtapositioning by transposing and de-contextualizing theatrical scenes and speeches to create a fractured narrative that explores a unique historical moment. By choosing particular scenes and lines from within the Shakespearean canon, the film constructs an intertextual dialogue between theater and cinema that implicitly comments on the cultural past and political present. These deliberately chosen bits and pieces of Shakespeare's texts function to construct the Bard's judgment regarding Indian political sovereignty. The film appropriates scenes and speeches from various plays so that they literally and metaphorically reinforce the breakup of Britain's colonial world. The transposed texts are de-contextualized from their own narratives and function as commentary on the political and cultural conditions within postcolonial India. Through these scenes, the film uses Shakespeare's words to reconstruct Indian nationalism and post-colonial culture.

An early scene sequence casts the film's characters into roles that explicitly echo Shakespeare's. In a scene that refers back to act two, scene two of *Hamlet*, the film sets up an Indian maharaja as the prince of Denmark. Like a modern day Rosencrantz or Guildenstern, the maharaja's servant informs the prince, "the Players have arrived." Cast as Hamlet's alter ego, the maharaja plays the saddened, disillusioned prince, and members of his acting troupe become his players. The dinner scene pushes these Shakespearean echoes further. Presiding over an elaborate dinner, the maharaja becomes the actor, playing multiple roles for his guests. He is the genial host, the theater buff, the international traveler, the educated lover of Shakespeare, and an actor himself. The maharaja comments on his stay in London during the coronation of Queen Elizabeth II, describing the ceremony as "theater ... magical in every way." The maharaja fancies himself a drama enthusiast for whom attending the theater outranks all other activities. He remembers that while in London he would often "slip away ... from the round of banquets and what not and spend an enjoyable and instructive evening in the theater." He reveals that his "great love of Shakespeare was first aroused" by a performance of *The Merchant of Venice*, and his interpretation of that production is directly coded in Aristotelian language. He was "held spellbound literally in accordance to Aristotle's precept, purged with pity and terror." The Maharaja reveals a propensity to recite, launching into Portia's signature speech: "'The quality of mercy is not strain'd.'" He states that in India Shakespeare is valued as both poet and teacher: "We go to Shakespeare not only for his poetry but also for his wisdom." In this crucial line, the pronoun "we" implies an identification with fellow Indians although the antecedent remains unspoken. However, as the film reveals, the inclusive identification applies only to the "we" who still love Shakespeare; it rejects the emerging part of Indian culture that embraces a more indigenous lifestyle (Ivory 97–99).

During the dinner scene, the political and cultural tensions accompanying the waning of the British Raj are alluded to with lines from Shakespeare's history plays. The maharaja asks who but Shakespeare "could have written so profoundly on the cares of kingship?" He answers himself using Shakespeare's own words, "'Uneasy lies the head that wears a crown.'" The film appropriates and contextualizes Shakespeare's language so it reflects the maharaja's loss of wealth and power. "In the old days," the maharaja had jewels and influence, but today, "half [his] palace has been turned into offices." Acknowledging the loss, Tony appropriates *Richard II*: "'Let us sit upon the ground / And tell the sad stories of the death of kings.'" Carla adds, "'How some have been depos'd, / some slain in war, / Some haunted by the ghosts they have deposed'" (Ivory 99). These key lines from both *II Henry IV* and *Richard II* positions the maharaja as India's counterpart to British royalty. By deliberately re-contextualizing these lines, the film shrouds the dissolution of the British Raj in the elegiac and mournful words of kings Henry IV and Richard II.

Throughout the dinner scene, Shakespearean dialogue seeds the conversation, reflecting differences between the colonial past and the postcolonial present; however, these differences are also refracted through the Shakespearean plays performed by the troupe. The first play is a command performance of *Antony and Cleopatra* for the maharaja. The film's viewers are treated to a highly condensed and revised version of the drama intended to reflect the loss of empire. Viewers encounter the play beginning with Enobarbas' famous description of Cleopatra:

> Cleopatra? I will tell you.
> Age cannot wither her, nor custom stale
> Her infinite variety. Other women cloy
> The appetites they feed: but she makes hungry
> Where most she satisfies… .

The barge she sat in, like a burnish'd throne.
Burn'd on the water: the poop was beaten gold;
Purple the sales, and so perfumed that
The winds were love-sick with them: the oars were silver,
Which to the tune of flutes kept stroke, and made
The water which they beat to follow faster,
As amorous of their strokes. For her own person,
It beggar'd all description: she did lie
In her pavilion —cloth-of-gold of tissue — on each side her
Stood pretty dimpled boys, like smiling Cupids,
With divers-color'd fans; at the helm
A seeming mermaid steers: the silken tackle
Swell with the touches of those flower-soft hands ... [Ivory 99–100].

The opening lines of the play text, Philo's assessment of Marc Antony, are transported in *Shakespeare Wallah* so that they come immediately after the description of the Egyptian queen:

Nay, but this dotage of our general's
O'erflows the measure: those his goodly eyes,
That o'er the files and musters of the war
Have glow'd like plated Mars, now bend, now turn,
The office and devotion of their view
Upon a tawny front: ... Look, where they come:
Take but good note, and you shall see in him
The triple pillar of the world transform'd
Into a strumpet's fool: behold and see [Ivory 100].

Having given viewers descriptive evaluations of Antony and Cleopatra, the film showcases their love for one another. Antony answers Philo's announcement, "News my good lord, from Rome," with "Let Rome in Tiber melt, and the wide arch / Of the ranged empire fall! Here is my space / Kingdoms are clay (for such a pair as we!)" (Ivory 101). From here the film jumps forward to Antony's death scene, and the production concludes with Cleopatra's euology:

Noblest of men, woo'd die?
Hast thou no care of me? Shall I abide
In this dull world, which in thy absence is
No better than a sty? O, see, my women,
The crown o' the earth doth melt. My lord!
O, wither'd is the garland of the war,
The soldier's pole is fall'n: young boys and girls
Are level now with men; the odds is gone,
And there is nothing left remarkable
Beneath the visiting moon [Ivory 101–102].

The film's appropriation of *Antony and Cleopatra* creates a parallel between Shakespeare's tragedy and the contemporary political and cultural conditions within post-colonial India. By aligning India with "tawny" Cleopatra, the film reifies the idea of the feminized, exoticized, and racially dark East. The film's reshuffling of Philo's lines subordinates them to Enobarbas' description of Cleopatra. Through this revision, Antony has been "transform'd / Into strumpet's fool" because of Cleopatra's "infinite variety." Tony and Carla's own foolish obsession with remaining in the Indian "space" after the colonial empire has fallen is refracted through Shakespeare's characters. The film invites the viewer to conclude that "there is nothing left remarkable / Beneath the visiting moon" because of the death of British culture. Furthermore, by concluding the on-screen production with Antony's death, *Shakespeare Wallah* prompts the viewer to connect his passing with the decline of British cultural influence. Like Cleopatra mourning a world without Antony, the maharaja mourns the demise of empire. Re-contextualized within an alternate cultural frame, Shakespeare's texts critique contemporary political conditions and reflect the passing of the British colonial civilization in India.

Moreover, the film's inclusion of a maharaja draws on the deeply embedded political relationships between Indian princes and the imperial government. Historically, the Indian princes were used by the colonizers as strategic bulwarks against the move towards independence. Prem Chowdhry writes in *Colonial India and the Making of Empire Cinema*,

> In imperial politics, the princely states had come to dominate more and more London's strategic thinking about the subcontinent. In the early twentieth century they served as an important break-water not only against armed rebellion ... but also against the menacing political consciousness that threatened a move towards democracy in British-administered India. They were used repeatedly by the British at every stage of political concession as a counterpoint to the growing nationalist demands [200].

A carefully constructed character, the maharaja represents both ancient, bygone India and the appreciative, colonial audience. Visually, he symbolizes the exoticized Indian native. He wears a jeweled turban, the salwar kameez, slippers with curled toes, and a sash around his waist. His palace, though reduced in size by recent events, is nonetheless magnificent with brocade furnishings, servants, and Eastern artifacts. Throughout these scenes, it is clear that the maharaja is intimately knowledgeable about Shakespeare's plays and characters. The maharaja's appreciation for Shakespeare and the Buckinghams' art makes him a member of that pre–1947 audience. For the maharaja, political sovereignty has not meant the abandonment of culture. The maharaja, the film implies, continues to be loyal to the theater and to Shakespeare and has not changed as others have. He is thus made familiar at the same time he is exoticized. A symbol of nostalgia for both the comfortable British past and the traditional Indian elite, the maharaja ignores the rising Indian film culture and all it represents.

As the maharaja represents India's colonial aristocracy, the character of Sanju provides the film's audience with a representative of India's postcolonial elite. Like the maharaja, Sanju belongs to the monied upper class, but he knows little about Shakespeare. Introduced to the film audience as a wealthy playboy, Sanju's primary attraction to the Buckingham actors is their daughter, Lizzie. During one of their early encounters, he recites "'Romeo, Romeo, Wherefore art thou?'" before admitting, "That's all I remember" (Ivory 107). Fascinated by Lizzie and her itinerant and artistic lifestyle, Sanju pursues her, even promising to attend a performance. However, as the dramatic production concludes, it becomes apparent to the viewers that Sanju is absent from the theater. The next scene reveals Sanju watching a Hindi film being shot.

The juxtapositioning of these scenes emphasizes the predominant tropes of theater and cinema as they represent the growing division between British and Indian cultures. The theatrical performance that Sanju skipped is physically marginalized by the film. The entire production takes place offscreen, the viewer seeing only the final curtain call, entering the stage performance at its extreme conclusion, never even learning the show's title. The indoor theater is darkly lit, and the only sounds are whispered dialogue reacting to Sanju's absence and the audience's applause. The next scene takes place outdoors, revealing a young woman singing and dancing exuberantly in a sunny, lush woodland setting. Loud, insistent Hindi film music accompanies the woman's exaggerated, highly stylized gestures and dance steps. As the scene unfolds, it becomes evident that we are watching a rehearsal for a Hindi movie. Camera men, lighting and sound technicians, and production staff closely monitor the actress. The light, sound, and energy of the film shoot contrasts with the dark, sedate quiet of the theatrical curtain call. The energetic Hindi film intrudes on and replaces the somber Shakespearean theater. More particularly, the contrast that *Shakespeare Wallah* constructs between the theater and the cinema is revealed through the presentation of specific parts of the production processes. The theatrical curtain call signals the conclusion of the production and performance process, whereas the film shoot rehearsal signals the beginning. This represents the move away from the cultural legacy of British colonialism to the cultural preferences of Indian modernity. The

Merchant Ivory's *Shakespeare Wallah*: Manjula (Madhur Jaffrey) rehearses her dance moves with an unidentified actor during the Hindi film shoot.

moribund British theater, carrying the cultural mark of colonialism, is symbolically preempted by the energy, sensuality, and sheer volume of the Hindi film.

The two very diverse worlds reflected through these juxtaposed scenes are connected via Sanju, who as the film progresses finds himself attracted to Lizzie as well as to the Hindi film actress, Manjula. Sanju's attraction to Lizzie extends to his developing appreciation for Shakespeare at the expense of Hindi films. He attends a performance of *Hamlet* and is clearly captivated by it. He describes the performance to Manjula as, "What a play! What acting! I wish I could remember the words. Such poetry!" and then asks, "Don't you get tired of your films? Always the same singing, dancing, tears, love?" He describes Lizzie as a "fine artist," igniting Manjula's jealousy (Ivory 117).

Sanju's growing attraction to Lizzie and Shakespeare and his seeming rejection of Manjula and cinema sets up *Shakespeare Wallah's* literal and cultural conflict. Angered over Sanju's change of heart, Manjula strikes against Lizzie.[3] Forcing Lizzie to come into her home, Manjula out–Englishes the English girl by staging an elaborate tea service where the film star flaunts her wealth and popularity, saying, "We have so much in common. Two artists. You have been in films also? Oh, then never mind. Stage must also be very interesting" (Ivory 127). The deepening romance between Sanju and Lizzie also worries Carla, who fears that her daughter might wed the Indian boy. She asks, "You wouldn't marry him, would you Lizzie?" Lizzie's response, "If he asked me, you don't know what I wouldn't do" (Ivory 134), fuels Carla's anxieties and steels her resolve to send her daughter "home" to an England she has never seen.

Although the romance between Sanju and Lizzie disrupts the racial and cultural codes that define conventional relationships, their union also deepens the cultural divisions brought to the foreground by the film's metaphors of theater and cinema. As the Buckinghams struggle ever harder to find audiences, the ultimate rejection of theater art comes to a head because of Manjula and her reputation as Hindi film star. In this narrative sequence, *Shakespeare Wallah* appropriates Shakespeare's own play-within-a-play technique to put theater and cinema into direct conflict. As the troupe performs *Othello*, Manjula stages her own production in the seats, deliberately courting the theater audience's attention. She arrives very late with the performance nearing its conclusion and forces the audience to notice her. She enters with an entourage, accompanied by servants and a photographer who snaps flash pictures of her. The audience for *Othello* immediately transfers its attention to her. People ask for her autograph; others leave their seats to get closer to her; the general buzz regarding her presence grows ever louder, finally disrupting the "real" performance on stage. Manjula's play-within-a-play disrupts *Othello*, but more significantly, it simultaneously endorses as it inverts *Othello's* racial and gender codes. Manjula's deliberate "killing" of the production reverses Othello's masculine domination of Desdemona, but it also reifies the image of the dark Other destroying white innocence on the stage.

The viewer enters the Buckinghams' performance during the crucial bedroom scene. We see and hear Tony in blackface recite Othello's lines over the sleeping Desdemona: "It is the cause, it is the cause, my soul —/ Let me not name it to you, you chaste stars! —/ It is the cause... / Yet she must die" (Ivory 136). As Manjula enters the auditorium, the latter half of the final line, "or else she'll betray more men," is inaudible to the film viewer. The fanfare accompanying her late arrival dominates the screen; the production is pushed off the screen visually and marginalized narratologically. Desdemona's death scene unfolds on the stage, and the film's audience continues to hear Shakespeare's words, but Manjula's drama draws our attention. By juxtaposing Othello's language with Manjula's actions, *Shakespeare Wallah* applies Shakespeare's words to a new visual text. We hear Othello say, "If I quench thee thou flaming minister / I can again thy former light restore," but the words now apply to Manjula's literal disruption of the production and metaphorical destruction of the theater (Ivory 136). As Othello believed that killing Desdemona would her "former light restore," so Manjula acts to "quench" the romance between Lizzie and Sanju.

Another technique *Shakespeare Wallah* uses to convey Manjula's disruptive presence during the *Othello* sequence is the split screen. The film divides the screen between both dramas. We see Manjula eating, waving to fans, signing autographs, and talking while we simultaneously watch Othello and Desdemona's final moments together. However, although visually Manjula's play-within-a-play and *Othello* share screen space, our attention is manipulated by camera angles, lighting, and perspective so that we remain focused on Manjula's actions. The shot subordinates Shakespeare's play to Manjula's. *Othello* may be on stage, but Manjula's play is on screen. Othello's murder of Desdemona, the dramatic climax of the play, is subsumed and lost under Manjula's preparations to leave the theater. Othello's plaintive cry, "Not dead? Not yet quite dead?" (Ivory 139) which in the play text refers to Desdemona's last gasps for life, here apply to the production's final moments. Although spoken by Othello, the words could accurately reflect Manjula's own thoughts: despite her efforts to destroy the production, the Buckinghams have continued with their performance. They, like Desdemona and Shakespeare, are "not yet quite dead" either.

Abandoning the split screen technique and again pushing *Othello* off screen, the film directs the audience's gaze to Manjula, who prompts Sanju to leave, saying "Let's go," and as Manjula exits the auditorium, the camera follows her out. Visually, the film leads its audience out of the auditorium and narratologically, Manjula's play-within-a-play takes *Othello's* audience away as well. As the theatergoers surround Manjula, we hear

Othello's line, "Where art thou now?" In the play text, this line refers to Emilia entering Desdemona's bedroom after the murder, but in the film, the line has a more metaphoric meaning. Re-contextualized within the film's alternate frame, "Where art thou now?" translates into a nostalgic longing for the loyal theater audiences of the past. As Manjula literally draws *Othello's* audience around herself, the film's audience is treated to one final line from the play. The production, which has already been pushed off screen, is now barely audible; only broken phrases of dialogue filter through the buzz generated by Manjula's actions. We hear the words "sweet revenge grows harsh." In the play text the line conveys Othello's sorrowful reaction to the news of Roderigo's death at the hands of Cassio. In Shakespeare's drama, Roderigo was to emerge the victor after slaying the adulterous Cassio; Cassio's death was Othello's goal. The line here applies to Manjula's defeat. Although she successfully disrupted the production, her actions ultimately result in pushing Sanju further away from herself and closer to Lizzie. Like Othello, Manjula's success is only partial; she fails to achieve her desired goal of attracting Sanju. He refuses to leave with her, shutting the theater's doors in her face. Embarrassed and ashamed of her disruptive behavior, Sanju later apologizes to a wearied but resigned Tony. Their exchange recalls the conflict between theater and cinema. Tony tells Sanju to think of the situation as "a victory for the motion pictures over theater" (Ivory 139).

As the film continues, the direct conflicts between theater and cinema are pushed into the background, and the relationship between Sanju and Lizzie begins to dominate the narrative, calling our attention to the uneasy balance between traditional culture and post-colonial modernity. Sanju's anger towards Manjula drives him closer to Lizzie, and the couple share their first night together. Their romance solidifies, further worrying the already anxious Carla, and becomes much more public. We see Sanju and Lizzie kissing in a dressing room, in an auditorium, during a rehearsal. In each of these scenes, they are interrupted as Lizzie's obligations to the theater intrude upon them. In one scene, Carla comes to fetch Lizzie for a practice session, and in another, a rehearsal is already in progress behind them. Bits and pieces of dialogue can be heard, irritating Sanju, who leaves, telling Lizzie, "I'm not used to living in public" (Ivory 146).

As Sanju's difficulties coping with the highly public aspects of Lizzie's life grow, his appreciation for Shakespeare and theater are challenged. Here again, the film appropriates Shakespeare's own text to reflect the emerging cultural conflict between the couple. *Shakespeare Wallah* complicates the romance between Sanju and Lizzie through a production of *Romeo and Juliet*. Like Shakespeare's "star crossed lovers," Sanju and Lizzie's romance

Shakespeare Wallah: Sanju (Shashi Kapoor) and Lizzie (Felicity Kendal) share a lighthearted and public moment in the Buckingham's dressing room.

must end, but *Shakespeare Wallah* does not draw simple analogies between the two sets of lovers. *Shakespeare Wallah's* re-contextualizing of *Romeo and Juliet* within the film's larger narrative allows the audience to explore the means by which the individual relationships reflect the contradictory nature of post-colonialism. The film audience enters the performance on Friar Lawrence's line, "So smile the heavens upon this holy act / Love moderately," and the camera's pan of the theater audience reveals Sanju in the seats (Ivory 147). On the Friar's cue, "Here comes the lady," Lizzie as Juliet comes on stage and on screen (Ivory 148). Upon seeing her, audience members whistle and holler catcalls, angering Sanju who reacts physically against those nearest him. Although *Romeo and Juliet* continues on stage, the audience becomes engulfed in a fight. The last lines audible over the violence are Juliet's: "My true love has grown to such excess." The Friar responds, "Come, come with me" (Ivory 148, 149). Although visually the performance continues, the dialogue can no longer be heard, leaving unspoken the Friar's lines, "You shall not stay alone / Till holy church incorporate two in one" (Ivory 149). Like the troupe's production of *Othello*, *Romeo and Juliet* ends prematurely due to the spectators' behavior.

As in earlier instances, *Shakespeare Wallah* uses the Bard's dialogue to highlight the film's narrative. *Shakespeare Wallah* appropriates act two, scene six of the play; it is in this scene that Romeo and Juliet meet in the Friar's cell to be married. In the film, the stage marriage is interrupted by the audience. In the play as written, the lovers are symbolically and visually reunited in death at the play's conclusion; however, Sanju and Lizzie are separated by the film's end. The film's final scenes, in which Sanju and Lizzie are driven apart, can be read as an alternate ending for *Romeo and Juliet*. Following the premature end of the performance, Sanju lashes out at Lizzie, saying, "I don't care. I'll do it again. Do you hear me? Again and again! Standing there like that — letting all those goondas whistle at you…. I can't stand the way you live" (Ivory 149).[4] Lizzie responds with, "You don't know anything about it. I couldn't ever give it up" (Ivory 150). Then, hugging Sanju, she retracts her statement: "But for you I would give up anything. You only have to ask" (Ivory 151). As they continue holding one another, Sanju remains silent, a silence that speaks to his decision. As they separate, Sanju says, "I'll see you tomorrow" (Ivory 151), but the subsequent scenes show Lizzie on a ship's deck ready to sail for England. Sanju reappears only in her daydreams. As Lizzie waves good-bye to her parents and to India, the scene dissolves to show her sitting at a piano playing scales with Sanju, who plays the Indian musical notes of Se-Re-Ga-Ma to Lizzie's English Do-Re-Mi. Only in Lizzie's dreams do India and England unite. Unlike Romeo and Juliet, Sanju and Lizzie do not "with their death bury their parents' strife."

The "glooming peace" achieved by the film's conclusion reveals the cultural divisions that exist between Sanju and Lizzie / India and England. Sanju cannot accept Lizzie's artistic, and to his eyes, English, way of life. Moreover, even though Lizzie was born and has lived her entire life in India, her future lies at "home" in England. Although the ideas of home and belonging to a place are alluded to throughout the narrative, the characters are all displaced individuals, searching for their cultural positions. The actors' creation of fictional worlds and their itinerant lifestyle underscores their rootlessness. The Indian characters are Westernized and modern but also deeply traditional. Thematically and visually evocative, *Shakespeare Wallah* reflects the demise of "old India" even as it reveals the conflicted culture of the new.

Works Cited

Chowdhry, Prem. *Colonial India and the Making of Empire: Cinema Image, Ideology and Identity*. New York: Manchester University Press, 2000.

Ivory, James. *Savages / Shakespeare Wallah*. New York: Grove Press, Inc., 1973.

Jackson, Russell. "Introduction: Shakespeare, Films, and the Marketplace." In *The Cambridge Companion to Shakespeare on Film*. Edited by Russell Jackson. Cambridge: Cambridge University Press, 2000. 1–12.

Kendal, Geoffrey. *The Shakespeare Wallah: The Autobiography of Geoffrey Kendal*. London: Sidgwick and Jackson, 1986.

Long, Robert Emmet. *The Films of Merchant-Ivory*. New York: Harry N. Abrams, Inc. Publishers, 1991.

Rothwell, Kenneth S. *A History of Shakespeare on Screen: A Century of Film and Television.* Cambridge: Cambridge University Press, 1999.

Wayne, Valerie. "*Shakespeare Wallah* and Colonial Specularity." *Shakespeare, the Movie: Popularizing the Plays on Film, TV, and Video.* Edited by Lynda Boose and Richard Burt. New York: Routledge, 1997. 95–102.

Notes

1. For more details on the Shakespeareana family circle, especially information regarding Shashi Kapoor and Jennifer Kendal's marriage, please see Geoffrey Kendal's *Shakespeare Wallah.*

2. All quotations are from James Ivory's published screenplay, *Savages/Shakespeare Wallah.* There are minor discrepancies between the screenplay and the film.

3. For a more detailed exploration of the film's construction of gender, please see Valerie Wayne's article, "*Shakespeare Wallah* and Colonial Specularity."

4. Goondas is a Hindi perjorative for lower class, uneducated men.

4

Suture, Shakespeare, and Race: Or, What Is Our Cultural Debt to the Bard?

Ayanna Thompson

> How is it that we know who we are? We might wake up in the night disoriented, and wonder where we are. We may have forgotten where the window or the door or the bathroom is, or who is sleeping beside us. We may think perhaps that we have lived through what we just dreamed of, or we may wonder if we are now still dreaming. But we never wonder who we are. However confused we might be about every other particular of our existence, we always know that it is us—that we are now who we have always been. We never wake up and wonder "who am I?"
> —*Suture*

A type of modern film noir set in the glaring bright light of Phoenix, *Suture,* an independent film written and directed by Scott McGehee and David Siegel, examines the connections between personal identity, societal perceptions, and cultural memory. Two brothers, who have never met, unexpectedly discover each other at their father's funeral. One brother, Vincent Towers, has lived a life of opulence and luxury in Phoenix, Arizona, while the other brother, Clay Arlington, has lived a life of poverty and manual labor in Needles, California. Yet they immediately discover their secret kinship because their "physical similarity is disarming." Vincent mysteriously invites Clay to Phoenix for a weekend visit following the funeral. After dressing Clay in his own clothes and furtively swapping their driver's licenses, Vincent attempts to fake his own death by blowing Clay up in his car. We later learn that Vincent has been the chief murder suspect in his father's death and seeks to evade the law by substituting his

brother's body for his own. Clay, however, survives the blast only to lose
his memory. Everyone assumes that he is Vincent because of his clothes,
car, and photo identification, and they attempt to reconstruct Vincent's
identity and memory for him. Prominently featured within the film are
two doctors—a psychiatrist who hopes to cure "Vincent's" memory loss
and a plastic surgeon who hopes to heal "Vincent's" facial scars. In the end,
Vincent returns to kill Clay, but is instead killed by him. Although this
violent deed helps to restore all of Clay's memories, he nevertheless decides
to live his life as the wealthy and privileged Vincent Towers, forever for-
saking his identity as Clay Arlington.

Suture depicts amnesia as more than the loss of one's memory: it is
also the loss of one's identity socially, politically, and culturally. Although
Suture does not explicitly link itself to the early modern period, Shakespeare's plays provide an interesting perspective on this film because they
are singled out as a litmus test for cultural literacy and cultural memory.
Shakespeare, through Hamlet, is presented as a universal text that everyone should have knowledge of and access to. In this essay, I explore Suture's
bond to Shakespeare (the film's most identifiable signifier of a cultural
memory cue) and the larger notion of the construction of and belief in a
universal cultural debt to the bard.

Complicating these issues in the film is an unexplained veil of color.
While on paper the film's plot reads like a standard double plot, Suture
muddies matters by employing a salt and pepper cast: Vincent is white;
Clay is black; and they look nothing alike. No one within the film notices,

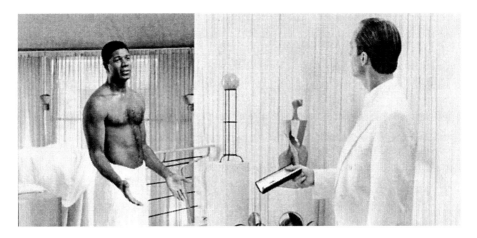

**Dennis Haysbert and Michael Harris play identical brothers in Suture. No one
in the film ever mentions their racial difference.**

or at least no one comments on, the color discrepancy, leaving the audience in the awkward position of experiencing something entirely different from the characters in the film. Because *Suture* visibly highlights the importance of color while it then deconstructs this emphasis through its actions (i.e., the lack of verbal attention to Clay's—or is it simply supposed to be the actor's?—blackness), the film brings something new to the discussion of cultural memory and literary / cultural appropriation. I examine *Suture* through its discussions of race and its references to Shakespeare in order to complicate a simplistic notion of borrowing. At its heart, this paper asks what it means to substitute an open discussion about race relations for a presentation of a universal color-blind world (as represented by Shakespeare's themes and plots). Although Shakespeare does in fact have a great deal to say about the connections between race and cultural memory, the film's selective borrowing from Shakespeare substitutes any of these discussions for a presentation of his "universal" themes. Thus, my examination of *Suture* explores the construction of racial identities and the notion of racially coded cultural memories as a challenge to the simplistic notion of a universal cultural debt to the bard.

The essay begins with a discussion of suture theory as an investigation of substitution and absence, and their effects on cultural memory. From there it analyzes the film directors' persistent representation of racial differences in terms of color rather than culture, a substitution of visible surfaces for invisible cultural memories. Included in the discussion is August Wilson's uncanny call and response to McGehee and Siegel's film, his assessment of color-blind casting that appeared in print the same year as *Suture*'s release. Despite McGehee and Siegel's claims to the contrary, the film does not eschew all cultural cues by examining its debt to psychoanalysis and Shakespeare. While psychoanalysts argue that their theories and methods are universal, the practice's debt to Shakespeare in general and *Hamlet* in particular necessarily raises questions about cultural memories and debts. By using *Othello* to interrogate the complex relationships between race, culture, and memory, however, the essay reveals that suture theory's investment in substitution serves to block discussions of cultural and racial differences.

Because the audience can never be sure whether or not they are supposed to see Clay's blackness (Has *Suture* employed colorblind casting? Is the audience culpable for constantly seeing Clay's blackness? Or is there something wrong with the characters in the film who cannot see color?), the film disrupts the audience's ability to suture.[1]

Although suture theory is often deemed Lacanian, Jacques Lacan never mentioned suturing. Instead, Jacques-Alain Miller introduced the concept into the field of psychoanalysis. Suture theory describes the difficulty of having to fit oneself into society's discourse. In order to participate in society, one must acquire language, but that language limits one's ability to exist, to think, freely; without governed constructions. A doubleness exists in which the subject realizes that there is a gap between his/her individual (and yet inexpressible) view of him/herself and his/her (expressible and yet alienating) pronoun/name. Jean-Pierre Oudart helped appropriate suture theory for film studies, arguing:

> Every filmic field is echoed by an absent field, the place of a character who is put there by the viewer's imaginary, and which we shall call the Absent One. At a certain moment of the reading all the objects of the filmic field combine together to form the signifier of its absence. At this key-moment the image enters the order of the signifier, and the undefined strip of film the realm of the discontinuous, the "discrete." It is essential to understand this, since up to now film-makers believed that, by resorting to cinematic units as discrete as possible, they would find their way back to the rules of linguistic discourse, whereas it is cinema itself, when designating itself as cinematography, which tends to constitute its own *énoncé* in "discrete" units.

Kaja Silverman, a critic who helped solidify suture theory in film studies, goes on to explain that certain film-shot rules are derived "from the imperative that the camera deny its own existence as much as possible, fostering the illusion that what is shown has an autonomous existence, independent of any technological interference, or any coercive gaze." Thus, "Lacanian" suture theory identifies the necessary loss or absence of a private and personal identity in order to function within a communicable society. In film, the camera must help the audience suture over their own absence from the events depicted in order to communicate the plot effectively. It is interesting to note that this "Lacanian" theory itself sutures over the absence of this theoretical discourse in Lacan. Not only the theory, but also the critics expose the necessity of substitution — Miller for Lacan, Oudart for Miller, etc.

Commenting on the title of their film, McGehee and Siegel have discussed their interest in suture theory:

> The name came early on, as a joke. You don't want to make a film that's about theory from that end: it would be very dull. This film's very loosely about suture theory; it's more about identity and identification.... We might have come up with some elaborately structured system where point-of-view shots were reserved for certain situations about suture, but we didn't do anything like that. It's really on a metaphorical level that you can talk about suture in film [quoted in Romney 33].

Interested in the larger issue of identity formation, McGehee and Siegel refer to suture theory because it provides a shorthand metaphor for their project's theme. McGehee and Siegel also declared that their use of a racially mixed cast was not a "casting issue" because it was "integral to the film and the story [they] were trying to tell" (quoted in Grundmann 25). And yet, according to them, the presence of a black man in *Suture* is a metaphor for all identity issues: "We didn't set out to make a film about black experience in America. How we've attempted to control those social metaphors in the film is pretty broad—we've attempted to keep the film more in the parameters of sociology than race, the way the homogeneity of society affects the construction of personal identity" (quoted in Romney 34). McGehee even declared that the film deliberately did not employ references to black history and black culture, stating that "the soundtrack features Johnny Cash, not James Brown" (quoted in Grundmann 26). As Roy Grundmann has noted, the film depicts "a black man, not an African-American" (24).

Despite the disavowal that their film investigates the differences between surface (blackness) and culture (African-Americanness), *Suture* raises many questions about the nature of and relationship between color, culture, and memory. While McGehee and Siegel argue that color can be separated from cultural memory, it is important to question what this substitution entails. In addition, it is important to question whether they portray all cultural memories as equally valuable and/or problematic.

The same year that *Suture* appeared nationally, August Wilson created a firestorm with his views on the politics of race and culture in contemporary film and theater. In "I Want a Black Director," Wilson publicized his belief that race and culture are inseparable entities. Discussing the fact that *Fences*, his 1986 play which won the Pulitzer Prize for drama, had been optioned by Paramount Pictures, Wilson unapologetically declared that he would only agree to give his support if a black director made the film. Wilson concluded his article with the argument that he desired a director "who shares the same cultural sensibilities of the characters. The last time I looked, all those directors were black" (204). Two years later, in "The Ground on Which I Stand," Wilson poured gasoline on this fire by declaring that

> colorblind casting is an aberrant idea that has never had any validity
> other than as a tool of the Cultural Imperialists who view their American
> Culture, rooted in the icons of European Culture, as beyond reproach in
> its perfection. It is inconceivable to them that life could be lived and even
> enriched without knowing Shakespeare or Mozart.... To mount an all
> black production of *Death of a Salesman* or any other play conceived for

white actors as an investigation of the human condition through the specific white culture is to deny us our humanity, our own history, and the need to make our investigations from the cultural ground on which we stand as black Americans [498–99].

For Wilson, black skins are never just a surface but instead represent a cultural history that is far too often denied.[2]

Although Wilson never comments on *Suture* (he does not watch television or movies and rarely goes to the theater except to see his own plays), one can easily recognize the application of his words to McGehee and Siegel's creation: "America often expects blacks to be carbon copies of whites and white culture" (quoted in DiGaetani 280). Wilson has argued that there is a desire in white America to ignore and even eradicate the differences between races and cultures, and it is possible to read McGehee and Siegel's film as both employing and exposing this desire. In *Suture*, is Clay supposed to be a "carbon copy" of his white brother? Is it desirable to ignore their racial differences? Because *Suture*'s characters persistently remain silent on the issues of race, it is difficult to determine when the desire to eradicate racial differences is exposed and when it is merely employed. In one of the film's more disturbing scenes, Renee Descartes, the plastic surgeon, comments on Clay's "elegant" (imagistically malleable) features:

> You have what they call a Greco-Roman or American nose, sleek with a small prominence at the bridge and point. Physiognomists were sure that people with Greco-Roman noses were inclined towards music and literature and the arts. Definitely not deviant behavior like killing people…. And your fine, straight hair — almost always a sign of good mental temperament, not to mention digestion. And your mouth — thin, smooth lips, slightly open. Lips that are a sign of an affectionate, kind-hearted, and generous person.

Dr. Descartes pulls the sutures from Clay's black face and strokes his curly hair, all the while creating him anew in her own image — white, slender nosed, thin lipped, and straight haired. Far from promoting the philosophy her namesake declared 350 years earlier — "I think, therefore, I am" — Renee echoes something closer to Genesis:, "I declare, therefore, you are." As one critic has noted, "Renee sutures over the difference between her desired vision of Clay and what we, the audience, can see" (Burns 74). *Suture*'s ambivalence about the connections or disconnects between color and culture makes reading this scene difficult. It is possible to understand these events as the exposure of white society's attempt to ignore racial differences (and thus to see society narcissistically).

Dr. Renee Descartes (Mel Harris) sutures together Clay's wounds while suturing over the differences between her desire and reality.

And yet, *Suture* resists taking this notion in a cultural direction — that is, as a constructed category made up of many historical factors, beliefs, and discourses, not just a visual expression of difference. Insisting on the primacy of the visual over the cultural, *Suture* makes race an issue of color only. Although the audience may expect and even desire Clay to acknowledge his racial difference when he finally remembers his past (as Clay Arlington and not Vincent Towers), he actually envisions himself and his past history in the white working class town of Needles, California. He remembers sleeping next to a white woman and driving past little white children playing in the road. Just when the audience is confident that color, culture, and consciousness cannot be separated successfully and that cultural differences will explode the lacuna about race in the filmic world, culture is exchanged for something else, like economics or aesthetics.[3] As Clay slowly reconstructs his own history, the attribute of his past that troubles him most is the poverty and ugliness of his town and his life, not the blackness of his skin. "Dirt. Junk. Just run down. It seems I have this fantasy life of being poor," he remarks to his psychiatrist before realizing that his dreams of Needles are memories and not fantasies. Maintaining its silence about Clay's racial difference from the blindingly white inhabitants of Vincent's social network in Phoenix, *Suture* constantly pulls a bait and switch, by substituting a poor (and white) background for one informed by black culture.

The notion of culture and cultural memory is not completely absent in the film, however. It is only absent for the lone black character. Culture and cultural memory are explored for the white characters. As one critic has pointed out, the film explodes "the Hollywood cinematic tradition of presenting whiteness as an 'invisible'.... [It] presents a critical reading of whiteness as a dominant social and cultural construction" (Giroux 65, 67). We see whiteness and markers of white, European culture throughout the film, which includes snatches of Wagner, Brahms, Auden, Freud, and Shakespeare floating.

Dr. Max Shinoda, the film's parody of a psychoanalyst, whose office is framed by two giant paintings of Rorschach blots, seems most attuned to the importance of cultural memory. Although McGehee and Siegel repeatedly declared in interviews that Shinoda embodies the shortcomings of psychoanalysis, the problem of sacrificing the exterior for exclusive focus on the interior, there is an ambivalence in the film about the value of cultural memory. Dr. Shinoda, for example, is the only character in the film who employs cultural markers to help spark "Vincent's" memory. Weaving quotations from the great books into his discussions with Clay, Shinoda implicitly trusts that these works have something valuable to say about "Vincent's" condition: "Learn from your dreams what you lack." "Dreams appear like a coded puzzle." "To sleep — [perchance] to dream." "Nothing is insignificant." "[That's] for remembrance."

While Shinoda's pedantic nature is grating and grossly inappropriate at times, his method is not all madness. Favoring both Freud and Shakespeare, and in particular *The Interpretation of Dreams* and *Hamlet,* the psychoanalyst cites passages that have the most cultural significance for him. And it is no accident that these texts do since Freud, as the father of psychoanalysis, revered Shakespeare above all others. Analyzing the modern fascination with debunking Shakespeare's identity as the genius dramatist of the Renaissance, Marjorie Garber has argued that Freud was thinking about *Hamlet,* a play about remembrance, when he penned *The Interpretation of Dreams.* "While Freud thus confers upon Oedipus a primacy he denies to Hamlet," Garber writes, "Hamlet remains a half-hidden center of preoccupation throughout Freud's work.... [The] writings of Freud himself seem uncannily to circle back upon the subject — the subjects— of Hamlet" (169). More recently, in *Hamlet in Purgatory,* Stephen Greenblatt examined the play as a commentary on the problems of cultural memory. It is no accident, Greenblatt argues, that Western civilization is obsessed with *Hamlet* because it both addresses and creates our cultural memory.

These texts, however, do not spark any memories for Clay. While McGehee and Siegel suggest that Shinoda's method is flawed for not paying more attention to surface issues (for not seeing Clay's blackness), the film does leave room for the idea that the flaw resides not in the method itself but in the texts employed. Although we cannot expect a Freudian to forgo favoring Freud or Shakespeare, perhaps the good doctor could have employed *Othello*'s discussion of cultural memory instead *Hamlet*'s, thereby acknowledging the possible schism between surfaces and interiors.

Although *Hamlet* beautifully and painstakingly presents the problems facing memory, mourning, and action, *Othello* presents more clearly the problems facing the individual's internalization of society's prejudices. In Venice, Shakespeare creates a town obsessed with racial, cultural, and religious differences, a town afraid of "turning Turk" through the advances of the Ottoman Empire. Othello is employed by the Venetians to fend off the Turkish advances on Cyprus and Rhodes. Iago manipulates Venice's conflation of racial and religious differences by initiating a racist discourse in which the phrases "thick lips," "black ram," "lascivious Moor," "sooty bosom," "pagans," "erring Barbarian," and "black Othello" are bandied about.

But as critics have pointed out, Othello seems to have internalized the fears of difference, miscegenation, and cultural contamination.[4] The "story of [his] life" (I.iii.128), which won Desdemona's attention and affection, is a compilation of fantastical travel tales crafted by various European explorers.

> And portance in my traveler's history,
> Wherein of antres vast and deserts idle,
> Rough quarries, rocks, and hills whose heads touch heaven,
> It was my hint to speak — such was my process —
> And of the cannibals that each other eat,
> The Anthropophagi, and men whose heads
> Do grow beneath their shoulders. These things to hear
> Would Desdemona seriously incline [I.iii.138–145].

Iago, of course, recognizes Othello's internalization of Venice's racism and capitalizes on this to spark Othello's jealousy. He plans to turn Desdemona's "virtue to pitch" (II.iii.334) by making Othello question her unwillingness to marry one "Of her own clime, complexion, and degree" (III.iii.235). After taking Iago's bait, Othello more clearly verbalizes his internalization of the society's intolerance, questioning whether his blackness is the cause for Desdemona's purported adultery ("Haply, for I am black" [III.iii.267]) and blaming himself for her affairs ("I am to blame" [III.iii.286]). And in the end when he commits suicide, Othello most clearly verbalizes and enacts his understanding and acceptance of intolerance:

> And say besides, that in Aleppo once,
> Where a malignant and a turbaned Turk
> Beat a Venetian and traduced the state,
> I took by th' throat the circumcised dog,
> And smote him, thus. [*He stabs himself*] [V.ii.361–365].

Enacting both roles— the Turk and the defender of the Christian state — Othello eradicates that which Venice could not fully integrate in its society, the Moor of Venice.

    Othello, however, is not a play that blindly promotes racial essentialism. While Iago successfully highlights the perceived differences between racial surfaces (as a sign of essential distinctions), he simultaneously deconstructs them by becoming the "demi-devil" of the tale (V.ii.307). As critics like Anthony Barthelemy have shown, the devil in medieval morality and mystery plays was often depicted in blackface. Although it is not clear that these blackened figures were specifically racialized, the importance of their color was emphasized both in action and verbally. Emilia borrows from this older theatrical tradition by referring to Othello as a "blacker devil" when she discovers Desdemona's body (V.ii.140). But it is Iago who is most often referred to as a devil in the play. Demonstrating his ability to manipulate the slippage between the use of *black* symbolically and literally, Iago proclaims himself a devil early on:

> When devils will the blackest sins put on,
> They do suggest at first with heavenly shows
> As I do now [II.iii.325-327].

By the end of the play, Othello acknowledges his former inability to distinguish between the symbolic and the literal as he "look[s] down towards [Iago's] feet" for Satan's cloven hoof and realizes "that's a fable" (V.ii.292).

    Othello further deconstructs the essentialist belief that surfaces reveal interiors through the use of the word "slave" for Iago (V.ii.298,341). In an era when slavery increasingly became tied to the burgeoning business of transporting West Africans to the New World colonies, Africans and blacks were more readily identified as slaves than any other group. Far from merely identifying a status of bondage, "slave" began to connote a racial designation as well. By 1680, in fact, this point was made explicit by the evangelist Morgan Godwyn: "These two words, *Negro* and *Slave*, being by custom grown Homogeneous and Convertible; even as *Negro* and *Christian, Englishman* and *Heathen*, are by the like corrupt Custom and Partiality made Opposites." By associating Iago with the devil and referring to him as a "slave," however, *Othello* deconstructs the importance of surfaces. This Venetian, who understands and manipulates the pitfalls of internalizing society's prejudices, replaces the Moor as the devil and slave in this tale. In other words, although Iago hopes to capitalize on the belief that surfaces reveal essential differences, his mere presence undermines this project.

As critics have noted, *Othello* is a play obsessed with the notion and nature of proof. How does one know if one's wife is having an affair? How can one differentiate between a liar and an honest man? How can one discern a devil in one's midst? Stanley Cavell has suggested that *Othello* anticipates and promotes a theory of skepticism. "My intuition," Cavell writes, "is that the advent of skepticism as manifested in Descartes' *Meditations* is already in full existence in Shakespeare, from the time of the great tragedies in the first years of the seventeenth century, in the generation preceding that of Descartes" (3). *Suture* is also interested in the nature of proof and reveals an anxiety about an individual's internalization of society's views, but the directors never make the connection with *Othello's* skepticism. We can be thankful that Renee Descartes, the plastic surgeon who repair's "Vincent's" face, does not fulminate on the nature of being and deception (i.e., she does not verbalize and make literal the connections with her namesake), but the film does ask the audience to question identity.

Suture asks its audience to question identity through the lens of certain cultural models that do not account for cultural or racial differences: Descartes, *Hamlet*, Freud, Lacan, and others. Because McGehee and Siegel favor color over culture ("sociology [over] race"), *Suture* silences any discussions about the possible connections and disconnects between them. It is almost as if McGehee and Siegel willfully substitute certain cultural texts, which explicitly do not ask or answer questions about the connections between identity and race, ethnicity, and/or culture, for texts that would question these relationships. Despite the fact that the black Clay replaces the white Vincent, *Hamlet* replaces *Othello*; Tom Jones replaces James Brown; and even more disturbingly, Lacan replaces DuBois.

Lacan's suture theory describes the difficulty of having to fit oneself into society's discourse and the realization that there is a gap between the individual's unique view of him/herself and his/her expressible pronoun/name. While Lacanian suture theory treats this double consciousness as universal, several decades earlier W.E.B. DuBois expressed a similar theory that was unique to the "Negro." Not focusing exclusively on the role language plays in identity formation, DuBois nevertheless wrote extensively about double consciousness. In *The Souls of Black Folk* (1903), DuBois declared:

> the Negro is a sort of seventh son, born with a veil, and gifted with second-sight in this American world, — a world which yields him no true self-consciousness, but only lets him see himself through the revelation of the other world. It is a peculiar sensation, this double-consciousness, this sense of always looking at one's self through the eyes of others, of measuring one's soul by the tape of a world that looks on in amused contempt and pity. One ever feels his twoness, — an American, a Negro; two souls, two thoughts, two unreconciled strivings; two warring ideals in one dark body, whose dogged strength alone keeps it from being torn asunder [45].

Like Shakespeare's depiction of Othello as a man plagued by his internalization of Venice's dividing discourses (and the only man in the play plagued by this problem), DuBois identified the split between one's view of oneself and one's view of society's view of oneself as unique to the "Negro."

It is interesting to note that Clay Arlington's situation in *Suture* is closer to DuBois than Lacan. As McGehee and Siegel have declared, *Suture* is "more about identity and identification," and it is only "on a metaphorical level that you can talk about suture in the film" (quoted in Romney 33). But the double consciousness that DuBois describes exists on more than a metaphorical level in the film. After Clay shoots Vincent in the face, ensuring that his brother cannot be identified as the true Vincent Towers, Clay's memory is fully restored. But he explains to Dr. Shinoda that he will not return to living as the poor, working class Clay Arlington because the world still sees him as "Vincent."

> I am Vincent Towers.... Who was hounded by the police? Who was dragged through a line-up.... When I look in the mirror, I see Vincent Towers. When I go to the club, people call me Vincent Towers. Renee's in love with Vincent Towers.... There's a dead body that cannot be identified, and in a most real way it is not the body of Vincent Towers. I am Vincent Towers.

The world's treatment of Clay as "Vincent" becomes more important than the memories that have been restored to him. Society's projection of Vincent's identity onto Clay has been fully internalized by "Vincent"; despite the fact that Dr. Shinoda repeatedly calls him Clay, "Vincent" can only respond, "I am Vincent Towers." Clay's adoption of Vincent's identity enacts DuBois's theory perfectly: he has "no true self consciousness" and only sees himself "through the eyes of others."

Of course, the fascinating twist in *Suture* is the fact that the society's projection of Vincent onto Clay actually affords him wealth, power, acceptance, and love, the exact opposite of the "contempt and pity" that DuBois identified as white America's projection onto blacks. But of course, the real twist occurs for the audience members who are never sure they can trust what they have seen. The film does not make it clear (since no one in the film remarks on the racial differences between Clay and the white society that surrounds him) whether we should be able to ignore Clay's blackness (true color-blind casting) or whether there is something wrong with the society depicted (they are too blind to surfaces). And because McGehee and Siegel strive to employ a black man as a metaphor for the construction of identity, surfaces are emphasized above all else.

And yet there are moments in the movie when Clay's/"Vincent's" blackness exists as more than a metaphor, more than a deniable surface. There are moments in the film where his language exposes the cultural and social memories connected with blackness: a true double consciousness. Because Vincent is the prime suspect in his father's murder, the police are following "Vincent" closely after the accident. Aware that the police watch him constantly, "Vincent" tells Renee: "All the police want to do is put a noose around my neck." And the "policeman's not there for my protection. He's there to hunt me, to hound me." As one critic has pointed out, "Some viewers may also realize that the plot they've just watched has some unsettling parallels to one of the more recent American social traumas" the Rodney King video" (Grundmann 24). The notion of being hounded and hunted to be fitted for a noose has undeniable racial and cultural connotations, demonstrating that race is more than a surface color. A social and cultural history accompanies blackness in America, a history of violence and brutal oppression that was fresh in Americans' minds after watching the riots in Los Angeles. Despite the fact that McGehee and Siegel sought to repress all cultural connections between color and race, Clay's language reveals the full extent of his double consciousness as an African-American (and not just a black man).

Suture ends with "Vincent" marrying Renee. A photo essay of their travels together is projected on the screen while Dr. Shinoda's voice intones a harsh criticism of Clay's attempted internalization of Vincent's identity.

> He is not Vincent Towers; he is Clay Arlington. He may dress in Vincent's fine clothes, drive Vincent's expensive car, play golf at Vincent's country club, or use Vincent's box at the opera. But this will not make him Vincent Towers. He can never be Vincent Towers, simply because he

is not. Nothing can change this, not the material comforts his life may afford him, nor the love Renee may provide. And if by some chance over the cries of his true ego, he is able to achieve happiness, it will be false, empty. For he has buried the wrong life, the wrong past, buried his soul. He has lost all that makes life worth living. Of this we can be completely certain.

Suture, of course, has made the audience doubt everything that they have seen; "completely certain" is not a phrase that means much by the end of the film.

Suture seeks to substitute a black man for a white one in a fictional world that has no language to describe race or racial difference. Although the filmic world created in *Suture* sees and treats Clay and Vincent as uncanny doubles, the movie allows its audience to question the very notions of substitution, commensurability, and equality through its disruption of the audience's ability to suture. The film's own use of substitution, however, creates an even graver sense of the uncanny. Is it fair to substitute black for white, color for culture, memory for consciousness, metaphor for theory, *Hamlet* for *Othello*, and universality for cultural specificity? McGehee and Siegel attempt to employ Shakespeare as shorthand for the universal experience they want to depict, but in the end, perhaps *Suture* resembles Shakespeare's *Measure for Measure*, which also seems obsessed with the problems of substitution and commensurability, more than anything else: a problem play with no clear resolution. Claiming that a text produces indeterminate responses is a well-worn commonplace in literary criticism today — yet here we have a profound indeterminacy that gets to the core of America's troubled relationship with race. The film's indeterminacy (between treating race as merely a surface or visual matter versus treating it as a cultural matter), however, merely reproduces this problem. In order to move the discussions about race in America forward, we need to do more than present ambivalence. Suture theory and the borrowings from *Hamlet* provided too convenient a way to prize color over culture and consciousness in McGehee and Siegel's cinematic debut. It is interesting to note that their next film (*The Deep End*) landed them in more comfortable territory: the all white and privileged town of Tahoe, in which color and culture could be collapsed comfortably without discussion. It is also interesting to note that McGehee and Siegel no longer needed to borrow from Shakespeare in order to represent the universal in *The Deep End*— the film's all white cast was enough to depict this in their minds. Appropriating Shakespeare to represent the universal, however, necessarily raises the question of just who is included in "our" cultural debt to the bard.

Works Cited

Barthelemy, Anthony. *Black Face, Maligned Race: The Representation of Blacks in English Drama from Shakespeare to Southerne*. Baton Rouge: Louisiana State University Press, 1987.

Brustein, Robert. "Subsidized Separatism." *American Theatre* 13 (1996): 26–27, 100–107.

Burns, Christy. "Suturing over Racial Difference: Problems for a Colorblind Approach in a Visual Culture." *Discourse* 22 (2000): 70–91.

Cavell, Stanley. *Disowning Knowledge*. Cambridge: Cambridge University Press, 1987.

The Deep End. Dir. Scott McGehee and David Siegel. Fox Searchlight, 2001.

DiGaetani, John. "August Wilson." In *A Search for a Postmodern Theater: Interviews with Contemporary Playwrights*. New York: Greenwood Press, 1991. 275–284.

Drake, Chris. Review. *Sight and Sound* 5.2 (Feb. 1995): 54.

DuBois, W.E.B. *The Souls of Black Folk* (1903). New York: Signet Classics, 1969.

Freud, Sigmund. *The Interpretation of Dreams* (1900). Edited by and translated by James Strachey. New York: Avon Books, 1965.

Garber, Marjorie. *Shakespeare's Ghost Writers: Literature as Uncanny Causality*. New York: Routledge, 1987.

Gates, Henry Louis, Jr. "The Chitlin Circuit." *The New Yorker* 3 February 1997: 44–55.

Giroux, Henry. "White Noise: Toward a Pedagogy of Whiteness." *Race-ing Representation: Voice, History, and Sexuality*. Edited by Kostas and Linda Myrsiades. Lanham: Rowman & Littlefield, 1998. 42–76.

Godwyn, Morgan. *The Negro's and Indians Advocate, suing for their Admission into the Church: or a Persuasive to the Instructing and Baptizing of the Negros and Indians in our Plantations...* London: prtd. for the author by J.D., 1680.

Greenblatt, Stephen. *Hamlet in Purgatory*. Princeton: Princeton University Press, 2001.

_____. *Renaissance Self-Fashioning*. Chicago: University of Chicago Press, 1980.

Grundmann, Roy. "Identity Politics at Face Value: An Interview with Scott McGehee and David Siegel." *Cineaste* 20 (1994): 24–26.

Massachelein, Annaleen. "Double Reading/Reading Double: Psychoanalytic Poetics at Work." *Paradoxa: Studies in World Literary Genres* 3 (1997): 395–406.

Miller, Jacques-Alain. "Suture (elements of the logic of the signifier)." *Screen* 18 (1977): 24–34.

Newman, Karen. "And wash the Ethiop white: Femininity and the Monstrous in *Othello*." In *Shakespeare Reproduced: The Text in History and Ideology*. Edited by Jean Howard and Marion O'Connor. New York: Methuen, 1987. 143–162.

Oudart, Jean-Pierre. "Cinema and Suture." *Screen* 18 (1977): 35–47.

Romney, Jonathan. "How Did We Get Here?" *Sight and Sound* 5.2 (Feb. 1995): 32–34.

Shakespeare, William. *The Tragedy of Hamlet, Prince of Denmark*. In *The Norton Anthology of Shakespeare*. Edited by Stephen Greenblatt. New York: W.W. Norton & Co., 1997.

_____. *The Tragedy of Othello, the Moor of Venice*. In *The Norton Anthology of Shakespeare*. Edited by Stephen Greenblatt. New York: W.W. Norton & Co., 1997.

Silverman, Kaja. "(On Suture)." In *Film Theory and Criticism: Introductory Readings*. Edited by Leo Braudy and Marshall Cohen. New York: Oxford University Press, 1999. 137–147.

Suture. Dir. Scott McGehee and David Siegel. Metro Goldwyn Mayer, 1993.

Wilson, August. "The Ground on Which I Stand." *Callaloo: A Journal of African-American and African Arts and Letters* 20 (1997): 493–503.

_____. "I Want a Black Director." *May All Your Fences Have Gates: Essays on the Drama of August Wilson*. Edited by Alan Nadel. Iowa City: University of Iowa Press, 1994. 200–204.

Notes

1. Several critics have written about this disruption. See especially Massachelein and Drake.

2. The firestorm about colorblind casting was enacted publicly in print and in person between August Wilson and Robert Brustein, the artistic director of the American Repertory Theatre, which often employs color-blind casting techniques. Brustein responded to Wilson's speech in the journal *American Theatre*, which allowed Wilson a rebuttal as well. Wilson and Brustein then met to debate publicly in New York (mediated by Anna Deavere Smith). Henry Louis Gates, Jr. then entered into the debate, writing a fascinating article for *The New Yorker*.

3. Interestingly, Burns herself sutures over the whiteness of Clay's past; she reads Clay's past as culturally black despite the fact that his memories include nothing black. She writes: "Blackness and poverty are merged in Clay's past as that which will be sutured over.... [The] Freudian analysis focuses on the recovery of Clay's personal history, but I am suggesting that the elision of Clay's blackness, within the film, extends that commentary as well to a reflection on the necessity and/or desirability of rediscovering one's cultural roots. Clay is cut off from both personal and cultural history, and Max's inability to see his visual difference (his blackness) allows Clay and those around him to reconstruct his memories (and body) as those of Vincent Towers" (76–77).

4. Despite the fact that they reach radically different conclusions, the following books and articles present the most persuasive arguments about Othello's internalization of Venice's racism: Greenblatt's *Renaissance Self-Fashioning*, Newman's "And wash the Ethiop white: Femininity and the Monstrous in *Othello*," and Cavell's *Disowning Knowledge*.

5

Cinema in the Round: Self-Reflexivity in Tim Blake Nelson's O

Eric C. Brown

With the success and ubiquitous endorsements of Peter Jackson's *The Lord of the Rings* (2001, 2002), symbolic "O's" proliferate in cinema at present. Nearly lost in this fetishization of metallic roundness is Tim Blake Nelson's Shakespearean adaptation *O*, a contemporary retelling of *Othello* set against the backdrop of Carolina high school basketball. As Jackson's adaptation of Tolkien lingers over various visualizations of the One Ring— held up close in dirty hobbit palms, dropping with resonant thuds upon their floors— so too Nelson's remodeling of Shakespeare centers itself around filmic representations of "O," at once suggesting the long vowels of Othello, Iago, Cassio, and Desdemona, and a violent emptiness evident in the film's marketing, where "O's" become wounds and bullet holes. Refashioning *Othello* into the prolific genre of teen Shakespeare films, Nelson joins a trend of such adaptations and borrowings, all set in the salad days of adolescence — *10 Things I Hate About You*, *Get Over It*, and *Never Been Kissed*. Most have tended towards the comic, these three deriving from *Taming of the Shrew*, *A Midsummer Night's Dream*, and *As You Like It* respectively. But while all these films alternately trumpet and mute their Shakespearean echoes, none are as self-conscious about their heritage as Nelson's *O*. The film's near obsession with the visual and aural properties of "O" generates a self-reflexivity that both aligns it with its precursor and, ironically, creates a series of discontinuous moments that sever bonds with Shakespeare's play. The title itself seems to draw on a comparably self-reflexive moment in *Henry V*, when the Chorus asks, "Can this cockpit hold / The vasty fields of France? Or may we cram / Within this wooden

O the very casques / That did affright the air at Agincourt?" (Prologue, 11–14). This "wooden O" of the Globe theater, which is also the globe, has become an even more encompassing trope in Nelson's work, where "O" suggests a self-contained drama, the world at large, and the circulating interplay between these spheres.

Adapting *Othello* as a high-school tragedy was both impelled and impeded by Columbine and other school shootings, all of which were redefining the notion of "high-school tragedy" at the turn of the twenty-first century. The film's 1999 release date was moved back several times despite Nelson's championing of the film's immediate relevance. Indeed, the director credits violent high school students across the country as influences on this work, noting that his final scenes are "absolutely mirroring" news footage devoted to high-profile school shootings—at least five of which immediately preceded the film. Finally released in 2001 after several years of suspension, *O* uses none of the play's Shakespearean language, distinguishing it from other teen-genre tragic adaptations such as Baz Lurhmann's *Romeo + Juliet* and Michael Almereyda's *Hamlet 2000*.[1] *O* rather acknowledges its debt to Shakespeare in brief asides, as when Hugo, Josh Hartnett's Iago figure, is asked by his teacher whether he can tell his class anything about Shakespeare's work: he responds, "I thought he wrote movies." The film thus constructs a self-reflexive circuit in which high school students are teaching us about tragedy; filmic imitations of these tragedies teach us about Shakespeare; and the film itself claims that Shakespeare is writing the script in the first place. Nor is the circuit a purely fictive concoction: in a video made by the Columbine murderers before the shootings, one quotes from Shakespeare's *Tempest*: "Good wombs have born bad sons" (I.ii.140).[2]

But by involving itself so self-consciously in a cycle of prominent American tragedies, the film also risks self-parody. Odin James, the Othello figure, shares with another athletic O.J. those initials that for many in the 1990s became synonymous with a new American Othello. As Kenneth Rothwell has supposed, it is the surface of *Othello* which "shares in soap opera motifs such as jealousy and misunderstanding" and which has "inspired several mirror-like derivatives, not the least being the real-life O.J. Simpson case" (222). The O.J. Simpson trial provided abundant fodder for Shakespeareans looking for ways to make Othello relevant, and the parallels—a famous black man accused of killing his white wife in a jealous rage, mitigated only by a plaintive suicide note claiming he loved too much, "not wisely but too well" (V.ii.344)—have been extensively explicated.[3] Yet these often superficial markers have by now sagged into cultural cliché, and Odin himself claims this namesake only as he disavows it: at his best, when he is most celebrated in the film, he is simply O — no J, as if that other half, that Elizabethan "I" of "Iago," needs to be truncated for the good "O" to prosper. Similarly, the specter of O.J. Simpson seems raised only for exorcism, a gesture representative of the film's simultaneous enshrinement and desacralization of its contextual moments.[4] For instance, a sequence of white doves at the beginning, and then throughout, makes perhaps an unintentional homage to Columbine and the latinate dove suggested by the school's name. Meanwhile, the background music for this sequence — the subdued strains of Verdi's *Otello*— is gradually displaced by energetic rap music — Kurupt and Roscoe's "We Riddaz." Such techniques are typical of the film's cultural ambivalence; Nelson seems to want the authorization of Shakespeare, but he often establishes O's pointedness by distancing it from all things classically Shakespearean.

Several other initial directorial gestures evince the highly wrought nature of the film, a self-conscious artistry that nearly overruns the picture in the use of "O's" and other circular emblems. Nelson's DVD commentary emphasizes two recurrent motifs: birds and the American flag. The direction scrupulously incorporates these images even when their placement is serendipitous: when Hugo imagines the success of his murder plot, Desi and O are given a closeup against a blue sky, across which flutter a flock of black birds. Nelson remarks, "I can't claim that to have been intentional, but editorially it was intentional … to make sure the birds made it into the sequence." The red, white, and blue, meanwhile, are intended to underscore the nationalism of this *Othello*, "to say that this was an American version of Shakespeare's tragic tale, and that right now in the United States … maybe high school is not only a credible place to tell the story but the most appropriate one, as well." Nelson joins his film with an American culture increasingly self-aware of its own capacity for, and susceptibility to, the very violence Shakespeare once tried to contain in that "wooden O" of the theater. Other colors crucial to Nelson's vision are more informed by the play's thematics: Shakespeare's "green-eyed monster" of jealousy, for instance, gets glossed as the green walls of Hugo's dorm room, which he shares with Roger. O also makes a mock proposal to Desi, placing a green rubber band over her finger to pretend an engagement, even as the constricting green band suggests both O's jealousy and Desi's eventual suffocation. But the reflexivity of this American version of *Othello* is nowhere more explicit than in the iconography of the letter "O" itself.

Shakespeare's title comprises an almost palindromic use of "O," as the letter forms the alpha and omega of the name "Othello." Stephen Greenblatt has observed the "big, open Os that are sounded so hauntingly through the play," and "that vowel in all its expressive power" speckles the entire work, culminating in Othello's "painfully simple line 'O, O, O!'" (54).[5] Nelson, in an effort to make "O" visible and audible, begins his picture with Verdi's *Otello* playing as white doves perch around the circumference of a wooden, O-shaped railing. Hugo offers a brief, somewhat mawkish voiceover set to the *Otello* opera: "All my life, I always wanted to fly. I always wanted to live like a hawk." This, by the way, is only one musical device in the film that self-consciously addresses the subject's past. Nelson points out that the score for the film includes the use of "Elizabethan instruments ... so that even musically this film ... is always referring to its antecedents." (He might have added that the students contributing post-production sound to several scenes, including crowd noise at the basketball games, attended Sir Francis Drake high school in San Anselmo, California.) As noted above, however, this reference to antecedents is always a problematical one for the film: opera gives way to rap even as the cooing doves are supplanted by a close shot of a hawk abruptly bursting the initial scene as the film proper begins.

We then see a close up of Odin James as he sweats in a basketball huddle. Like Lawrence Fishburne in the 1996 film of *Othello* (directed by Oliver Parker), Mekhi Phifer plays the character bald, lending his silhouette a prominent "O" shape. Nelson may have combined his bird and patriotic symbolism to construct Odin as a kind of peremptory bald eagle. The contours of Odin's closeup give way in this scene to shots of the crowd gathered to watch the closing seconds of the game, during which we see many fans holding aloft handmade "O" signs. We also see the team mascot, a live hawk, reiterated in the midcourt design — a red hawk surrounded by two concentric circles. The basketball huddle includes Michael Cassio and Hugo, who happens to be the son of the coach, Duke Goulding, played by Martin Sheen. This character has no direct counterpart in Shakespeare's play, though his name maintains the long vowels, and is intended to provide motivation for Hugo, since Odin has replaced him in his father's affections. Indeed, as O has deposed Hugo, so too Hugo will transfer and multiply his anxieties over his father onto O. In this opening (a kind of microcosm for the film narrative), Coach Goulding designs the final play for either Odin or Michael, while Hugo serves as "decoy." The coach's term for his son continues the bird imagery. Not only is Hugo not yet a hawk, as his voice-over expressed, he is not even a real bird. Instead he is a wooden construct, a "decoy," whose primary purpose is to lure other birds to their death, or in this case, other teams to their defeat. When O puts up the winning shot (and this recurs several times in the film), we get a scan of the scoreboard clock reading "triple zero" as time expires, as if winning and expiring were both synonymous with O. The crowd then surges onto the court; players and spectators alike embrace O while Hugo is left on the outskirts, embraced by no one. This alienation will return at the finale, when after the carnage, Hugo is driven off in a police cruiser, determined that "one of these days, everyone's gonna pay attention to me, because I'm gonna fly too."

Following the game, the scene shifts to a school pep-rally, at which O not only receives the team MVP award, but is given an ovation, a "standing O," by the student body. When Duke Goulding begins, "I am a man of few words," echoing Othello's "Rude am I in my speech" (I.iii.81), Hugo quips, "Except when we're late to practice, right Pop?" His father responds with characteristic insouciance, "I'll pretend I don't know who said that," a moment of theater that suggests he has been both pretending and actualizing that ignorance for some time. On the other hand, with his introduction of Odin, the coach becomes, like Othello, suddenly comfortable with civic discourse: "I'm very proud to say this publicly.... I love him like my own son." Or rather, were he his son, he would not be Hugo. Odin shares the award with Michael Cassio, further infuriating Hugo, who we learn shortly is a four-year "utility" man on the team, capable of improvising any part. He tells Roger, the Roderigo foil, "I rebound, I can shoot, I play guard, forward, power forward ... I'm the MVP of this team." The unwitting pun here, on shooting basketballs and shooting guns, making hoops and bullet holes, is one of several gestures that link games and violence, though the more emphatic connection in the film is between violence and sex.

The sexual dynamics of the letter "O" are pervasive in the film, nearly turning this into a second *Story of O*. In the most expressive scene, Desi and O have arranged to drive to The Willows, a motel named for the play's "Willow song," and with the prosodic suggestion of "Will-O," where the two have planned an evening in which Desi will lose her virginity. Patricia Parker has pointed to Shakespeare's agreement with Renaissance medical texts in his use of the letter "O," and its position too as a cipher, to suggest "the female sexual orifice" (114). She notes that "the 'O' or 'nothing'" was "printed in early Shakespeare texts as a graphically smaller 'o'" and that the female anatomy is described in Helkiah Crooke's *Microcosmographia* (London, 1615) as "like the letter, o, small and wondrous narrow, yet capable of being 'more open' according to 'the woman's appetite'" (114). Parker highlights Desi's very desire at The Willows, where she tells O, as they kiss, "I want you to be able to do anything. I want you to do what you want with me. I want you to have me however you want. I want to give myself to you the way you want me, Odin. Don't hold back." Thus the virginal Desi seeks not only to become "more open," but in transforming her "small o" and especially in seeking the euphemistic "big O" of orgasm, she seeks literally to become one with O.

The pledge of openness returns to haunt her, when O later accuses her, in her own bedroom, not only of infidelity but of being, as Hugo puts it, one of those white girls who are "horny snakes": "If you a virgin like you said you were, how come when we were doin' it you actin' all freaky and stuff, tellin' me I can do whatever I want with you?" The scene captures what Edward Snow sees as broader male anxiety in *Othello*: "The play consistently insinuates that Othello is apt to believe in Desdemona's unfaithfulness with Cassio because a part of him is convinced of the sinfulness of her sexual appetite" (389). Thus Desi, capacious and rapacious, becomes a source of male anxiety constructed in the Willow sequence as a moment of *coitus interruptus* rapidly disintegrates into rape. As O and Desi begin to have sex, Desi abandons the role of submissive incumbent, climbing on top of O, a position that seems more pleasurable for her as she begins to moan "O, O, O," apparently on the path to orgasm. The intonations recall an earlier basketball game in which the crowd produced a rhythmic chant of "O," punctuated by O dunking the ball and winning the game, as the clock once again unwinds to "triple zero." Whether Desi's throaty "O's" remind him of that game, at which he first noticed the intimacy between Michael and Desi, or whether Desi's enjoyment of the sex itself disturbs him, O switches his own position. Reflected in the O-shaped bedroom mirror, Odin sees himself transformed into Michael Cassio lying atop Desi; the vision enrages him, and he brings the lovemaking to a violent conclusion while Desi pleads with him, three times, to stop. His aggression thus overtops her own, and her loss of virginity becomes not an openness, but a closure, effectively isolating the lovers from one another.

O's anxiety is crosscut with Hugo's; when Emily arrives at his room with the handkerchief token, a scarf, and tells him she "has something" for him, he counters, "you have things for lots of guys." Hugo places the scarf over Emily as they have sex, first draping it like a shroud over her face, a clear foreshadowing of the final death scene, and subsequently, forcing the scarf into her mouth. The makeshift gag silences Emily — anticipating his later attempts to "shut her up" before he kills her, to "close up" that other O, the mouth, which Parker sees as recurrent motif in Shakespeare's version: "The sense of closing, or attempting to close, what has been 'opened,' in this linking of the 'o' of a woman's 'secrete' place with the openness of her mouth, gathers force as the tragedy moves to its own close, in the increasingly insistent references to the stopping of woman's mouths: in the desire to keep Bianca from railing in the streets (IV.i.163) and in Iago's command to Emilia" (123). Hugo's use of the scarf, then, is yet another movement geared to closing off vulnerable exposure.

Paralleling the sex sequence is the subsequent slam-dunk contest, which O wins by shattering the glass backboard. Here, Desi's repetitive "O's", as she joins the crowd in chant, are drowned out by the sound of the bouncing basketball, until O smashes the glass and the crowd erupts in consummate delight. However, much like the sex between Desi and O, these frissons shift into something horrific, and O's smashing of the backboard seems to fulfill his rage at the hotel mirror. When a boy comes to retrieve the ball for other contestants, O pushes him aside, throws the ball at the glass, shattering it completely, and hoists the hoop into the air, now to the boos of the disgusted onlookers. The primal "O" raised above his head challenges the crowd: do they worship O the person or O the hoop? And this replicates the love scene between Desi and him: does she love O the person or O the orgasm?

The most self-reflexive moment, however, occurs not in the bedroom or basketball court, but in an English class. The scene begins with a dissolve from another faux-literary scene, what Nelson terms his "*Pelican Brief* sequence," when Hugo gives the scarf to Michael amidst "supreme court building-like columns." The drone of the English teacher (played by Lisa Benavides, the director's wife) fades in with the voice over, "she purposefully uses this maternal imagery to get him into doing this dirty work," and the image dissolves to a classroom in which Hugo and Odin are engaged in a whispered discussion under the cadence of their instructor. The teacher is lecturing, of course, on *Macbeth*, and specifically the manipulations by Lady Macbeth of her husband. She reinforces the lesson with a line of iambic verse on the chalkboard, along with the act and scene under discussion. The teacher's quotation of Lady Macbeth shows the "maternal imagery" that nourishes the murder of Duncan: "I have given suck, and know / How tender 'tis to love the babe that milks me" (I.vii.54–5). As Hugo and Othello discuss the missing silk scarf, the teacher interrupts: "Gentlemen ... Mr. Goulding, Mr. James, would either of you care to name one of Shakespeare's poems for me?" Hugo's response to this, "I thought he wrote movies," is met with amused condescension: "Perhaps you two should pay attention. That way, after you win this nationally televised championship you'll have something more profound to say than — "but her words are cut off before we hear what this profundity might be.

The scene is particularly interesting in its canonization of Shakespeare as a writer not of plays but "poems," an arguable critical stance, but it is not clear how Hugo or Odin might have gleaned this from the lecture. Her query implies a broader scholastic ignorance: not only are these students currently inattentive, they apparently have not read anything by Shakespeare since they cannot even name a title. Perhaps there is a mischievous trickery in the question, too, and they have not read enough to recognize him as a writer of plays; or perhaps the teacher actually expects a work of pure verse: *Venus and Adonis, The Rape of Lucrece,* or, with the rampant avian imagery, *The Phoenix and Turtle.* At any rate, Hugo and O are consumed with their own separate theater — the basketball court, ostensibly, but even more the Shakespearean tragedy they are currently enacting in the film. In this scene more than any other, Nelson's production reveals an awareness that it is the Shakespearean film, rather than his "poems," that is the medium most recognizable to high school students, and that O itself will soon be perpetuating the pedagogical practice of substituting celluloid for text. Still, the teacher's interrogation is a bit bewildering. In this moment, the film, despite its pretensions to literacy, cannot quite convince its audience that the characters are in control of their readings; thus it reinforces the illiteracy of its main character.

With Hugo, Nelson seems conflicted, torn between presenting a condemnable villain and recuperating Iago's perfidy, as well as the high school genre itself. Indeed, this Hugo bears none of the "motiveless malignity" of some other Iagos, and Nelson makes a point of describing Hartnett's character as both physically appealing and intellectual, unlike the characters in other teen genres. We hear Hugo inform his father, "By the way, I'm getting an 'A' in English again," a success belied by his earlier clueless moment. Nelson once again emphasizes his villain's intelligence when he points out the Loeb Classical Library Latin text on Hugo's desk: "This is a smart kid, a sophisticated kid, who does well in school." An earlier scene in which Hugo and Michael discuss the merits of reputation in a biology lab is supposed to convey a similar trait — studiousness— but the scene never quite communicates this idea. Setting Iago before a dissecting pan has some thematic resonance, but as with the scene in the English class, we see Hugo doing anything but studying — rather, he is acting, his entire curriculum becoming one extended drama class. His father is notably oblivious to Hugo's latent talent for the liberal arts, as he apparently is for Hugo in general, and responds dismissively to Hugo's "A" work: "That's great, son.... You know I don't ever have to worry about you.... But Odin is different." Duke's final salvo, "You know, your mother just doesn't understand us," perpetuates a cycle of misunderstanding and admits Duke to the fraternity of anxious males in the film. Beyond this appeal to face and intellect, Hugo is cast by Nelson as something of a Byronic hero, an individual mistreated and repressed by family and society who celebrates his own rebellion and aberrance.

Indeed, Hugo invokes Byron at a crucial moment, saying "So we'll go no more a-roving" as he plots to stamp Michael's fingerprints upon an incriminating glass. Hugo actually paraphrases the line, "we shall go no more a-roving," another quirky suggestion that not only Hugo's, but Nelson's, view of the character as a scholar does not quite add up, but the sentiment is lost entirely on Michael, who, like Hugo's father before, neither acknowledges Hugo's budding literacy nor picks up on the tragic subtext. We should not expect more from Michael, whose lucubrations are limited to sexual liaisons with Brandy (the Bianca figure) in the library. But Byron's poem, composed in Venice, the setting for Shakespeare's play, provides a rich intertextual moment with the film's denouement:

> So we'll go no more a-roving
> So late into the night,
> Though the heart be still as loving,
> And the moon be still as bright.
>
> For the sword outwears its sheath,
> And the soul wears out the breast,
> And the heart must pause to breathe,
> And Love itself have rest.
>
> Though the night was made for loving,
> And the day returns too soon,
> Yet we'll go no more a-roving
> By the light of the moon.

Thus Hugo, with an ironic gesture at fellowship, offering Michael one final drink before their "last game" together, spells the end of their carousing and foreshadows the tragic murders to come. Under a full moon that seems drawn from Byron's Italian night, Hugo and Michael drive off down the dark Carolina road. The full moon, yet another self-reference to "O," works in two ways here. Beyond continuing the mood of Byron's lament, the paleness of the moon clearly sets off the blackness of the O below and works to configure an O that is always above Hugo—like the hawk that soars always "above us"—and that draws him on to lunacy.

The endgame is set up with a discussion between Duke Goulding and another Division I representative, in this case the "head of the Gamecock's athletic department." This school may have been chosen to continue the bird imagery of which Nelson seems so proud and which prompted one critic to ask, "What's with all the hawk metaphors?" (Ansen 67). But we are once again back to *Henry V*, where the "cockpit" of the Globe has been subsumed by the Gamecock athletic director: if the cockpit can contain the vasty fields of Agincourt, can the promises embodied by this figure —

fame, prestige, NCAA basketball—contain the violence of O? (Indeed, the University of South Carolina's student government website describes one section of its sports arena as the "cockpit," and a "bunch of crazed fans sit here during home basketball games.")[6] The athletic director seems determined to sustain the violence: "I saw him in the North Charleston semis, and he just lacerated their defense.... He'd sure look good in that garnet and black." The assessment of O as a "lacerator" provides an uncomfortable subtext, since the A.D.'s words become a voice-over as we see O scaling the ladder to Desi's room. In this sequence, O and his coach have been conflated for the last time: we see that Duke has been living through O as much as Hugo has; he angles for a coaching position with South Carolina, promoting his own "good coaching," while the camera focuses on O climbing to his tragic fall.[7]

The fall, in Nelson's version, is precipitated partly by drugs. Though Nelson is aware that this added substance undermines the "purity" of Othello's jealous rage (at least as he reads Shakespeare), the director nevertheless decides that drugs are hallmarks of modern high school life and, therefore, ought to be included. In an interview included in the DVD edition, Phifer describes O's cocaine use as his "spiraling downwards," a circular effect which Nelson recreates in the film with the spiral staircase and the twisting camera work and which culminates in the scene in which Hugo and O pledge to carry out the murders. Drug use also has a part in Shakespeare's play: Iago growls to Othello, after setting the wheels of jealousy in motion, "Not poppy, nor mandragora, / Nor all the drowsy syrups of the world / Shall ever medicine thee to that sweet sleep / Which thou ow'dst yesterday" (III.iii.330), and in fact O first seeks drugs before the dunk contest because "I just ain't slept in a couple of days, that's all." O's cocaine high during his rampage supplements the tragic fall: when O finally realizes his grievous error, he crashes physically as well as dramatically.

The death of Desi unfolds as O climbs through her window to find her sleeping in a white gown. In Hugo's fantasy of the plot, we never see O killing Desi, only that she lies still on the bed while O phones Hugo, signaling that he can now have Roger kill Cassio. This too, in Hugo's vision, comes off cleanly. Hugo and Michael pull their car over to help a stranded motorist, the feigning Roger, who then shoots Michael through the stomach in revenge for their earlier fight when Roger was stabbed in the abdomen with a broken bottle. The actual murders are less easily accomplished, though Nelson seems to prefer single shots to the stomach as Hugo's signature method. His acts of violence recycle earlier self-inflicted violence, when he is injected through the abdomen with the steroid needle. Cassio, in keeping with Shakespeare's play, is only unconscious and wounded, while Roger reverts to a blubbering child, afraid he will be exposed if Cassio ever regains consciousness. Meanwhile, O strangles Desi with a prolonged grip, forming a circle around her with both hands and thereby mimicking a pose he struck earlier in the film, after sinking a game-winning shot. He reinvests the gesture with a new sense of annihilation, ending Desi's life even as he once capped off basketball contests.

When, at the end, the *Otello* opera returns, the film has come full circle. This tempting rhetorical device, in fact, was actually used in the trailer for the film: a tagline reads menacingly, "everything comes full circle." Although this undoubtedly suggests the cycles of violence and revenge in the play ("what goes around comes around"), the expectation from the appearance of a final, granite "O" is that the energies instantiated by this circular letter motivate the revenge itself. Hugo bookends the narration, once again expressing how "All my life, I always wanted to fly ... I always wanted to live like a hawk," even as his dreams of playing for the Tar Heels have plummeted.

The post-production marketing for this film continues many of the above ideas. The properties of "O," including both self-contained inviolability (a premise undermined in the film's very plot, where physical violation plays prominently) and dilated openness, are intimated by the video cover design. Nelson has carved a niche in the alphabetical inventory of video stores everywhere, since his other major contribution to film recently was a starring role in *O Brother Where Art Thou* (dir. Joel and Ethan Coen, 2000), an adaptation of the *Odyssey* that Nelson was shooting at the same time he was editing *O*. For the cover of *O*, the central, story title is pockmarked with either erosion or bullet holes. This ambivalent design, at once defiant and wounded, insulated and perforated, reproduces the self-reflexivity of the marketing itself. Such recent Shakespeare adaptations as Branagh's *Love's Labour's Lost* (2000), a title which for the general viewer might plausibly escape recognition as Shakespearean, have avoided any mention of Shakespeare in their covers: *Love's Labour's Lost* offers only "sexy and glamorous ... a new spin on the old song and dance" and credits exclusively Branagh's non-Shakespearean parts: *Celebrity* (dir. Woody Allen, 1998) and *Wild, Wild West* (dir. Barry Sonnenfeld, 1999). The marketing seems to have eschewed completely the Shakespearean enthusiast — though given the nearly total lack of enthusiasm for this Branagh adaptation among Shakespeare-on-film critics, the abandonment may be mutual.[8] Has Shakespearean cinema become too unsettling, too insufficient, or too uncomfortable straddling high art and box office poison? In Nelson's film, which wants to remind us of and make us forget Shakespeare, the circulations of play and film, theater and globe, literate and unstudied, are all bound up in a series of invitations and dismissals. *O* captures the play even while perhaps mocking the meat it has fed on, and so finally reproduces the anxieties it has sought to dramatize: it becomes another in a lengthening line of recent adaptations that ask audiences to love Shakespeare wisely, but not too wisely.

Works Cited

Ansen, David. "Final Score: O, What a Pity: The Bard Gets Sent Back to Warm the Bench." *Newsweek* (September 10, 2001): 67.

Burt, Richard. "Shakespeare and the Holocaust: Julie Taymor's *Titus* Is Beautiful, or Shakesploi Meets (the) Camp." *Colby Quarterly* 37.1 (March 2001): 78–106.

Byron, George Gordon, Lord. "So We'll Go No More A-Roving." *Romantic Poetry and Prose*. Edited by Harold Bloom and Lionel Trilling. New York: Oxford University Press, 1973. 314–15.

Fineman, Joel. "The Sound of O in *Othello*: The Real of the Tragedy of Desire." In *Critical Essays on Shakespeare's Othello*. Edited by Anthony Gerard Barthelemy. New York: G.K. Hall, 1994. 104–23.

Greenblatt, Stephen. "Racial Memory and Literary History." *PMLA* 116.1 (January 2001): 48–63.

Hodgdon, Barbara. "Race-ing *Othello*, Re-engendering White-out." *Shakespeare, the Movie: Popularizing the Plays on Film, TV, and Video*. Edited by Lynda E. Boose and Richard Burt. New York: Routledge, 1997. 23–44.

Janofsky, Michael. "Student Killers' Tapes Filled with Rage." *New York Times* 14 Dec., 1999: A10.

Martinek, Jeffrey. "'An Ebullition of Fancy': *Othello*, Orenthal James Simpson, and the Play of the 'Race Card.'" *Studies in the Humanities* 25.1–2 (1998): 66–100.

Nelson, Tim Blake, dir. *O*. Miramax, 2001. DVD ed.

Osborne, Laurie. "Introduction: Screening Shakespeare." *Colby Quarterly* 37.1 (March 2001): 5–14

Parker, Patricia. "*Othello* and *Hamlet*: Dilation, Spying, and the 'Secret Place' of Woman." In *Shakespeare Reread: The Texts in New Contexts*. Edited by Russ McDonald. Ithaca, NY: Cornell University Press, 1994. 105–46.

Rothwell, Kenneth S. *A History of Shakespeare on Screen: A Century of Film and Television*. Cambridge: Cambridge University Press, 1999.

Shakespeare, William. *The Riverside Shakespeare*. Edited by G. Blakemore Evans et al. 2nd ed. Boston: Houghton, 1997.

Snow, Edward. "Sexual Anxiety and the Male Order of Things in *Othello*." *ELR* 10 (1980): 384–412.

Notes

1. Hodgdon insightfully argues how appropriation of Shakespeare's "language" can be especially problematic in adaptations of *Othello* "when that language represents a sign of Anglo-European dominance and has high cultural status. Always already perceived as a transition from a 'master text,' black Othellos' 'rude speech' positions them as imperfect slaves who perform disservice to Shakespeare's canonical word" (35). While Hodgdon discusses the ways in which black and white actors alike have navigated these presuppositions

of "correctness," Nelson's film seems to resist that "high cultural status" by discarding the "canonical word" altogether and permitting the entire cast to speak "rudely" in order to liberate the story of Othello from its formal English constraints.

2. Quoted in Janofsky, who takes the phrase as an attempt by the killers to exculpate their parents.

3. See especially Hodgdon and Martinek.

4. Burt points to a broader "desacralization" of Shakespeare, one dependent on "a larger transformation in Shakespeare's reproduction.... . Most people ... now come to Shakespeare first not through his texts but through some visual representation of them, a film, an advertisement, or a subgenre of fiction such as teen comedies, science fiction, or Harlequin romances" (89). Hugo's witticism on Shakespeare as a writer of movies, then, joins that of "the character Cher in *Clueless*" (dir. Amy Heckerling, 1996) and a number of critics who "use the same cliché that Shakespeare is a screenwriter" (Burt 89).

5. See also Fineman.

6. http://www.sg.sc.edu/abc/c.htm

7. The fictional prep school of Palmetto Grove, where most of the action transpires, is placed near Charleston, South Carolina. Filmed on location at the College of Charleston, the story places Carolina basketball as a central motif: Duke, the University of North Carolina, and the University of South Carolina are all invoked. O has options to play virtually anywhere, as his coach informs one recruiter: "every conference in the country's been after this kid ... the ACC, the Big 12, the Pac Ten, Big Ten." But Hugo apparently has dreams of Chapel Hill. During a scene in which he is injected with steroids, Hugo is exhorted by Dell, the dealer, "When you start playin' for North Carolina don't forget about me." Duke University is incorporated by a banner on Desi's wall. While this support for the Blue Devils may be a nod to the "demon" in "Desdemona," the banner also ironically suggests the basketball coach, Duke Goulding. While this seems an infelicitous conflation, Duke and O do share other parts of the Othello character, though presumably this does not include Desi's affection.

8. See Osborne, for instance, who writes that "Kenneth Branagh's *Love's Labour's Lost* proves the importance of Shakespearean box office duds" partly because it "inadvertently raises the issue of whether Shakespeare's plays might actually be essentially at odds with film traditions and strategies" (11).

6

Sex, Lies, Videotape — and Othello

R.S. White

This paper is part of a larger project to assess the significance of Shakespeare's presence behind film genres (not plots) in the twentieth century and beyond, particularly in films dealing with love. The idea of "genre" understood here is both more and less specific than the usual dramatic or film categories (comedy, tragedy, pastoral; Western, gangster, horror, musical, etc.) and is more like a characteristic narrative action, generating a certain predictable range of feelings. Some terms of literary theory that at least open up the territory are "fabula" and "histoire," or "sujet," all covering the basic shape of a story, recurrent plot structure, standard character types, predictable outcomes, and comparable manipulation of reader or viewer into certain subject positions. When genre is defined in this way, a good case can be made that Shakespeare initiated, or at least embedded in the cultural mix, a repertoire of certain plots and narrative patterns that have come to dominate modern films. Some examples of Shakespeare "inventing" Hollywood subgenres about love would be *Midsummer Night's Dream* and love triangles, *The Tempest* (or *As You like It*) and holiday romance, *The Shrew* and misogynistic, violent courtship, and perhaps even *All's Well* and the "she got her man" film. *Romeo and Juliet* may not be the first but is certainly the greatest antecedent of "star-crossed lovers" whose young love is doomed by their being in the wrong families (or religions, countries, political factions). At least one among many reasons for the pervasiveness of Shakespeare in film may be that over the years there must have been thousands of English literature graduates working in Hollywood as scriptwriters, and they must have been tempted to re-contextualize dramatic situations that they already found familiar from their studies. There must at times be a conscious decision to conceal the primary Shakespearean reference, since although he has regularly given prestige to films, his name has also been seen as the kiss of death at the box office. The example to be explored here is the relationship of *Othello* to modern "jealousy" films, which it is tempting to rename the "sex, lies, and video" genre.

A strand of psychoanalytical-based film theory argues that the experience of cinema-going is inescapably linked to scopophilia, an illicit pleasure in watching (Levine; Copjec). Voyeurism, prying into the intimate lives of others or eavesdropping on social classes either above or below our own, is central; as is fetishism, an unhealthy dwelling on objects of desire or parts of the gendered body made significant to the viewer by the mesmeric gaze of the camera. Such uncomfortable pleasures are not confined to genres like horror film and psychological thrillers. The most innocent of Shakespeare's plays, *A Midsummer Night's Dream*, has, since Reinhardt's 1930s version, always been filmed with erotically charged fairies, and in the 1999 Hoffman/Klein version, the producers strategically aimed to avoid a general classification, thereby depriving thousands of schoolchildren of the opportunity to see it by inserting a scene of completely gratuitous nudity at the end (Daileader 192ff).

We would all probably resist the argument about viewers' motives since they expose us in a rather unpleasant light. We try to find an escape hatch into something more apparently healthy and communitarian, but it is extraordinarily difficult to escape the mesh woven by a skilled advocate. After all, here we are, sitting in the dark, watching people in compromising or extravagant situations, acting as though they are not being observed. If we are at home watching an endlessly repeatable video, the situation is even more clear. We are vaguely aware of the fact that the image is a crafted artifact, and yet we are seeing real bodies in real settings so clearly that we are persuaded to think the behavior is unscripted and natural, a disposition based on the assumption that what we can see must actually have been there when the camera started rolling and is now happening in front of our eyes. Some directors, most notably the Englishman Mike Leigh, enhance these effects by allowing the actors to make up the script as they go along. An even starker example is the "reality TV" genre, like *Big Brother*, where the whole point is voyeurism on the side of the camera and exhibitionism on the part of the participants. The viewer's satisfaction derives to some extent from waiting for the unusualness, not to mention perversity, of the observed people's responses, since humdrum activity would be boring, ungratifying, and anticlimactic. At the same time, these embodied images unleash sentiments that suggest we too have the latent potential for such feelings and actions. Hitchcock, time and time again, relies on exactly this response, even evoking it deliberately so we will feel

as guilty and implicated as the protagonist. We watch in isolation, even if
the cinema is full — more so if it is empty — and we can share responses
with others even after the event, seeking no more than post factum
verification rather than going through an elevating or educational experience with others. Whether we like it or not, at least with certain kinds of
film, we are Iachimo in *Cymbeline*, concealed as in a trunk, mesmerized
by nakedness and transferred sexual desire.

If there is any truth in this murky approach to film, then Shakespeare's
Othello provides the quintessential movie experience, building into its
very structure and spectacle the tug of scopophilia, voyeurism, masochism,
fetishism, and worse. Moving inexorably toward the marital bed on which
is enacted sex and death, it taps into semi- or unconscious impulses of
solipsistic envy, issuing into violent fantasy based on jealousy. And more
sinister still, it provides us, in the figure of Iago, with a character who is
the quintessential moviemaker, orchestrating this material for our "pleasure." He is the "supervisor" of "ocular proof," standing close to the role
of an exploitative director, gaping on while making a salacious film:

> OTHELLO: Be sure of it. Give me the ocular proof ...
>
> IAGO: You would be satisfied?
>
> OTHELLO: Would? Nay, and I will.
>
> IAGO: And may. But how? How satisfied, my lord? Would you, the super-
> visor, grossly gape on, Behold her topped? [III.iii.365, 398–401]

And Oliver Parker's version, unable to resist the box-office temptation,
does literally this, allowing both Othello and the viewer to witness Desdemona "topped." In general, some issues considered by theorists to be
central to the medium of film itself are explicitly raised in the play. There
is fetishism (the handkerchief), and the construction of the female object
as target of the male gaze. In fact, reading the female body as text may
have been initiated in Othello's lines, "Was this fair paper, this most goodly
book, / Made to write 'whore' upon?" Internal, illicit gazing (associated
with scopophilia — the desire for looking) is central to the plot from its
first scene devoted to sexual speculation, innuendo, and voyeurism by
characters and by audience. The play also gives us the persecution of innocence expected in screen melodrama. The emphasis on these aspects is
orchestrated by the figure of Iago and highlighted by his role in the play.

Voyeurism turns as much on what is not seen as what is — on the
inferred or imagined as much as on the directly viewed. This is the
keynote — or keyhole? — Shakespeare sets up from the beginning of his
play. Significantly, it is Iago who introduces the salacious imaginings: "Even

now, very now, an old black ram / Is tupping your white ewe" (I.i.89–90), "making the beast with two backs" (I.i.107); and he infects Othello with statements like "Would you, the supervisor, grossly gape on? Behold her topped?" (III.iii.400–01), and so on, compulsively. Presumably he is lying when he speaks of Cassio's dream-talk and again reveals what seems pure scopophilia. He exploits the power of suggestion over visual evidence, or rather, the construction of an imagined scenario from random scraps of neutral evidence. This is a central trick of the film medium, and the evidence that Shakespeare understood it lies not only in the Dark Lady sonnets, but also *The Rape of Lucrece*:

> For much imaginary work was there;
> Conceit deceitful, so compact, so kind,
> That for Achilles' image stood his spear
> Gripped in an armed hand: himself behind
> Was left unseen save to the eye of mind:
>   A hand, a foot, a face, a leg, a head,
>   Stood for the whole to be imagined.
> [1422–8]

Desdemona's handkerchief gradually becomes not a handkerchief, but a symbol of marital fidelity and infidelity, and a fetish, both in the primary sense ("intimate object worshiped by savages for its magical power")— "there's magic in the web of it"—as well as the secondary sense of "sexually symbolic" (Rycroft 51–2). The loss of it, with its suggestive strawberry marking, becomes associated with the loss of Desdemona's virginity and inferred adultery, standing "for the whole to be imagined." Already, it is emerging that *Othello* could have been written by a twentieth century film theorist, and in fact, this anticipates my very conclusion.

Othello has been filmed many times. Depending on how we count, there have been up to 20 versions, more if we count Verdi's *Otello* and other close, conscious adaptations. The major silent version made in Germany in 1922, directed by Dimitri Bucherowetzki, does not respect the visuality of film, as it is overloaded with inserts of intertext (strange how Godard returned to early avant-garde effects). By no means essential to understanding the plot, some are quotations from Shakespeare and others are paraphrases, but there seems to be a conscious attempt to make film respectable by implying its primary literary worth, a common use of Shakespeare in the cinema. Visually, there is much rolling of the eyes from Othello, and, from our point of view, Iago (Werner Krauss) is conceived, at least in makeup and demeanor, as a comic villain, complete with long tapered moustache, portly frame, and wickedly malicious glances. He has been described as "near manic" (McKernan and Terris 120), and "more a stage manager than a rhetorician, but the character's malevolent brilliance survives" (Buhler 16). To this extent, he establishes the filmic centrality of this Iago as a figure of vice and a mischief-maker, with a special way of appealing directly to the camera. Kenneth Rothwell (*passim*) has suggested that the discovery of the closeup was the most significant breakthrough for Shakespeare films, and this one makes ample use of it, suggesting that Shakespeare himself created, through Iago's soliloquies and asides, a stage anticipation of the closeup. This buttonholing of the audience is exploited particularly by the unctuous and affable Iago of Kenneth Branagh, frequently filmed in closeup (Coursen 23), in the version directed by Oliver Parker with Laurence Fishburne as Othello (1995), and by the used-car-salesman approach of a terribly plausible Bob Hoskins in the version made for television by Jonathan Miller (1981). Lynda E. Boose says that in this production, Iago's "prurient lewdness is complicit with a distinctly puritanical sexual morality that 'hates the slime / That sticks on filthy deeds,'" and she highlights the centrality of this character to the film's gaze in Miller's production: "As Lodovico gives the final voyeuristic order of the play to 'look upon the tragic loading of the bed, Bob Hoskins leans forward to look, his face wreathed in loving smiles" (Boose 193–4). Hoskins' success on the small screen suggests that the play, or at least the Iago-experience, is even more potent on video than on the big screen, which is different again from staging the play. For example, I have forgotten any detail from Frank Finlay's Iago, playing alongside Olivier, in a film made from the stage (1965), though I recall vividly Olivier's Othello, red rose in mouth, swaggering like a West Indian cricket bowler, even though his performance was quite disappointing and even racist. Similarly, Yutkevic's Russian version (1955) is conceived as a screen epic, and again Iago's presence is somewhat diminished. On the other hand, Orson Welles built into his film (1952) a cramping indoors feeling at odds with the Moroccan sunshine outside, and the camera often descends literally to the sewers. As Kathy Howlett suggests, much of the film's atmosphere is generated by Welles' knowledge of Michaél MacLiammóir's offscreen homosexuality, in creating a "voyeuristic pleasure of pain" that marks Iago here (Howlett 52–91). Howlett's account finds the same emphasis on voyeurism in the play itself that I am exploring, but her account is more focused on visual sources.

This essay is not intended to examine film versions of *Othello* but adaptations at one remove from the play: derivative films that are not Shakespeare adaptations but clearly consistent with the Shakespearean model and consciously or unconsciously based on it. In this case, *Othello* has proven so fertile as a source for films that it has arguably created a sub-genre in film, the "jealousy thriller." The most recent one, *O* (2001), is set in the world of American high school basketball. Odin James (Mekhi Phifer), a young African American student, is persuaded by his scheming best friend, Hugo Goulding (Josh Hartnett), that his girlfriend Desi (Julia Stiles) is unfaithful. Hugo is in fact motivated by his own jealousy of Odin. Arguably, it fails as an adaptation and shows by contrast the importance of Othello's age in creating his insecurity. A high school student is not a plausible vehicle for the insecurities that the play represents, which are those encountered within marriage, not juvenile courtship. The film gained brief notoriety by being withdrawn from release after the Columbine school killings. This in itself reminds us of the sensational contemporaneity that *Othello* can take on, as in depicting miscegenation in Janet Suzman's stage and screen version made during the apartheid years in South Africa, and in the uncannily similar (alleged) facts of domestic violence in the O.J. Simpson case.

Both *A Double Life* (1947) and *Les enfants du paradis* (1948) include a central character who is an actor playing Othello, and his life takes on tragic similarities to the play. In both, the "Iago impulse" seems to be present within the Othello character, rather than represented as a separate persona. In *A Double Life*, the method actor character (Ronald Coleman) suffers from multiple personality disorder and becomes a psychopathic murderer, killing a prostitute and then, on stage in full view of the audience, attempting to smother the actress playing Desdemona. In this disturbing film noir, a new psychoanalytical dimension is found in the play and highlighted by devices reminiscent of 1940s psychological thrillers (Wilson 84–93). Meanwhile, in *Les enfants*, the actor finds his own love life taking on a similarity to that of the character he is playing. All the characters involved in the various love triangles react, however, with selfless generosity rather than vindictiveness in this gentle and lovely film. Another example of a "real" Othello entangled with a stage performance is *Men Are Not Gods* (1936).

There are other examples of meta-cinema in which a Shakespeare play is an inset or "play within a film": notably *Romeo and Juliet*; *The Tempest* in the 1940s *Love Story*; and *A Midsummer Night's Dream* in *Dead Poet's Society*. There have been eight screen versions of the life of Edmund Kean, the earliest in 1922 and the most recent, *Kean* (1982), starring Ben Kingsley, made for television. In these, the role of Othello is invariably featured, although Kean played on stage both Othello and Iago alternately, both with distinction. The films compare the roles with biographical details in Kean's life, since he was notorious for his own professional jealousy (Hillebrand 127–31). His Iago always attracted more critical attention, perhaps because of Hazlitt's memorable phrase, "a lighthearted monster, a careless, cordial, comfortable villain," conveying "the extreme grace, alacrity, and rapidity of the execution" (90–101, 205–11). The attention, which might be unfair to Kean's versatility, also highlights the disturbing centrality of the Iago role.

At a further remove lie the derivatives based on the *Othello* plot (which by this time can be seen as a genre in its own right) without necessary reference to the play. Without the precedent of Shakespeare's play, however, it is difficult to see how each film could have been conceived. *Jubal* (1956) is, unexpectedly, a Western, one genre where we do not expect fully developed themes like sexual jealousy or psychological complexity. In this sense, it might be classified as an extrinsic adaptation, where the Shakespeare plot is placed within an apparently distant and even irrelevant Hollywood genre, distinct from an intrinsic adaptation like *A Double Life*, where a plot involving jealousy and murder is adapted to a film genre (noir or psychological thriller) where we expect such narratives. In *Jubal*, the cattle-king Shep (the Othello figure played by Ernest Borgnine) is persuaded by his usurped foreman Pinky (Iago, Rod Steiger) that his wife (Mae, Valerie French) is sleeping with the man whom Shep appointed over him as the new foreman, Jubal (Cassio, Glenn Ford). A significant difference from *Othello* is that the wife is frustrated and flirtatious and tries to seduce Jubal without success. Unlike Desdemona, Mae is far from innocent, and her name might be a pun indicating that she "may" commit adultery, given half a chance. Shep's actions are like Othello's in his rapid descent from good-humored emotional security to a frenzy of jealousy, culminating in his attempt to kill her. The scene is replete with Shakespearean references such as the carrying of a candle to the offending lady's bed. Mae, under provocation, confesses her love for Jubal, and Shep then tries to kill him. Instead, Jubal tragically kills his boss in self defense. Despite the incongruities between the Western genre and Shakespeare's play, there are many important parallels, right down to the "put out the light" imagery, and the narrative source is undeniably *Othello*, especially in the portrayal of the devious Pinky who is motivated by his own desire for Mae and his envy of the usurping Jubal (Wilson 122–9).

In *All Night Long* (1961), the events are transported into the world of a 1960s jazz band. The drummer, Johnnie (Patrick McGoohan), fabricates evidence of an extra marital affair involving his friend's wife in order to pry her away from her black husband, Aurelius Rex (Paul Harris VI) and lure her into his own band. Johnnie's closeness to Iago is evident in all salient plot features, including the fact that his wife calls him a "congenital liar." In jealousy, Rex tries to strangle his wife, but before she dies, Johnnie's lies are exposed. They all survive, Johnnie left alone with just his drum for a companion. *All Night Long* makes the judgment that is kept ambiguous in *Othello*, showing that Rex is already possessive at the beginning of the film and ripe for Johnnie's manipulation. In a technological updating of the "ocular proof," Johnnie uses a taped recording edited to fabricate evidence, rather than facilitating an opportunity for eavesdropping.

This trope points us toward the final part of this paper which addresses a film where the manipulation of video is central. *All Night Long* shows its 1960s origins, not only in having jazz musicians such as Charlie Mingus and Dave Brubeck playing themselves, but also in the psychoanalytical references and explanations that are given liberally. As an intrinsic adaptation of *Othello*, *All Night Long* seems skillful, in that the Shakespearean source is not essential to understanding the plot and character motivation, yet is palpably and pervasively present. Other recognized film analogues, in varying degrees of distance from the play, are *Carnival* (1921, remade in 1931), *Catch My Soul* (1973, which appears to be a musical version of *Othello*), *Une histoire inventee* (1990), *True Identity* (1991), and *The Playboys* (1992).

sex, lies, and videotape draws more subtly upon the *Othello* genre, a claim which requires argument since the film makes no reference — explicit or implicit — to the play itself. I am not arguing for a source relationship but an analogical one. (The need for a more precise generic description is signaled by the film's bland classification on Web sites as "classic, comedy, drama.") The film suggests Shakespeare by its placement, as one reviewer put it, "back in the days when speech was an erogenous zone" (Ebert) and when conversation could be erotic, phrases that could be just as true of *Othello* and *Much Ado About Nothing*. The film comes closest of all to centralizing the "Iago experience"; this character becomes a kind of director within a play, creating triangles of jealousy and sexual insecurity. Film itself as a medium, or at least videotape, is the central subject, and lurking close to the foreground is the disturbing exchange between Othello and Iago when they discuss the "ocular proof." In this film, an Iago-like character exaggerates the role of Iago as plotter, stage manager, director of films, and voyeuristic "supervisor."

A surprise hit of 1989, the film was written in eight days by Steven Soderbergh, unexpectedly grossing $100 million for an outlay of only $1.8

million. Soderbergh said in an interview that it was a "personal" film and that he is all four characters—"I cut myself in quarters"—which is again suggestive of Shakespeare's play as a kind of collective experience shared between Othello, Desdemona, and Iago in various vicarious ways. The comment also establishes that it is a genuine auteur film, in the sense that *Othello* can be presented as under Iago's auteur directorship. At first, one could not imagine a more unlikely derivative of *Othello* than *sex, lies, and videotape*, and yet on reflection, it seems to mirror Shakespeare's play in its central concerns.

The character roles bear comparison with the four main characters in *Othello*, but again, as in *Jubal*, there are creative variations. This film centralizes the Iago figure, Graham (James Spader), making him danger-ously subversive of marital trust. Like Iago, the character is presented as

The cast of a modern *Othello*? A self-aggrandizing braggart, John (Peter Gal-lagher), complacently claims possession of his wife; Bianca smoulders (Cyn-thia played by Laura San Giacomo), while "honest Iago" (Graham played by James Spader) snuggles up to Desdemona (Ann played by Andie MacDowell) and ingratiates himself to the viewer. No, it is the cast of *sex, lies, and video-tape*.

(at least superficially) sympathetic and is liked by the other characters, partly because he adopts a confiding and apparently vulnerable tone, mixed with a kind of honest frankness. The Othello figure, the lawyer John (Peter Gallagher), fades in the background as something of a gull, and instead the riveting attention falls on the process of insidious subversion of an admittedly unsatisfactory marriage by the voyeuristic best friend who thinks of himself as honest. John has given up on sex with his wife but is having an affair with her sister. Othello and Desdemona are, by contrast, newlyweds, but the facts of their sexual relations ("have they or haven't they") have been solemnly debated by critics: the couple may not have consummated their marriage, or Othello may be impotent. John himself emerges as something like the Othello of T.S. Eliot and F.R. Leavis—a self-deceiving egotist and braggart—rather than, for example, that of brooding Orson Welles. However, just as Eliot and Leavis construct this character by implicitly adopting an Iago-perspective (Bayley 181), so John is viewed early on through the eyes of Graham, who clearly despises his old college friend, calling him, quite openly, a liar. The four characters are driven by different obsessions that include voyeurism, masochism, lies and honesty, and fetishism. John accuses his wife Ann (wonderfully played by Andie MacDowell) of frigidity. She challenges him as unfaithful, a charge he denies even though he is sleeping with her sister, Cynthia (Laura San Giacomo), who is, in Ann's coy euphemism, "outgoing." Into this triangle comes Graham, whose hobby is video-interviewing women about their sex lives. A true Iago, he stakes a claim to honesty by leaving his door always open ("It's open," he keeps saying), by guaranteeing confidentiality, and by referring to John as a liar while saying of himself that he "used to be a liar." He also, like Horner in the *Country Wife*, claims to be impotent and no threat to women or marriages. Ann is as innocent as Desdemona, both in the sentimental sense and in the legal or moral sense. She tells her analyst that sex is "no big deal," but she uses housework, which she attacks with a masochistic zeal, as her outlet from repression and frustration. Cynthia could be seen as akin to Bianca, at least in her sexual openness, and she obliges Graham by visually revealing in her interview that she is not wearing underclothes, and then (apparently) masturbating for the camera (that is, if we believe that Graham is impotent). Significantly, we do not see this, as if the voyeuristic potential for the film is heightened (like Othello's jealousy itself) by withholding the "ocular proof" and instead offering an inference which "stands for the whole to be imagined." It is Ann's shocked reaction to Cynthia's revelation that implies the act: "You didn't! ... Oh, you're in real trouble."

Videotape itself is as important to this film as the tape recorder was in *All Night Long*. The apparently truth-telling medium of the camera conceals and implies more than it shows, requiring the viewer's imagination to extend the frame into neurotic self-projection. The handkerchief is replaced by Cynthia's earring, which enables Ann to get evidence of her husband's infidelity. In retaliation against both John and Cynthia, she storms off to be interviewed. She uses the occasion to break up Graham's fantasy life by intruding physically upon him and forcing him to shut off his video camera, leading him, presumably, out of impotence into a sexual encounter and into the smashing his videos one by one. The similarities between the roles of Iago and Graham seem strong. John, in a moment of heavy irony, describes Graham as "Mr. Honesty, Mr. Apostle of Truth," portraying him as an "honest Iago" at last unmasked. Ann literally turns the camera on him and extracts the confession that not only did he used to be a "pathological liar," but he still is one. In this unexpected peripeteia, we can imagine Desdemona turning on Iago, or even more aptly, think of Ann at this point as Aemilia. She calls Graham "pathetic" and repeatedly asks, "Why do you do this?" receiving only the unsatisfactory answer that he is getting over a much earlier failed relationship with a woman who, he discovers, was bedded by John at the time, a detail very close to one of Iago's suspicions about Othello and Aemilia.

"Give me the ocular proof." Ann (Andie MacDowell) turns the video camera on Graham (James Spader) as Emilia turns the tables on Iago in Steven Soderbergh's *sex, lies, and videotape*.

Unfortunately, the ending of *sex, lies, and videotape* is disappointing, and not the one that Soderbergh originally wrote, which was completely indeterminate and open (Soderbergh). The producers, for box-office reasons, persuaded the director to imply strongly that a relationship between Ann and Graham develops: we see them holding hands at the end of the film. This union seems to be much more than Graham deserves. The real ending comes earlier, as an alternative and perhaps more rigorous ending of *Othello*, where Iago is "outed," not, however, by Aemilia, but by Desdemona. "You have a lot of problems," says Ann to Graham, and we wish Desdemona had been given the opportunity to say the same to Iago.

Graham's psychology is pure Iago. On the surface, he is baby-faced, tactful, sensitive, passive (often viewed supine and, once, asleep), honest, and open, claiming a special understanding of women, just as Iago does. Underneath this surface, however, he is envious, jealous, psychologically sadistic, intrusive, devious, a peeping-tom, scopophilic, and a fetishist of the video machine. Like Shakespeare, Soderbergh leaves it ambiguous whether Graham genuinely changes the situation in the triangle of John, Ann, and Cynthia, or whether he is just a catalyst for processes that would have happened without him. Each of the others is to some extent either infected by his congenital jealousy of heterosexual couples (he confesses his own sexual failure before he became impotent), or else so receptive to his presence that he clarifies that emotion within them.

When we closely inspect this disarming and unsettling film, we find ourselves well and truly in Othello-country, making *Sex, Lies, and Videotape*, at least arguably, a sophisticated and accurate contemporary derivative of Shakespeare's play. Intrinsic connections between videotape, jealousy, and voyeurism make *Othello* seem as though Shakespeare had made it prophetically with this modern medium, and perhaps—who knows?—with this very film in mind.

Works Cited

Bayley, John. "Love and Identity: *Othello*." In *The Characters of Love*. London: Constable, 1960.

Boose, Lynda E. "Grossly Gaping Viewers and Jonathan Miller's *Othello*." In *Shakespeare the Movie: Popularizing the Plays on Film TV, and Video*. Edited by Lynda E. Boose and Richard Burt. London: Routledge, 1997. 186–97.

Buhler, Stephen M. *Shakespeare in the Cinema: Ocular Proof*. New York: New York University Press, 2002.

Copjec, Joan. *Read My Desire: Lacan Against the Historicists*. Cambridge, Mass.: MIT Press, 1994.

Coursen, H.R. *Shakespeare in Space: Recent Shakespeare Productions on Film*. New York: Peter Lang, 2002.

Daileader, Celia R. "Nude Shakespeare in Film and Nineties Popular Feminism." *Shakespeare and Sexuality*. Edited by Catherine M.S. Alexander and Stanley Wells. Cambridge: Cambridge University Press, 2001. 183–200.

Ebert, Roger. "*Sex, Lies, and Videotape.*" *Chicago Sun Times*, 11 August 1989.

Hazlitt, William. *Hazlitt's Criticism of Shakespeare*. Edited by R.S. White. Lewiston: Edwing Mellen Press, 1996.

Hillebrand, Harold Newcomb. *Edmund Kean*. New York: AMS Press. 1966.

Howlett, Kathy M. "The Voyeuristic Pleasures of Perversion: Orson Welles's *Othello.*" In *Framing Shakespeare on Film*. Athens, Ohio: Ohio University Press, 2000. 52–91.

Levine, Michael. "Depraved Spectators and Impossible Audiences." *Journal of the Society for Philosophical Study of the Contemporary Visual Arts: Philosophy and Film: Edition on Horror* (2001): 63–71.

McKernan, Luke and Olwen Terris, editors. *Walking Shadows: Shakespeare in the National Film and Television Archive*. London: British Film Institute, 1994.

Rothwell, Kenneth. *Early Shakespeare Movies: How the Spurned Spawned Art*. Chipping Campden: International Shakespeare Association, 2000.

Rycroft, Charles. *A Critical Dictionary of Psychoanalysis*. London: Penguin, 1995.

Sammons, Eddie. *Shakespeare: A Hundred Years of Film*. London: Shepheard-Walwyn, 2000.

Shakespeare, William. *The Norton Shakespeare*. Edited by Stephen Greenblatt. New York: Norton, 1997.

Soderbergh, Stephen. Interview in *The Guardian*. 22 February 2003. Online at http://film.guardian.co.uk/interview/interviewpages/0,6737,900407,00.html.

Wilson, Robert F. Jr. *Shakespeare in Hollywood: 1929–1956*. Cranbury, N.Y.: Fairleigh Dickinson University Press, 2000.

7

"The Time Is Out of Joint": *Withnail and I* and Historical Melancholia

Aaron Kelly and David Salter

Uncle Monty: "It is the most shattering experience of a young man's life, when one morning he awakes, and quite reasonably says to himself, "I will never play the Dane."
— Bruce Robinson, *Withnail and I*

Although the specter of *Hamlet* lurks behind — and gives shape and meaning to — *Withnail and I* (Bruce Robinson's cult classic from 1986), the film's complex set of allusions to and quotations from Shakespeare's play has received very little critical attention. In many ways, this is hardly surprising, since to its legion of die-hard fans, the film's principal appeal lies in its comic evocation of the squalor and decadence of late-1960s London, with all its alcohol- and drug-fuelled excesses. "I must have some booze. I *demand* to have some booze" (Robinson 16), announces the eponymous Withnail — played by Richard E. Grant — near the beginning of the film, and much of the story's comic energy is bound up with his relentless search for, and seemingly endless consumption of, drugs and alcohol. So, in the popular imagination at least — and for very understandable reasons — *Withnail and I* has come to be seen as almost a paean to Bacchanalian indulgence and excess. And it is this spirit of Dionysian revelry that lies behind the game played by many of the movie's more fanatical devotees, the purpose of which is to emulate the characters on screen by attempting — when watching the film — to match them drink for drink (an undertaking fraught with danger, not least because it involves the consumption of lighter fuel, which according to Withnail, is "a far superior drink to meths" [Robinson 16]).

But while the film's prevailing mood is undoubtedly a comic one, its writer and director, Bruce Robinson, is nonetheless keen to point out that the comedy is decidedly bittersweet in nature (Owen 127). Withnail is certainly a brilliant comic creation, but his is a comedy of frustration, stagnation, inertia, and ultimately of failure. So alongside the strongly celebratory element evident in *Withnail and I* (to which its fans respond with such enthusiasm), there is also a powerful strain of sadness, and to a very great extent the film both registers and expresses this melancholy note through its allusions to, quotations from, and intertextual dialogue with Shakespeare's *Hamlet*. Indeed, *Hamlet* can be said to haunt *Withnail and I*, and in the pages that follow, we shall explore some of the different ways in which the spectral presence of Shakespeare's play inflects the mood and atmosphere of the film, creating a tangible sense of disillusionment and melancholy.[1]

As was suggested above, since the time of its release in 1986, *Withnail and I* has enjoyed a cult following, particularly in Britain, but as the term "cult" suggests, the film has always remained something of a curio, inspiring fanatical devotion among its loyal fans, but never really entering mainstream popular culture.[2] Because *Withnail and I* is so little known outside the relatively small circle of its admirers, we shall first offer a very brief description of its reasonably simple and straightforward plot, before going on to consider the role and function of *Hamlet* within the film.

Set in the dying months of 1969, the film follows the unhappy fortunes of two unemployed and down-at-heel actors: Withnail and Marwood (the "I" of the film's title, played by Paul McGann). Seeking a temporary respite from their life of desperate squalor and penury in London, the pair leave their rancid and vermin infested flat to spend the weekend in the country cottage of Withnail's Uncle Monty (a part brilliantly played by Richard Griffiths). Hoping for a pastoral idyll, their expectations are immediately shattered when they find themselves confronted by the inhospitable reality of a cold, damp, and virtually derelict building, completely lacking in the comforts and amenities of the consumer age. Ill equipped to deal either with country life — or with the colorful "local types" they encounter — the protagonists are further troubled by the unexpected arrival of Uncle Monty, who has taken a shine to Marwood, and who fully intends to "have" him, "even if it must be burglary." Narrowly avoiding "a buggering," Marwood insists that he and Withnail beat a hasty retreat back to London. On their return, Marwood hears that he has been offered a job as an actor in Manchester, and the film concludes on a strikingly melancholy note with Withnail — having said goodbye to Marwood — standing on his own in the pouring rain, reciting Hamlet's great speech of sadness and disillusionment: "I have of late — but wherefore I know not — lost all my mirth…" (II.ii.293–308).

Of course, such cursory plot summaries inevitably fail to capture the richness and complexity of the works they describe, and this is especially true in the case of *Withnail and I,* where so much of the atmosphere and humor of the film emerges from the craft of the actors and the skill and artistry of the dialogue. But even from this bare summary of the plot, the importance of *Hamlet* to the film is immediately apparent. For in the climactic scene of the film, Withnail gives vent to his intense feelings of frustration, disillusionment, and melancholy, not through his own words, but through Hamlet's speech. The emotional impact of these words is all the more powerful because they are the last to be spoken in the film and are uttered in such desultory surroundings: Withnail standing outside the wolf enclosure of London zoo in the pouring rain, his only audience consisting of the bored, wet, and — in the words of the screenplay — "pissed off wolves" (Robinson 127).

In addition to using Hamlet's actual words to articulate Withnail's personal sense of dejection and loss, the melancholy film is informed by Shakespeare's play in other ways. Both Withnail and Marwood are unemployed actors to whom Hamlet represents the most exacting and demanding of theatrical roles and thus the pinnacle of actorly ambition. (Earlier on in the film, Withnail indicates that Hamlet is "a part I intend to play" [Robinson 34].) So for Withnail, the dawning realization that — in the words of Uncle Monty — he "will never play the Dane" represents his thwarted desires and aspirations. And perhaps it is for this reason that his final soliloquy assumes such poignancy and emotional force; for his is a masterful rendition of one of the most powerful speeches in the classical actor's repertoire, and yet he performs it before an audience of captive wolves. Ironically, then, the moment at which he proves his worth as an actor occurs at precisely the same time that he — and we — realize that he is destined never to make it on the stage. This paradox is beautifully conveyed through Richard E. Grant's moving performance, but is also explicitly articulated in the screenplay:

> [Withnail] looks at the wolves in wonder that the bastards aren't clapping…. Albert Finny never felt so good. He takes a last final slug of the bottle and casts it aside. By Christ, that was the best rendition of *Hamlet* the world will ever see. The only pity was it was only wolves that saw it. They stare at Withnail through the bars. He bids them a silent good afternoon and walks away [Robinson 128].

Of course, this tone of simultaneous triumph and failure is perfectly expressed by Hamlet himself in the speech that Withnail recites:

I have of late — but wherefore I know not — lost all my mirth, forgone all custom of exercise; and indeed it goes so heavily with my disposition that this goodly frame, the earth, seems to me a sterile promontory. This most excellent canopy, the air, look you, this brave o'erhanging firmament, this majestical roof fretted with golden fire — why, it appears no other thing to me than a foul and pestilent congregation of vapours. What a piece of work is a man, how noble in reason, how infinite in faculty, in form and moving how express and admirable, in action how like an angel, in apprehension how like a god — the beauty of the world, the paragon of animals! And yet, to me, what is this quintessence of dust? Man delights not me — no nor woman neither [II.ii.293–308].

In this speech, Hamlet first asserts an optimistic belief in the innate dignity of humanity, only to subject that same belief to a powerful critique: "And yet to me, what is this quintessence of dust? Man delights not me." What is more, Hamlet is using the principal goal and instrument of humanist education — eloquence — not to sing the praises of humanity, as conventional usage would dictate, but rather to sow the seeds of doubt and dissatisfaction. So these lines are ideally suited to convey Withnail's predicament not simply because they capture a sense of melancholy and disenchantment, but because that note of sadness is imperceptibly blended with one of confidence and authority. In a sense, both Hamlet and Withnail are rejecting — or being rejected by — that which they have mastered.

Bruce Robinson has pointed out that he originally intended to conclude the film with Withnail committing suicide, but that on reflection he felt that such a violent dénouement would provide too abrupt and emotionally jarring a note on which to end (Owen 127). Instead, the more subtle "sweet and sour" quality that he sought was — as we have seen — achieved by sustaining and bringing to fulfillment an intertextual dialogue with *Hamlet* that is initiated earlier in the film. However, the disillusionment to which the film gives such powerful expression goes well beyond the mere disenchantment of its principal protagonist, and once again, it is *Hamlet* that provides the interpretative key to understanding this phenomenon. Central to *Hamlet* is a sense of temporal disjuncture and dislocation, the feeling — in Hamlet's famous phrase — that "The time is out of joint" (I.v.196).

Of course, for Hamlet, the profound disorientation he experiences is bound up with his nostalgia for the past as he looks back fondly on his father's reign from the context of his corrupt uncle's politically and emotionally restrictive regime. This almost tangible sense of social and political upheaval — of a world of liberty giving way to one of repression and entrapment ("Denmark's a prison" [II.ii.242]) — is paralleled in *Withnail and I.* Set at the end of the 1960s—that self-proclaimed decade of political freedom and social experimentation—the film is increasingly overwhelmed by a pervasive melancholy at the passing of an era:

> London is a country comin' down from its trip. We are sixty days from the enda this decade, and there's gonna be a lota refugees. We're about to witness the world's biggest hangover, and there's fuck all Harold Wilson can do about it…. They'll be goin' round this town shoutin' "Bring out your dead" [Robinson 119–120].

But although the film deliberately seeks to evoke the end of the 1960s, *Withnail and I* nonetheless tells us as much — if not more — about the time in which it was made. The late 1960s are implicitly placed alongside, and viewed from the perspective of, the Thatcherite 1980s, and in the remainder of this essay, we shall use *Hamlet* and its meditations on historical disjuncture to explore how, in Robinson's own words, "the horror of Thatcherism" (*Empire* 81) haunts the film's recreation of the past.[4]

So the film's disenchantment may be politicized by examining how it deploys Shakespeare's *Hamlet* to ground a series of meditations on temporal disjuncture, most specifically the end of the 1960s and its negotiations, not merely with the onset of the 1970s, but also and most intricately with the film's contemporary context of the 1980s. Robinson himself appears to situate the film, ultimately, in the hindsight of a 1980s framework through which the arresting of 1960s radicalism is finalized:

> The whole generation, kids of the sixties who are now cabinet ministers and Prime Ministers, did think there was something new and that it couldn't possibly revert to the old order. It did feel for a while that something fundamental had changed, like at Grosvenor Square, 150,000 young kids saying, "Fuck the war in Vietnam." And then, of course, it all fell to bits and turned into Margaret Thatcher [Owen 123].

With this sense of a generational negotiation between old and new orders in mind, Albert Camus postulates that tragedy is generated by a particular kind of historical transition: "Tragedy is born in the west each time that the pendulum of civilization is halfway between a sacred society and a society built around man…. Man frees himself from an older form of civilization and finds that he has broken away from it without having found a new form which satisfies him" (quoted in Dollimore 8). Following from Camus' reading of the social symbolism of tragedy, the 1960s can be interpreted as signaling a rupture in the postwar social settlement that precipitates a crisis of identity, society, and historical memory, and is perhaps best theorized by Antonio Gramsci as an "interregnum" for which tragedy, as defined in Camus' terms, becomes a paradigmatic form:

> [I]f the ruling class has lost its consensus, i.e. is no longer "leading" but only "dominant," exercising coercive force alone, this means precisely that the great masses have become detached from their traditional ideologies, and no longer believe what they used to believe previously, etc. The crisis consists precisely in the fact that the old is dying and the new cannot be born; and in this interregnum a great variety of morbid symptoms appear [Gramsci 275–276].

However, we want at this juncture to demonstrate, through an understanding of *Hamlet* as a representational deep structure in the film's political unconscious (to employ Frederic Jameson's term) that the constitutive disappointment or disillusionment of *Withnail and I* resides not in its avowed complaint that the emancipatory spirit of the 1960s is exorcised by the harsh realities of Thatcherism, that the new social potentiality struggling in vain to be born is eventually overcome by the old order. Rather, the film's disillusionment is located in its realization that it is precisely the underlying political and socioeconomic logic of the 1960s and its Gramscian "morbid symptoms" that produce the 1980s.

So in unraveling the temporal mediations of *Withnail and I*, we are positing that the 1960s, rather than being readily periodized as an oppositional vista in an otherwise dreary postwar capitalist realignment, is actually the ghost that haunts the neoliberal economics of the 1980s. Notable is the fact that the film itself is produced by George Harrison's HandMade Films, funded by the millionaire former Beatle's supposedly dissident counterculture activities of the 1960s: a succinct transfusion of 1960s countercultural capital into 1980s entrepreneurial investment. In particular, Fredric Jameson has averred that:

> [T]his sense of freedom and possibility...which is of course in the 60s a momentarily objective reality, as well as (from the hindsight of the 80s) a historical illusion—can perhaps best be explained in terms of the superstructural movement and play enabled by the transition from one infrastructural or systemic stage of capitalism to another. The 60s were in that sense an immense and inflationary issuing of superstructural credit; a universal abandonment of the gold standard; an extraordinary printing up of ever more devalued signifiers [*Ideologies* 208].

What we are proposing in this essay, therefore, is that the film's political unconscious discloses a generational affinity between the two decades rather than a formative struggle. Robinson argues that the discussion at the end of the film about the selling of hippie wigs in Woolworth's suggests that by the end of the decade, "the sixties are now being marketed rather than lived" (Owen 112).

But while this process demonstrates reification, the political debilitation of commodity fetishism, and the capacity of capitalism as a system to absorb dissent, seemingly setting the sixties in opposition to commercialism, the film discloses a more profound affinity. For example, in one scene Withnail and Marwood pass an "Accident Black Spot" sign as they motor through London's Finchley borough — Thatcher's parliamentary constituency — where Withnail urges a pedestrian to "throw yourself into the road, darling, you haven't got a chance" (Owen 123). But this subtle adumbration of Thatcherism in the 1960s content of the film is part of a dialectical formal process whereby the two decades haunt and inform one another as a complex yet commensurate dynamic.

So in terms of the spectrality unleashed by *Hamlet*, what *Withnail and I* confronts is not the onset of the 1970s, but rather a haunting by the decade which fathered the 1980s, a Derridean "hauntology" in which the supposed freedoms of the 1960s are radically rewritten by the film's contemporary context in Thatcherite Britain. Indeed, it is noteworthy that Derrida's *Specters of Marx: The State of the Debt, the Work of Mourning, and the New International* takes as its epigraph Hamlet's complaint that "The time is out of joint." Derrida figures his concept of "hauntology" in the following terms:

> It would harbor within itself, but like circumscribed places or particular effects, eschatology and teleology themselves. It would *comprehend* them, but incomprehensibly. How to *comprehend* in fact the discourse of the end or the discourse about the end? Can the extremity of the extreme ever be comprehended? And the opposition between "to be" and "not to be"? *Hamlet* already began with the expected return of the dead King. After the end of history, the spirit comes by *coming back* [revenant], it figures *both* a dead man who comes back and a ghost whose expected return repeats itself again and again [10].

In the film, Marwood tells us that "Even a stopped clock gives the right time twice a day" (Robinson 14). This sense of repetitive dead time or what Walter Benjamin would term "homogeneous empty time" (*Illuminations* 252), which can be reiteratively prophetic precisely and only because of its stasis, divulges that the 1960s mark a constitutive historical breakdown in the Western world. The 1960s were the site not only of an oppositional movement, but also of a restructuration in the dominant economic and political organization of Western society and ultimately the contemporary world itself as a global economic totality. What seemed ostensibly to be a deterritorialization may ultimately have been a profound reterritorialization that unmasks itself finally in the monetarism of the 1980s, the avowed and speculative freedoms of the 1960s finding themselves materially grounded in the neoliberal economics of the eighties. Moreover, the haunting between the two decades in the film also permits the reformulation of the 1960s not as a moment primarily of political opposition and dissidence, but rather as the disorientation and disablement of political critique. The temporal disjuncture of the film signals that proclamations such as Francis Fukuyama's *The End of History and the Last Man* are to be understood not as evidence of a historical fulfillment, but as the culmination of an ideology denying collective historical change that emanates from the sixties and, again, establishes itself as a sociopolitical dominant in 1980s individualism.

The function of drugs in the film is to indicate a narcotization of social mapping and memory, to divulge that the 1960s were a "time out of joint," a blurring of identities and perceptions that disorients political mediations between the present and its past and futurity. Robinson observes that the only character recognizably associated with the sixties is the spaced-out drug dealer Danny: "It's interesting, though. Without Danny, the film would have no time frame at all. He is very much anchored in the age and they are not" (Owen 123). So the supposed time frame of the film is paradoxically a space of temporal disjuncture, wherein the dislocation and upheaval of the 1960s are shorn of their putative radicalism and repositioned as political debilitation, as are subsequent celebrations of altered states or fractured thought such as Deleuze and Guattari's "schizoanalysis."

As Derrida posits in elaborating "hauntology": "time is *disarticulated*, dislocated, dislodged, time is run down, on the run and run down, *deranged*, both out of order and mad" (18). Hence, when Withnail believes he is "making time" on the motorway on the journey back to London, he is arrested by the police, and this arrest itself symbolizes the running down of time, the iterative occlusion of historical possibility, of any temporal laceration of the enveloping and stagnant dead time of late capitalism. The film closes with Withnail's speech attesting to the breakdown of 1960s progressivism, and this splintering of the subject is confirmed by the absence of the "I" who narrates the film and who departs at its close. So the radical melancholia of the film does not merely harbor a nostalgia for the 1960s but also proffers a profound re-inscription of historical change that (to return to Camus' terms) desecrates the sacral aura of the 1960s by implying that it precipitates not dissidence but the very fracture of dissident political subjectivity. Withnail's final speech is delivered as a soliloquy, whereas in *Hamlet,* it is delivered to Rosencrantz and Guildenstern. Perhaps Thatcher's most notorious tenet was her assertion that "there is no such thing as society" (quoted in Lash and Urry 34). Notably the only experience of a community of sorts comes in the film's opening credits with the audience's applause during King Curtis' live cover version of Procul Harum's "A Whiter Shade of Pale." Yet here too the symbolism is ominous: the concert was recorded the night that Curtis was murdered, so the audience is a community ultimately formed around a death or an absence (Owen 127).

If tragedy is utilized as a representational deep structure in *Withnail and I* and indeed if Hamlet bewails the loss of an idealized kingdom, then there is also perhaps a more troubling aspect to the film's political unconscious, which concerns the tragedy of an England that has lost its imperial greatness. Thus, the primary tragedy in the film's political unconscious is not the end of the 1960s, nor the degradation of Thatcherism, but the specter of imperial decline and the end of an organic England. With regard to appropriations of tragedy, Raymond Williams has commented that "[i]n our century, especially, when there has been a widespread sense of ... civilization being threatened, the use of tragedy, to define a major tradition threatened or destroyed by an unruly present, has been quite obvious" (16).

What is interesting in this film about fragmentation and collapse, is that its dénouement very self-consciously evokes tragedy (and also the canonical figurehead of English literature and culture) both as an allusive resource and a formal structure that concludes the film. With reference to the formal politics or social symbolism of tragedy as a cultural mode (specifically both Camus' and Williams' reading of the form as denoting the extirpation of orders or civilizations), Friedrich Dürrenmatt asserts that it "assumes the existence of a world that possesses form," whereas "comedy ... is a world that is misshapen, in the process of becoming, of upheaval, of packing up, like ours" (82). Dürrenmatt's purpose is to assert that tragedy is no longer possible in our contemporary post–Second World War and supposedly post-imperial, post-historical, late capitalist and bureaucratized—and hence formless—world: comedy is now its most fitting mode. To this end, Dürrenmatt offers the following clarification:

> Tragedy assumes guilt, trouble, moderation, range of vision, responsibility. In the routine muddle of our century, in this last dance of the white race there are no longer any guilty people nor any responsible ones either. Nobody can do anything about it and nobody wanted it to happen. Things can really happen without anybody. Everything is dragged along

and gets caught in some sort of rake. We are too collectively guilty, too collectively embedded in the sins of fathers and forefathers. We are only grandchildren now [83–84].

It is this generational guilt, overlaying and decline that we wish to unpack and decode in our final reading of *Withnail and I*'s intertextual deployment of *Hamlet*. But despite asserting that pure tragedy is no longer possible in our degraded contemporary world, Dürrenmatt posits that "the tragic element is still possible, even if pure tragedy is no longer possible. We can extract the tragic from comedy, bring it forward as a terrible moment, as a chasm beginning to open, in this way indeed many tragedies of Shakespeare are already comedies from which the tragic factor rises up" (84). What is of interest here, according to Dürrenmatt's analysis, is that tragedy can now only function as a fragment of a former unity, as an allegorical device. As we have argued, *Withnail and I* itself is of course a comedic film structured by scattered tragic residues. The film is loaded with allegorical fragments gesturing to a former wholeness or indeed greatness: the clapped out Jaguar car, Withnail's suit tailored at Savile Row, Uncle Monty's Rolls Royce, the London housing being demolished, the once pure English countryside. In point of fact, the directions for the opening scene of the film make plain this allegorical impulse: "Despite the squalor the room is furnished with antiques ... heirlooms and other quality stuff.... A large Victorian globe of the world soars above bacon rinds" (Robinson 1). In one of the film's vertiginous final scenes, the reaction of a spaced-out Marwood to the black man, Presuming Ed, spinning Withnail's Victorian globe is telling in relation to Dürrenmatt's reference to a loss of European dominance and white imperialism: "He stares at the vast spade spinning Withnail's world around with all the dreadful connotations inherent in it" (Robinson 122). So when Dürrenmatt argues that tragedy is no longer possible, then perhaps the final tragedy in *Withnail and I* is precisely this: that tragedy, as well as the supposed civilization, empire, and aristocratic grandeur that produced it, is no longer tenable.

Consequently, the allegorical fragments strewn through the film — remnants of empire, Victorianism, aristocratic grandeur and grace, housing and social order — provide an instance of Patrick Wright's detailing of 1980s English culture's

> contemporary *orientation* towards the past rather than just the survival of old things. As so few guide-books ever recognize, this is not merely a matter of noticing old objects situated in a self-evident reality: the present meaning of historical traces such as these is only to be grasped if one takes account of the doubletake or second glance in which they are recognized. The ordinary or habitual perspectives are jarred as the old declares itself in the midst of all this dross [*On Living* 229–230].

For Walter Benjamin, the ruin is the paradigm of this allegorical imagination: "In the ruin history has physically merged into setting. And in this guise history does not assume the form of the process of an eternal life so much as that of irresistible decay. Allegory thereby declares itself to be beyond beauty. Allegories are, in the realm of thoughts, what ruins are in the realm of things" (*Origin* 177–178). While allegory acknowledges disintegration, it is nonetheless also a code of meaning that relies upon existing conventions of interpretation, its talismanic fragments gesturing to other signs and times. It thus opens up a dialectic between restoration and destruction, instigating an imaginative quest that attempts to equilibrate a sense of historical irretrievability with the reconstitution of complexes of collective meaning and value. Benjamin deems these contradictory temporal pressures "the antinomies of the allegorical":

> Any person, any object, any relationship can mean absolutely anything else. With this possibility a destructive, but just verdict is passed on the profane world: it is characterized as a world in which the detail is of no great importance. But it will be unmistakably apparent to anyone who is familiar with allegorical textual exegesis, that all of the things which are used to signify derive, from the very fact of their pointing to something else, a power which makes them appear no longer commensurable with profane things, which raises them onto a higher plane, and which can, indeed, sanctify them. Considered in allegorical terms, then, the profane world is both elevated and devalued [*Origin* 174].

Hence, the Thatcherite return to "Victorian Values," for example, sought both to indict and redeem the present, simultaneously bewailing the demise of an imaginatively ordered, filiative England while producing and convoking repositories of collective meaning. Robinson himself admits of the film that "[i]t's permeated with decay" (Owen 128). As Patrick Wright observes, "History is not just a matter of old relics: it also lies around as morbidly unfinished business, as ghosts and strange potencies that seep round the edges of every reforming design" (*Journey* 165). The 1980s lends a specific economic hue to Wright's concept of "morbidly unfinished business," given this haunting between sixties and eighties freedoms and investments, while also attesting to the residual lure of imperial grace and the Gramscian "morbid symptoms" of its interregnum. Most explicitly, this allegorical fragment demarcating the tragedy of imperial England is enacted when Monty and Withnail conduct the following exchange:

> MONTY (in Latin): ... but *old* now ... *old* ... There can be no beauty without decay.
>
> WITHNAIL (in Latin): A requiem for England." (Robinson 97)

Another submerged resonance of *Hamlet* in the film comes in the form of its discourse on Irishness and Ireland. It is significant in terms of English Renaissance discourse on Ireland that Hamlet swears by Saint Patrick (I.v.136) when intimating that his father's ghost comes from a place of purgation. This oath builds upon an established medieval discourse on Ireland (relating to translations and adaptations of *Saint Patrick's Purgatory* by Cistercians and Anglo-Norman Augustinian canons, among others), claiming that Ireland itself, specifically Lough Derg, was purgatory: "an entrance, perhaps the only entrance on earth accessible to mortals, to the otherworld" (Greenblatt 74). So this view of Ireland as purgatory is produced out of a long sedimented colonial discourse representing it as a place of hostile otherworldliness. This intertextual echo reverberates in *Withnail and I* in the scene in the Mother Black Cap Irish pub, which is graffitied with IRA slogans. For 1969 was not merely the final year of the sixties; it was also the year that the British army was deployed to the North of Ireland. In an interview, Robinson himself refers to his own experience of drinking in the Mother Black Cap with the Irish, whom he deems "The Wankers" from Camden Town and Kentish Town: "When arseholed, which was always, they were a pretty scary mob ..." (Owen 112)

This experience clearly informs the scene in the film in which Withnail and Marwood are accosted by an Irishman. The directions from the screenplay inform us that the "atmosphere is rank with smoke and Irish accent" (Robinson 18). So if the film is striving to suggest that there is something rotten in the state of Britain, then it is here projected onto the Irish and the "Irish problem." For those versed in English stereotyping of the Irish, Marwood's assailant is described in familiarly simian terms: "Get any more masculine than him and you'd have to live up a tree" (Robinson 20). In a film so concerned with playing roles and self-referential staging, here is a reworking of the stage Irishman promulgated most popularly in the Victorian period. The scene in this pub is vital to the plot of the film, for it is the moment when Withnail contacts Uncle Monty by phone to arrange a meeting to procure the keys to his country house; it must be endured for the journey to take place, for the transition from urban London hell to English pastoral (of sorts) to be accomplished. So if, as discussed, the film's use of tragedy mediates a sense of fracture between an older, imperial and more grandiose England and a new, infernal dispensation of decline, then in this instance, it is Irishness and the current "Troubles" in the North of Ireland that provide the purgatorial rite of passage. Ireland becomes not for the first time in history a desiring space through which Englishness rehearses its own problematics and disenchantments.

To conclude, then: If ever there was a figure who has been used to represent Britain's imperial glory it is Shakespeare, and despite the film's avowed iconoclastic chic, for Robinson, in terms of Englishness, Shakespeare is a figure both of mourning and of messianic redemption. Despite its veneer of social dissent and apparent celebration of countercultural values, the film in fact mourns what it affects to despise — the loss of England's high cultural greatness: "Shakespeare, to me, is a greater miracle than Jesus Christ. All the people that I've ever admired historically are as dwarves compared to this guy. Fuck Jesus, give me Shakespeare" (Owen 244–245). Nonetheless, we have also suggested that *Hamlet* does function in a more radical way in the film, providing an intergenerational haunting between the 1960s and the 1980s that divests the former decade of its radicalism and apprehends it instead as fathering the economic dynamic and individualism of the latter. For if tragedy as a form, from its classical precursors to the present, gives us access to a world that does not make moral sense, in which human beings are in thrall to systems beyond their control without logic or mercy, then surely tragedy reaches its apotheosis in the 1980s, the decade in which the "invisible hand" of the market dictated our lives as never before, where a naked monetarism and its spurious logic perversely offered themselves as the only explanation of our world.

Works Cited

Benjamin, Walter. *Illuminations.* London: Fontana, 1992.

_____. *The Origin of German Tragic Drama.* Translated by John Osborne. Introduction by George Steiner. London: NLB, 1977.

Deleuze, Gilles and Felix Guattari. *A Thousand Plateaus.* Translated and with introduction by Brian Massumi. London: Athlone Press, 1988.

Derrida, Jacques. *Specters of Marx: The State of the Debt, the Work of Mourning, and the New International.* Translated by Peggy Kamuf. Introduction by Bernd Magnus and Stephen Cullenberg. London: Routledge, 1994.

Dollimore, Jonathan. *Radical Tragedy.* London: Harvester Wheatsheaf, 1989.

Dürrenmatt, Friedrich. *Writings on Theatre and Drama.* Translated and with introduction by H.M. Waidson. London: Jonathan Cape, 1976.

Empire. Issue 81. March 1996. Interview with Bruce Robinson and Richard E. Grant. 79–82.

Fukuyama, Francis. *The End of History and the Last Man.* London: Penguin, 1992.

Gramsci, Antonio. *Selections from the Prison Notebooks.* Ed. and trans. Quintin Hoare and Geoffrey Nowell Smith. London: Lawrence and Wishart, 1996 (1973).

Greenblatt, Stephen. *Hamlet in Purgatory.* Princeton: Princeton U P, 2001.

Jameson, Fredric. *The Ideologies of Theory: Essays 1971–1986.* Volume II: *The Syntax of History.* London: Routledge, 1988.

_____. *The Political Unconscious: Narrative as a Socially Symbolic Act.* London: Routledge, 1996.

Lash, Scott and John Urry. *Economies of Sign and Space*. London: Sage, 1994.

Owen, Alistair, ed. *Smoking in Bed: Conversations with Bruce Robinson*. London: Bloomsbury, 2000.

Robinson, Bruce. *Withnail and I: The Original Screenplay*. London: Bloomsbury, 1989.

Shakespeare, William. *Hamlet*. Edited by G.R. Hibbard. Oxford: Oxford University Press, 1987.

Williams, Raymond. *Modern Tragedy*. London: Hogarth Press, 1992.

Wright, Patrick. *On Living in an Old Country: The National Past in Contemporary Britain*. London: Verso, 1985.

_____. *A Journey Through Ruins: The Last Days of London*. London: Radius, 1991.

Notes

1. As well as quoting *Hamlet* directly, the film invokes Shakespeare in other, often more allusive ways. For instance, there is a poster of Laurence Olivier as Othello in the bathroom of Withnail and Marwood's London flat, while Bob Dylan's lyrics to "All along the Watchtower" (the musical accompaniment to the boys' journey to the Lake District), recall I.iv. of *Hamlet*, in which the Prince awaits the visitation of the ghost: "All along the watchtower / Princes kept their view...." We are grateful to our colleague, Dr. Keith Hughes, for drawing our attention to this Shakespearean allusion.

2. In 1996, ten years after its initial release, the readers of *Empire* magazine voted *Withnail and I* their Favourite Cult Film.

3. See Walker, 163.

4. In an interview in *Empire* magazine to mark the tenth anniversary of the film's release, Robinson talks of Marwood's haircut at the end of film as symbolic of "the horror of Thatcherism coming on."

5. For a study of such stereotyping see L.P. Curtis, Jr. *Anglo-Saxons and Celts: A Study of Anti-Irish Prejudice in Victorian England* (Bridgeport, Connecticut: Conference on British Studies, 1968), and Liz Curtis, *Ireland: The Propaganda War, The British Media and the "Battle for Hearts and Minds."* (London: Pluto Press, 1984).

8

Horatio: The First CSI

Jody Malcolm

> Horatio, thou are e'en as just a man
> As e'er my conversation coped withal.
> —(*Hamlet*, III.ii.56–57)

Perhaps the most recent overt case of bardolatry on the small screen occurs on *CSI: Miami*, the sister-show to the hugely popular and well-established *CSI: Crime Scene Investigation*. Like its predecessor, the Miami show focuses on a group of crime-scene investigators whose daily lives are infused with mystery, violence, and dead bodies—lots of dead bodies. Leading the Miami group of sometimes blithe yet usually compassionate and earnest investigators is the competent and melancholy Horatio Caine (played by David Caruso), who shares much in common with *Hamlet's* Horatio. As Susan Baker writes in "Shakespearean Authority in the Classic Detective Story," when Shakespeare enters a text "as a convenient narrative device," his presence often becomes a "resonant narrative effect" (428). This Shakespearean presence may be manifested through direct or indirect discourse, and when a character is created within this parameter, "other descriptors will be applied to that character as well" (427). *CSI: Miami* and Horatio Caine have been developed within this Shakespearean presence, evolving immersed in the milieu of the classic film noir detective story.

Although *CSI: Miami* is not technically a noir crime drama, noir has had such an indelible effect on the development of fictional crime texts that most television detectives are indebted to Raymond Chandler's definition of what a detective is. Whereas Chandler's detective works outside organized law enforcement, television's investigators usually work from within, taking with them the traits of the hard-boiled private detective. As a group, modern television detectives possess astute powers of observation, uncanny

David Caruso as Horatio Caine in CBS's crime drama *CSI-Miami*.

insight into human behavior, and a strong, silent demeanor; in addition, many detectives exhibit the requisite noir problems with alcohol and women. Before Raymond Chandler, however, there was William Shakespeare. In "Dismember Me: Shakespeare, Paranoia, and the Logic of Mass Culture," Linda Charnes, after analyzing Renaissance revenge tragedies, asserts that *Hamlet* is the first noir literature and that Hamlet is the first noir detective/revenger (4). Thus in *CSI: Miami*, we witness the presence of two strong cultural presences: Chandler and Shakespeare.

Shakespeare's influence is confirmed in the episode "Case 22" when a character who is dying from radiation poisoning informs Investigator Caine that Horatio was the first crime-scene investigator. He looks at her quizzically, to which she responds, "You know, in *Hamlet*." Oddly, Horatio had obviously never considered the implications of his own name. In fact, if one did not know Shakespeare, one might associate the name with Horatio Hornblower, or as one *Slate* columnist has asserted, with both Hispanic and New England associations (Heffernan). However, it is clear that the writers of the series want the audience to associate this modern hero with Shakespeare's Horatio, and when we examine Horatio Caine's character and demeanor as well as the mood of the series, we find those descriptors that Baker articulates. One of the most convincing descriptors arises when we consider the function of Horatio in both works.

In *Hamlet*, it is only Horatio who is privy to Hamlet's plan, who knows how it went awry and, therefore, can explain why the stage floor is littered with corpses:

And let me speak to the yet unknowing world
How these things came about: so shall you hear
Of carnal, bloody, and unnatural acts,
Of accidental judgements, casual slaughters;
Of deaths put on by cunning and forc'd cause,
And, in this upshot, purposes mistook
Fall'n on the inventors' heads; all this can I
Truly deliver [V.ii.380–87].

On the series every week, Horatio Caine leads his colleagues step by step through the mystery at hand, making sense of the complexities of science and human nature to solve murders and atrocities similar to those Shakespeare's Horatio will recount. In his milieu, Horatio Caine has all the answers. Indeed, we get the sense that he is omniscient, that he has seen it all, that he knows how things happened before an investigation is completed. In Caine's biography at the *CSI* Web site, we are told that he "is a three-dimensional thinker, who easily sees how the pieces of a puzzle fit together," and that he "just doesn't trust science, he trusts his gut." Although we might think that he would be jaded by his journeys into violence and death, he remains compassionate toward the crime victims and their loved ones and understanding toward his staff who, he realizes, have not seen as much as he. His fierce determination and aggressiveness in the search for those responsible for committing such atrocities is equally matched by a sweet sadness and melancholy.

Although named Horatio, Caine takes over Hamlet's task of gathering evidence while retaining his predecessor's objectivity and ability to "tell the tale" of the corpses whose "guts are lugged" to his crime lab, this crime lab itself a veritable living illustration of Burton's *Anatomy of Melancholy*, a work which, of course, influenced Shakespeare's development of *Hamlet*. Like Burton in his seminal work, the Miami investigators' attempt to recreate the victims' consciousness, albeit by using high-tech devices Burton could not even have imagined. The high-tech devices used in Caine's crime lab combined with the digital technology now available serve to assist one of the latest trends in television crime drama: showing explicit investigations of corpses in order to recreate the circumstances concerning the victims' deaths. For example, digital technology allows the audience to follow a bullet from its point of entry on a body through its vital organs and out again.

Another trend in television crime drama is to show explicit scenes of bodily mutilation, just as Shakespeare broke from the decorum of the classics by showing such bodily mutilation on stage, complete with the spectacle of blood. Such displays are common on *CSI: Miami*. In one particularly gruesome episode, the Miami investigators sever a hand from a corpse and heat it in a microwave so that they can retrieve an object caught within its grip; in another episode, a bullet-riddled body is retrieved from the stomach of a shark. (So much, then, for Hamlet's quaint musings about the lives and fates of great and ordinary men in the graveyard scene.) Burton himself would be awed by the sophistication of Caine's crime lab in which human organs are sliced, diced, and dissected not only to discover the victims' causes of death, but also to recreate the minutiae of their lives: what they were eating, drinking, and sometimes even feeling shortly before their deaths.

The graphics utilized to illustrate these forensics findings are striking, and these spectacles most certainly engage the viewing audience's imagination, just as Shakespeare's stage blood did during his time. In addition, the offhand way in which some of the investigators approach these almost obscene investigations provides morbid comic relief from the grotesqueries presented every week. For example, Medical Examiner Alexx Woods talks soothingly to the corpses throughout her examinations, stopping to smooth back strands of loose hair or to caress a cheek, while cooing, "The poor baby never knew what hit her." At a scene of a sniper shooting, the following exchange between Caine and ballistics expert Calleigh Duquesne is representative of the sharp comic relief found in every episode of the series:

> HORATIO: So what do you get when a six-foot tall man lays down with a three foot long rifle?
>
> CALLEIGH: Hot flashes ... but that's just me.

The flip callousness of the remark reminds one of Hamlet's disdain for the gravedigger's singing while carrying out his unpleasant task, but as Horatio comments, "Custom hath made it in [the gravedigger] a property of / easiness" (IV.i.68–69). The *CSI* investigators approach their work as did Shakespeare's gravediggers and later as did Raymond Chandler's classic noir detective, "with a rude wit, a lively sense of the grotesque, a disgust for sham, and a contempt for pettiness" (15).

Although the writers exposed their affinity for the Bard in "Case 22," "Case 18" also provides clues to the writers' use of Shakespearean descriptors. This case, titled "Bunk" could be aptly subtitled "Something's Rotten in the City of Miami," as we find the investigators sealing off a suburban neighborhood threatened by the toxic fumes emitted from a home-based drug lab. In 1935, Caroline Spurgeon proposed that it is not Hamlet in particular who is diseased; Denmark itself is rotten, and in the series this rottenness is portrayed through the pervasive, debilitating effects of Miami's drug culture. The poisonous chemical nature of the drugs and the poisonous societal implications of making and dealing drugs evoke the "poison" that corrupts and kills in Elsinore. Dressed in biohazard suits, Caine and Speedle (another investigator) cautiously approach the bodies lying on the floor inside the otherwise normal-looking suburban home, a scene that reminds us of the bodies that litter the stage at the conclusion of *Hamlet*. To find the source of Elsinore's corruption, Hamlet must find the ghost; likewise, Caine comments to Speedle as they enter the home: "When we find the body, we find the source" of the poison that corrupts Miami.

Bodies continue to litter the stage in this episode of *CSI* as well. The violence escalates when a teenager dies from taking the tainted drugs, and the financial backer of the drug lab fears being exposed by his slacker chemist. The choice of weapon is interesting because it is a savage and messy way to commit murder, and certainly the choice of a dermatologist would be more tidy and less risky. However, *CSI*'s dermatologist uses a dagger, a dagger on which the camera and the storyline place much emphasis. Of course, most murder weapons are closely analyzed in a crime drama, but this dagger, because it represents such an odd choice of weapon and because of its ornate, aged appearance, suggests an era long past. Again, *CSI* evokes the violence that pervades Shakespeare's play: Hamlet, driven by primal rage, runs a sword through Polonius; later, after realizing that "the readiness is all," engages in what is supposed to be a civilized duel that results in four deaths. However, like Horatio Caine week after week on *CSI: Miami*, Shakespeare's Horatio remains standing at the end of the play, physically unaffected yet undoubtedly psychically changed by what he has witnessed.

The reason for Caine's melancholy has not yet been fully explored on the series; certainly, his line of work accounts for some of his pall, but the audience has recently been informed that his younger brother Raymond, a police officer, was killed during a drug bust gone wrong. It is not clear yet, but Caine was somehow involved in this operation and seems to feel responsible for his brother's death. During the "Dispo Day" episode, a police officer refers to the circumstances of Caine's brother's death. Caine laments his brother: "Yes. He was too good, too young," revealing the tragic sense of waste that characterizes Horatio's eulogy for Hamlet: "Now cracks a noble heart. Good night, sweet / Prince" (V.ii.359–60). Caine's brother, we can assume, possessed the virtue and sense of justice Caine himself displays and which Hamlet so desperately valued and sought in those he loved. It is obvious that Caine, although he faces and investigates death every day, has not come to terms with the death of his brother, and his adversaries take every opportunity to exploit his only apparent weakness. Hamlet, of course, comes to terms with death in the graveyard, commenting on how the gravedigger presses a skull into the ground as if were "Cain's jawbone, that did the first murder" (V.i.78). Perhaps then in *CSI*, Caine's name itself is an allusion not only to the fratricide that initiates the action in *Hamlet*, but also to the fratricide that Caine feels he may have committed.

However, in several episodes of the series' debut season, the integrity of Caine's brother is questioned. Was he really a good cop, or did he become an addict and a dealer himself during his undercover narcotics investigations? This possibility is alluded to in several episodes. In "Freaks and Tweaks," a drug dealer claims to have known Raymond, saying that he had "gotten high" with him many times. In "Case 18," the state attorney, conspicuously named Dante, becomes involved in the drug-house case, and the similarities to the situation that resulted in Raymond's death are apparent to both him and Caine. Dante assures Caine that Raymond was a good cop; however, he makes it clear that Caine should not push the current case as it would perhaps involve a look into Raymond's death that would tarnish the brother's image, as well as Caine's. "Let it go," he firmly tells Caine, for both professional and personal reasons, hinting at the ambiguity surrounding the circumstances of Raymond's life and death.

We, of course, are well aware of Hamlet's ambiguous nature. Was he really insane? Was he the "sweet prince" Horatio recalls? Or was he the "death bringer" as G. Wilson Knight identified him in 1930? Was he scourge or minister as debated by Fredson Thayer Bowers in 1989? The question of Hamlet's integrity remains unanswered, as do the questions we have about Raymond Caine at the end of the series' first season.

In future seasons, clues to Raymond Caine's integrity may be answered in part by his widow, Yelina, a character who has been a mysterious presence in at least five episodes. When she is first introduced, the audience is led to believe that she may be a love interest for Caine; however, in her second appearance, it is clear that she is his sister-in-law. There is an uneasy connection between Yelina and Caine, which may be a synthesis of sorrow, desire, and guilt. Because this series is new and the characters and their personas are being slowly revealed, it is difficult to speculate how the storyline with the sister-in-law may develop. Since she was married to the brother for whose death Horatio feels responsible, Yelina may represent a Gertrude-like figure, for there is clearly sexual tension between her and Caine. If this speculation proves true, especially if the two had consummated their attraction before the brother's death, the revelation would certainly add a new dimension to Caine's meta-virtuous character and provide solid justification for his allegorical name. Indeed, in the world of *Hamlet*, this coupling would be considered incestuous. Furthermore, according to Caine's biography at the *CSI* Web site, his mother was murdered by drug dealers when he was a young man, suggestive again of the poison that afflicts our culture and the poisoned drink that killed Hamlet's mother.

However, it may be that Yelina is an Ophelia-like figure, the even longer-suffering Ophelia who survives to be comforted or, as seems to be the case in *CSI*, discomforted by her lover's brother. Indeed, Slavoj Zizek asserts that the "femme fatale and the obscene-knowing father cannot appear simultaneously, within the same narrative space" (quoted in Charnes 6). As a possible object of temptation who could perhaps undermine Caine's patriarchal authority and unleash the libidinal obscene father, Yelina does appear with Caine in a few brief sequences, but the space they share is punctuated with an uneasiness suggestive of a personal history that neither wishes to confront. If Ophelia had survived the carnage of *Hamlet* and recovered from her madness, her relationship with Horatio likely would have been plagued by a similar dissonance. Although Yelina is seemingly self-possessed and is herself employed in law enforcement, she projects a fragility and femininity suggestive of Ophelia. Ultimately, Ophelia shares with Yelina the devastation of losing loved ones because of the errors in judgment of other loved ones.

Further complicating these complex relationships among mothers, brothers, and lovers, we have an absent father, instead of a dead one. According to Caine's biography, he was raised by a single mother who was herself killed by a drug dealer. The father's absence, perhaps even more so than his presence, mediates Caine's ontology in the symbolic order. Caine's father thus represents Lacan's "big Other," and as Charnes points out, the big Other

> is effective only when misrecognized as an essential "being" that guarantees the existence of subjective and social formations. In patriarchal culture the place of the big Other may be occupied by God, King, Pope, Lord, Father — placeholders who quilt a paternal allegory over a fundamentally antagonistic social formation and call things to order and account within it [2].

The function of the big Other in classic detective fiction assumes order and a teleology defined by logic and deduction; however, its function is transformed in noir so the big Other becomes an agent of "prurient pleasure, the obscene enjoyment that Lacan would claim always underwrites paternal

Law" (2). Referring to Zizek's discussion of noir, she adds that this "obscene father" is thus unable to function as the "guarantor of the symbolic" (2). In *CSI,* we have a protagonist whose fatherless past and personal life are suggestive of noir but whose public life is clearly ordered by the logic of classic detective fiction; thus the series itself synthesizes the two genres to satisfy the desires of the audience, who demands that all loose ends be tied up at the conclusion of each episode, and also to create an indeterminancy that differentiates *CSI* from the dozens of other crime dramas currently airing. Among those crime dramas that endeavor to make their characters' private lives part of the ongoing storyline, there have been very few that have introduced that personal information so subtly and provocatively. As Charnes says of *Hamlet,* "no one in this play 'knows' anyone else; and it is precisely this missing 'intersubjective' knowledge … that constitutes *Hamlet* as a *noir* tragedy" (6–7). Clearly, the viewers of *CSI* are missing this intersubjective knowledge in a medium that has the dubious honor of creating characters who are often more familiar than one's next door neighbors. As a result, the audience become detectives, putting together pieces of information in order to determine what tragedies lurk in this modern Horatio's past and what consequences those tragedies will have on his future. We know that the "rottenness of Denmark" ultimately consumed Hamlet, but will the poison of Miami in which Caine is immersed every day, the poison which claimed the lives of those closest to him, consume him as well?

As Horatio Caine's history slowly unfolds, we can be certain only that *CSI*'s creator Anthony Zuiker intended him to be a descendent of *Hamlet*'s Horatio and that he is molded in the style of Chandler's private investigator, of whom Chandler wrote:

> Down these mean streets a man must go who is not himself mean, who is neither tarnished nor afraid. The detective in this kind of story must be such a man. He is the hero, he is everything. He must be a complete man and a common man and yet an unusual man. He must be, to use a rather weathered phrase, a man of honor — by instinct, by inevitability, without thought of it, and certainly without saying it [14].

How Caine's personal and professional conflicts will be resolved on the series is uncertain, but from the frequent references to his brother's death, it does appear that revenge may be in his future. Indeed, his colleagues and adversaries alike seem to be anticipating an eruption of strong emotion from this unusually calm and composed man. Unlike Hamlet, however, who cursed that he was ever born to set his father's murder right, we would expect that Caine (like Chandler's detective) would "take … no man's insolence without a due and dispassionate revenge" (Chandler 14). Horatio, having learned from Hamlet the consequences of all passion spent, would instead put his noir talents to use in his classic detective environment. It remains to be seen if the paternal metaphor will succeed or fail on *CSI*; it is certain, however, that if it fails, the viewing audience will be introduced to the newest modern noir revenge tragedy.

Works Cited

Baker, Susan. "Shakespearean Authority in the Classic Detective Story." *Shakespeare Quarterly* 46 (1995): 424–48.

Bowers, Fredson Thayer. *Hamlet as Scourge and Minister*. Charlottesville, Va.: University of Virginia Press, 1989.

Burton, Robert. *The Anatomy of Melancholy*. New York: DaCapo Press, 1971.

Charnes, Linda. "Dismember Me: Shakespeare, Paranoia, and the Logic of Mass Culture." *Shakespeare Quarterly* 48 (1997): 1–16.

Chandler, Raymond. "The Simple Art of Murder." *The Second Chandler Omnibus*. London: Hamish Hamilton, 1962. 3–15.

CSI: Miami. Official Website. 25 March 2002. CBS. www.cbs.com/primetime/csi_miami.

Heffernan, Virginia. "Dial Miami for Murder." *Slate* 3 Oct. 2002 www.slate.msn.com. 22 May 2003.

Knight, G. Wilson. *The Wheel of Fire: Interpretations of Shakespeare*. 1930. London: Methuen, 1949.

Shakespeare, William. *Hamlet*. Edited by Edward Hubler. New York: Penguin-Signet, 1987.

Spurgeon, Caroline. *Shakespeare's Imagery and What It Tells Us*. 1935. Cambridge: Cambridge University Press, 1961.

Zuiker, Anthony E. *CSI: Miami*. Produced by Jerry Bruckheimer. CBS, 2002–2003.

9

Teen Scenes: Recognizing Shakespeare in Teen Film

Ariane M. Balizet

"I found [King Lear]...a Heap of Jewels, unstrung and unpolisht; yet so dazling in their Disorder, that I soon perceiv'd I had seiz'd a Treasure."
— Nahum Tate, introduction to *King Lear*,
"Reviv'd with Alterations," 1681.

Just 76 years after Shakespeare wrote *King Lear*, Nahum Tate's "Revision" attempted, as we see in his introduction, to bring forth from the text what Tate saw as the essence of the play. This process of identifying and, through alteration, illuminating particular aspects of Shakespeare's work is one with which contemporary directors, actors, and scholars struggle today, especially in the face of an increased presence of Shakespearean ideas and texts in popular media. Was Tate's revision a service to the text, we might ask, and to what degree did it deliberately obscure elements of the text that were perhaps controversial for the time? Using Tate's language, is the revised *King Lear* a new setting for the jewel that is Shakespeare's creation or does the revision change the nature of the jewel itself? The questions Tate's work poses offer a fresh insight into the resurgence of Shakespeare in popular cinema, specifically those films which depict teenaged characters.

This essay will examine a few of these teen films (*Romeo + Juliet* [1996], *10 Things I Hate About You* [1999], *Get Over it!* [2001], and *O* [2001]) and will argue that their process of identifying, extracting, and polishing the jewel of Shakespeare's text is directly related to their common integration of genre and popular culture. These films are connected through their production of a unique experience for the audience in which the figure of Shakespeare — as defined by his name, language, work, and/or broad cultural impact — appears with significant consequences for the adolescent world portrayed within the film.[1]

This particular experience can be summed up in what I term *recognition*. In certain instances, these films invoke recognition as a function of the familiar: the immediacy of the action on screen is highlighted when a film reveals a storyline or plot device as Shakespeare's. In this way, these films fit a Shakespearean lens over the modern world depicted on screen, offering an understanding of the high school prom through a familiar framework of Shakespeare's names and themes. *10 Things I Hate About You* and *Get Over It!* rely upon the praxis of *recognition-as-familiar*. The opposite perspective is equally important. A film like *Romeo + Juliet* (and others of this group, to a lesser degree) literally re-cognizes Shakespeare; that is, it uses a contemporary setting as a means to *know again* the play at the heart of the film. The audience peers through the conventions of a teen film to view "Shakespeare" on the other side. It is necessary for the concept of re-cognition, however, to distinguish between William Shakespeare, the author, and "Shakespeare," the landscape W.B. Worthen and others have identified as an inclusive phenomenon of encounters with the author. Worthen encapsulates the Shakespeare phenomena between quotation marks to define it this way: "'Shakespeare' ... demarcates a zone of cultural transmission that includes various sixteenth- and seventeenth-century texts, their textual and performative history, and our own labor and conversation with them" (12). Worthen's breadth here is not careless; the idea "Shakespeare" really must include centuries of text, performance, and scholarship given even the most basic examples of authorship debates and theater history. Re-cognition highlights Shakespeare's work, whereas recognition-as-familiar uses Shakespeare's work as a means of addressing contemporary concerns. Both forms of recognition shape, challenge, and add to "Shakespeare."

Compared with contemporary films such as Kenneth Branagh's *Henry V*, *Romeo + Juliet* and *10 Things I Hate About You* can be seen as active but peripheral elements of "Shakespeare." Their clearest distinction from Branagh's *Henry V* is their position as pop culture. In their recent collection *Shakespeare, the Movie*, Lynda Boose and Richard Burt construct a spectrum of "Shakespeare(s)" on film as a function of the popularization of the plays. Olivier, Zeffirelli, and even Branagh now appear as classic and authoritative — pure — interpreters, even though all three directors can be and are viewed as popularizers in their own time (Boose and Burt 2). Gil Junger, the director of *10 Things I Hate About You*, and Baz Lurhmann, the director of *Romeo + Juliet*, may never enjoy such status, if only because their films make the subtle but significant leap from "popular" to "pop." These films yoke the teen genre with the tradition of Shakespeare on film and can be examined as a coherent group. The Shakespeare teenpic[2] is characterized by two main elements: with respect to the cinematic tradition, the Shakespeare teenpic uses the authority of "Shakespeare" to legitimize a unique representation of adolescent life in the late twentieth and early twenty-first centuries; and within the realm of Shakespeare studies, this handful of films uses the malleable and colorful context of an adolescent world to extend boundaries of the "Shakespeare" phenomenon. These two constitutive elements of the Shakespeare teenpic thus replicate recognition-as-familiar and re-cognition, respectively. The Shakespeare teenpics reposition themselves around "Shakespeare" as a distinct object, including literary, historical, and poetic authority. The recognition of Shakespeare's play and its position relative to the film is essential to each film's effort to comment on adolescence.

Romeo + Juliet: Re-Cognizing the "Greatest Love Story Ever Told"[3]

Luhrmann's deliberate juxtaposition of the teen lovers and the rest of their world sets up the framework through which the movie re-cognizes Shakespeare's play. On the most basic level, Luhrmann depicts Romeo and

"Two blushing pilgrims ready stand": Romeo (Leonardo DiCaprio) first approaches Juliet (Claire Danes) in *William Shakespeare's Romeo + Juliet.*

Juliet as the ordered center of a cluttered world; the gangs, the families, and the rest of Verona Beach create an opaque and meaningless collage of human experience and emotion. Romeo and Juliet, however, are both the focus of our concern and the transparent subjects through which "Shakespeare" can be seen. Romeo and Juliet's stillness allow the audience to recognize them as familiar—familiar enough, that is, to provoke the re-cognition of their story. The Verona Beach of the film is a place of chaos. The patriarchs, unable to restrain modern outbreaks of their families' "ancient grudge," are sweaty, hulking, imposing men. Ladies Montague and Capulet are either garish and indulgent in a semi-incestuous relationship (Capulet) or dry and powerless in the face of her masculine family (Montague). Peers of the young lovers are senselessly angry and rebellious against society, but fiercely loyal to the family bitterness. People, cars, and conversations move with the reckless speed that marks the world of Luhrmann's film. While the world spins madly, however, the two main characters remain still and calm, like punctuation after a tirade. When we first see Romeo, he is brooding over a cigarette and a poem, framed in the decaying arch of a dilapidated theater. The sun sets behind him, and the weight of the camera pulling away from this figure of calm is highlighted by a series of slow motion shots of the beach. One shot — that of a prostitute dancing for a man as he reaches for his wallet — should fit in seamlessly with the established visual patterns of sexual excess, but because this brief scene does not have the swift energy of the film up to this point, it appears repulsive and embarrassing. The slowing, calming presence Romeo offers to the frenetic film makes the camera drag, and the carnivalesque space out of which our hero emerges becomes an exposure of obscenity.

The appearance of Juliet has a very similar effect. The camera focuses on her mother's clownish lips as she screams Juliet's name, then pans back into a wide shot of the Capulet mansion, the Lady dwarfed (but not intimidated) by the estate. As Luhrmann's camera chases Lady Capulet around the house to find her daughter, the movement is suddenly interrupted by a portrait shot of Juliet, wide-eyed and framed by a halo of hair, face-down in her bathwater (we will see Romeo in the same view halfway through the party scene). Again, Juliet slows down the picture and draws the agitated movement to a point of focus. The audience is immediately aware of the fact that these two young people are unique — if only because they rarely scream or spin or shoot — and deserve our attention. At the expense of any real concern for the other characters, *Romeo + Juliet* makes it clear that the young lovers warrant concern far more than do their parents or cousins. They are the only true individuals of the movie, the most precious gems in Verona Beach.

Romeo (Leonardo DiCaprio) and Juliet (Claire Danes) exchange doomed wedding vows as a boys' choir performs the '90s dance hit *Everybody's Free (To Feel Good)*.

To say that Luhrmann is using Shakespeare to make a statement about contemporary pop culture and teen violence is not entirely unreasonable, but is perhaps backwards; *Romeo + Juliet* turns the focus of an exaggerated culture of youth back to William Shakespeare's play. Using a system of images and sounds that build upon an aspect of the "Shakespeare" landscape that interprets *Romeo and Juliet* as the quintessential tale of young, innocent love, Luhrmann's film creates a pop version of Verona that not only questions the traditional interpretation of the play, but also alters and re-frames the way audiences cognize *Romeo and Juliet*. This altered setting serves as the means for viewing and comprehending the jewel of Shakespeare's text, and the audience is invited to look through and beyond that symbolic world to see *Romeo and Juliet* anew. "Shakespeare" is the subject, and this MTV world is the lens through which it is accessed. For Luhrmann, "dazzling disorder" is the desired effect.

The question of which elements of the play are re-cognized is just as important as how this comes to be, although the answer must be somewhat reductive.[4] By isolating the title characters in a world of violence and lust, Luhrmann re-polarizes *Romeo and Juliet*. The symmetry of Capulet and Montague as equal and opposing forces shifts to the precarious vision of an entire world juxtaposed to Romeo and Juliet. Verona Beach is corrupt and irredeemable; parents are lustful, greedy, and domineering; and friends are murderous and lunatic. Even the kind friar (here, "Father Lawrence") is slow and irresponsible, and the nurse ultimately betrays her young charge by turning away from Juliet in her most desperate moment. No character deserves the love of Romeo or Juliet in the film, and the thought of their union canceling the "ancient grudge" between their families is rendered only in a brief and incoherent musing from Father Lawrence. Throughout Luhrmann's film, Romeo and Juliet carry with them the aesthetics of salvation but not the purpose. In the party scene, they are depicted as an angel and a chivalric knight, but both without a world to save. Luhrmann refuses to allow for the possibility that Verona Beach will ever change, but the figures Romeo and Juliet suggest that we may re-cognize *Romeo and Juliet* in *William Shakespeare's Romeo + Juliet* by putting aside the notion of doomed love and replacing it with an unfair expectation of civic redemption. Re-cognition, however, goes beyond a purely interpretive gesture by challenging a seemingly basic understanding of the play. Re-cognition is not the suggestion of new meaning, but the destabilizing of traditional modes of viewing the text and its manifestations in theaters, film, and even schools.

"I thought he only wrote movies": Shakespeare Goes to High School

In "The World According to Teenpix," Thomas M. Leitch defines the teen film of the 1980s as a cinematic space in which adolescents inhabit their own discrete world, where the crucial point of the characters' development is the act of accepting, applauding, and actually freezing that moment in time. Leitch takes as his examples the films of John Hughes (*Ferris Bueller's Day Off, The Breakfast Club, Sixteen Candles*) and a handful of slasher films of the day (*Halloween, A Nightmare on Elm Street*) to illuminate the pattern of teenaged subjects overcoming financial, parental, or institutional obstacles to reach their ultimate goal: each other. When characters kiss or embrace at the finale of Hughes's movies in particular, the audience is assured that the external factors holding apart the main characters have been eliminated, and the adolescent world has been resealed. Leitch addresses the shaping of that world by articulating the way teens in these movies confront the adult world and its inadequacies:

> Hughes's teens rise to this challenge by valorizing adolescence as an
> unchanging, self-justifying system of values which does not reaffirm or

renew standards of maturity but simply marginalizes the adult world by ignoring any possible continuities it might have with the world of adolescence and setting goals which can be reached without growth or change [45].

Leitch rightly constructs the teenpic as the best view of this arrested development, and when the evil principal has been bested, the forgetful father admonished, and the bullying senior humiliated, protagonists are rewarded with public acceptance of their heterosexual union. In the films, this union lasts only a moment (usually the film's final scene), but the protagonists' coming together appears to last forever, as they are frozen in perpetual adolescence.

The Shakespeare teenpix examined here owe as much to this tradition as they do to Shakespeare's plays. Films like *10 Things I Hate About You* and *Get Over It!* acknowledge (and complicate) this model in significant ways, thereby establishing themselves as heirs to Hughes's movies while making important departures from his formula. In his article, Leitch offers the precise point of departure at which my analysis begins. Leitch looks back to Shakespeare as a contrast to the Hughes love stories, thus anticipating the Shakespeare teenpic and its reworking of the arrested adolescent world in a way the teen movies of the 1980s never did: "The Beatrices and Benedicks of romantic comedy typically find themselves at odds with their destined romantic partners because of their own pride or prejudice — the limitations of their own identities from which romance can liberate them" (45). For the Hughes films, Leitch notes, obstacles remained definitively external. In Shakespeare's comedies — and, by extension, the Shakespeare teenpix of the 1990s — these obstacles are primarily internal. The adolescent process of realizing particular identity serves as a common obstacle for Katherina from *The Taming of the Shrew* and Kat from *10 Things I Hate About You*, although they both must engage this struggle in the face of misogyny and rigidly enforced gender roles.[5] This discussion examines *10 Things* and *Get Over It!* via the moments in which they harmonize with their Shakespearean counterparts (*The Taming of the Shrew* and *A Midsummer Night's Dream*, respectively), but the similarities and points of intersection should not be taken as indication of a complete correlation. To do so would marginalize the importance of these two films. The assumption that *10 Things* and *Get Over It!* are remakes of Shakespeare's unique work suggests that the text of *Taming* is the original and *10 Things* a lesser version. If Worthen's concept of "Shakespeare" has illustrated anything, it must be that the search for an absolute original on the spectrum of all things Shakespearean is futile.

10 Things and *Get Over It!* reverse the action of re-cognition in Luhrmann's film. *Romeo + Juliet* uses the movie as the medium through which the "jewel" of Shakespeare's play is made legible. In this pair of films, the audience is positioned on the other side of the movie-as-frame, in that we look through the conventions of Shakespeare's comedy to view Junger and O'Haver's message on contemporary youth culture. The process of recognition is one in which the audience apprehends the elements of Shakespeare's text in the films as familiar, and in acknowledging them as such, appreciates the film via a Shakespearean lens. Most importantly, however, the films employ "Shakespeare" to authorize the ultimate message of the film. That message, if it can be stated simply, is that the project of adolescence is self-awareness. When individuals (especially outsiders) are challenged to reveal their true identities and they successfully jettison the ill-fitting personality they had constructed to protect their "real" selves, they are rewarded with the same symbol of acceptance with which the Hughes movies conclude: heterosexual union, blessed by their small but influential community.

10 Things places in the foreground its gesture towards a "Shakespeare" icon. The film takes place in Seattle's fictional "Padua High School," and the key sisters in the movie are named Kat and Bianca Stratford. The mysterious new student paid to tame the equally rebellious Kat is Patrick Verona, and the two share an English class in which the teacher assigns Shakespeare's sonnets and asks his class to write their own. Kat's best friend treats Shakespeare like a pop idol by pasting posters of him in her locker and wearing a Renaissance costume to the prom. *10 Things* constructs a world in which Shakespeare as author is the touchstone of the high school English classroom and "Shakespeare" bleeds into everyday life. The characters never acknowledge the "Shakespeare" in their everyday world, yet they both study his works and reenact them. When preppy and vacuous Bianca asks her obstetrician father for permission to attend the prom, she is given the condition that she may when her sister, who openly expresses her distaste for men in general, agrees to go. This scenario allows the traces of *The Taming of the Shrew* to surface, and the audience sees the references to Shakespeare's work in both the details of the movie and the structure of Kat's story.

Kat, we quickly learn, is no "shrew." In fact, the audience immediately identifies with her as the sole character of substance in the film. Junger portrays her early in the film as a punk outsider, but as other characters are introduced — especially the superficial girls in her classes and her shallow, pretty sister — Kat's dress becomes increasingly conservative and her scowl is replaced with a look of intense thought. The introduction of

Patrick is our first complete look into the façade Kat has constructed. True to the *Taming* formula, the pair first meet with friendly fire, but soon Patrick follows Kat to a music store where he (and the audience) see her as no one can: strumming her dream guitar with headphones on and eyes closed. We see her completely vulnerable and lost in her own fantasy with Patrick's figure close behind her. Aided by Patrick's pursuit of Kat, the audience witnesses the tender artist beneath her aggressive exterior. Patrick, who up until this point has been aggravating Kat at every opportunity, respects her privacy by quietly slipping away before she can see him. Junger's camera lingers on her for a moment, and before it cuts away, Kat opens her eyes. Patrick's presence in Kat's life is allowing her to see an identity that she had been avoiding. Junger's formula for their romance is one in which Kat's eccentricities and rebelliousness are acceptable only in friendly competition with Patrick's. The audience watches Kat open up through Patrick's eyes, reinforcing the elemental trope that romantic union will be the culmination of their assertion of identity. Junger in fact insists on framing Kat through Patrick, confirming that the young woman in this story will not be complete until and unless a young man enables her self-discovery.

Towards the end of the film, Kat explains the nonconformity (albeit embraced and revered by Patrick) that earned her the "shrew" nickname and reveals that it grew out of an effort to protect her sister. She admits in a moment of crisis that one young man, now in pursuit of Bianca, sparked her "man-hating" persona. After one sexual encounter with him at a young age, she decided to refute her school's expectations of her as a young woman and found solace in the total dismissal of dating and the generic concept of fitting in. Here Junger offers the Kat character a monologue that explains her behavior, and indeed the reasons that Patrick brings out the best in her: he can see behind both masks. Through her relationship with him, Kat ultimately faces this moment in her past and thus overcomes her internal obstacles. The last scene of the film shows Patrick and Kat kissing in the school parking lot, crowded with cars and teenagers. That kiss, still and frozen in time, confirms her adolescent journey is complete, as the symbolic wedding of the two protagonists neatly concludes the structure of the film. Throughout *10 Things I Hate About You*, Kat is viewed from Patrick's perspective, and according to the teenpic tradition, his reward will be her. Kat, for all her feminist ambition, eventually reiterates the most literal sense of Katherina's final speech in *The Taming of the Shrew*:

> Why are our bodies soft and weak and smooth,
> Unapt to toil and trouble in the world,
> But that our soft conditions and our hearts
> Should well agree with our external parts [V.ii.169–172].

Kat has changed for Patrick, but the conventions of the film suggest that her change is really the exposure of her true self. The rebellious punk teen is really a front —created out of a crisis of peer pressure —for the "soft conditions" that truly constitute the Katherina character.

Tommy O'Haver's *Get Over It!* allows "Shakespeare" to affect the lives of its teen subjects much in the way *10 Things* does. Again, the focus of the film is on the adolescent world of the young protagonists, and "Shakespeare" is the vocabulary by which this world is made legible. As in Junger's film, the teens in *Get Over It!* are aware of Shakespeare's work as part of the high school classroom and stage, but unaware of "Shakespeare" as a shaping influence in their lives. The film depicts life imitating art as a high school musical production of *A Midsummer Night's Dream* inspires each character to take on his or her theatrical persona. The four main characters—cast as Hermia, Helena, Lysander, and Demetrius— grumble about the difficulty of the language as they replicate the play's plot. On stage, Berke (as Lysander) realizes that he does not want to choose his Hermia (the ex-girlfriend that was the object of his desire throughout the movie) but rather returns the affection of Helena, who has devotedly coached him through his bewildering confrontation with Shakespeare's text. In so doing,

"We cannot fight for love, as men may do": Kelly (Kirsten Dunst) and Basin (Mila Kunis) search for romance among their high school classmates in Tommy O'Haver's *Get Over It!*

he disrupts the expected finale of *A Midsummer Night's Rockin' Eve* by choosing Helena over Hermia. The film's adaptation of *A Midsummer Night's Dream's* structure, however, suggests that Berke is not standing in for Lysander but reproducing Demetrius; thus Berke must realize that he truly loves the young woman who has determinedly pursued him even in the face of his desire for another.

Although *Get Over It!* only loosely borrows its plot structure from Shakespeare's play, its dependence on "Shakespeare" is significant. The icon of Shakespeare serves as a legitimizing agent on the fickle love affairs of high school students. The audience's recognition of Shakespeare's play in the trials of these young men and women validates the internal struggle of adolescent self-realization. The film suggests these are not trivial quibbles of teen lust; the authority of "Shakespeare" offers profundity to the protagonists' interactions. When Lysander kisses Helena onstage, the parents and teachers in the film's internal audience are shown cheering and applauding enthusiastically. This brief moment not only illustrates Berke's reward for discovering himself through his affection for Kelly (Helena), but also creates a classic teenpic marriage between the two as their union is enthusiastically blessed by the entire community of adults and peers. In the final scene of the movie, Berke and Kelly wander out of the frame of the theater's backstage and into a beautiful, idealized forest in which tiny fairies twinkle over their heads. They freeze this adolescent moment by physically moving into the world of *A Midsummer Night's Dream*, a world in which marriage signals the end of the play. O'Haver's jewel is this idealized manifestation of adolescent bliss, and the frame of "Shakespeare" acts to prove that jewel is precious, indeed. Like *10 Things, Get Over It!* recognizes "Shakespeare" in the goings-on of young people, and celebrates their petty relations by invoking the familiarity of a cultural icon.

Conclusion: *O* and the Experience of Recognition

Tim Blake Nelson's *O* takes a different tone than *10 Things* and *Get Over It!* but is useful in further defining the contours of recognition. I have chosen to conclude with *O* because it demands the recognition of broader themes of violence and race in American culture along with its "Shakespearean" frame. *O* in fact suggests a third connotation of recognition directly tied to the cultural authority of "Shakespeare": by framing the film within William Shakespeare's *Othello, O* recognizes— validates— tropes of popular culture not yet fully articulated. The authority of "Shakespeare" recognizes contemporary intersections of race and youth violence and thus authenticates their unique potency in American popular culture.

Songwriter Kelly helps (Kirsten Dunst) Berke (Ben Foster) win back his ex-girl-friend Allison by gaining a role in the school musical.

Immediately after the April 1999 high school shootings in Littleton, Colorado, the release of O was postponed indefinitely. Finally opening at the end of August, 2001, the film's finale in which Odin "O" James strangles his girlfriend, shoots her roommate, and then kills himself played as a cringe-inducing reminder of recent incidents of large-scale youth violence at school.[6]

Apart from its recollection of the events at Columbine, however, O remains a disturbing and difficult film in relation to the Shakespeare teenpix I have examined thus far. This contemporary retelling of *Othello* takes place in an elite, basketball-obsessed South Carolina preparatory school. The title character is not only the sole black student at the school, but the basketball team's star player. At the beginning of the film, he is secretly dating the dean's daughter and gaining the admiration and love of the basketball coach. Coach Duke's real son, Hugo, becomes increasingly (but inwardly) envious of the charismatic high school superstar and sets in motion the infamous plot of deception that results in four deaths.

O adheres to many of the guidelines of the teenpic according to Leitch's construction. The protagonists are all teenagers struggling with both internal and external obstacles to self-understanding and community acceptance, and the high school in which the events take place is an adolescent world in which adults are oppressive, ineffectual, and clueless. Nelson highlights racism throughout the film to justify the film's tragic end. Racial tensions visually and thematically yoke *Othello*'s focus on the insider/outsider relationship with the more complex history of American racism. The girls' dorm is a remodeled plantation house, and a soundtrack of underground hip-hop jarringly imposes on nearly every scene. In *O*, the teenpic meets "Shakespeare," but the jewel framed by this overlap is a racialized system of American popular culture. The logical conclusion is to root Hugo's envy of Odin in the very fact that the popular manifestations of black culture (basketball, hip-hop) are never quite available to Hugo, and thus he hates Odin because he longs to be black. This conclusion of a young white man violently asserting his desire for black culture, however, can be seen as itself a trope for popular culture.[7] Odin James's initials, clearly, link his character to one of the most dynamic images of race in popular culture in the 1990s. Ultimately (and perhaps unfortunately), the coincidence of this film's release with the violence at Columbine and other schools points to a disturbing but prevalent theme growing in American popular culture: the terrifying possibility of acts of gun violence by young people in their homes and schools. *O* induces re-cognition by positioning these themes of race and violence as familiar aspects of contemporary American culture. Like *Romeo + Juliet*, *O* demands that the audience re-cognize the significance of *Othello* in the American South of the late twentieth century. Concurrently, like *10 Things I Hate About You* and *Get Over It!*, *O* uses the trope of a racialized youth culture in music and sports as a means of validating the adolescent lives of its characters. In *O*, however, these troubling additions to pop and popular culture — not only "Shakespeare" — emerge as the triggers of recognition-as-familiar.

We have moved from an analysis that places the jewel of William Shakespeare's text as a distinct object visible through the frame of popular culture to an analysis that suggests the recognition, by a film, of broad themes in American race relations. This movement highlights the essentially participatory nature of recognition as an action on the part of both the film and the audience. These Shakespeare teenpix suggest a process by which films frame a particular object dependent on the audience's recognition of concepts, themes, or texts extrinsic to that object. Tate's jewel is ultimately not an object at all, however, but rather the product of the viewing subject's participation in recognizing the frame. Moments of recognition — these films' nods to "Shakespeare" and popular culture — require the audience to both infer and imagine the object to be seen, and the audience itself constructs the jewel.

Again, it must be noted that re-cognition is not only an interpretive tool but also a mode of perception and an action that demands the audience's participation in that interpretation. This activity on the part of the audience thus directly impacts a broad expanse of the "Shakespeare" landscape. Re-cognition is a means of articulating the way these Shakespeare teenpix re-vision "Shakespeare," not only at its peripheries, but indeed at the core of late twentieth and early twenty-first century apprehension of the phenomenon. Re-cognition as outlined here, then, remains an inclusive process that demands films like *Romeo + Juliet, 10 Things I Hate About You, Get Over It!* and *O* be viewed, not as marginal offshoots, but as vital elements of the "Shakespeare" phenomenon. These films cohere in their expansion of the boundaries of "Shakespeare" by revealing new motives and methods to re-string, re-polish, and re-cognize his plays.

Works Cited

10 Things I Hate About You. Dir. Gil Junger. Touchstone Pictures: 1999. Videocassette.

Benton, Michael, Mark Dolan, and Rebecca Zisch. "Teen Films: An Annotated Bibliography." *Journal of Popular Film and Television* 25.2 (summer 1997): 83–88.

Boose, Lynda E. and Richard Burt, eds. *Shakespeare, the Movie: Popularizing the Plays on Film, TV, and Video.* London: Routledge, 1997.

Dryden, John, and William Davenant. *Five Restoration Adaptations of Shakespeare.* Edited by Christopher Spencer. Urbana: University of Illinois Press, 1965.

Get Over It! Dir. Tommy O'Haver. Miramax: 2001. Videocassette.

Hentges, Sarah Duncan. "Teen Girls and Pop Culture Come of Age." In *The Image of the Twentieth Century in Literature, Media, and Society.* Edited by Will Wright and Steven Kaplan. Pueblo, Colo.: Society for the Interdisciplinary Study of Social Imagery, University of Southern Colorado. 134–42.

Hodgon, Barbara. "William Shakespeare's *Romeo + Juliet*: Everything's Nice in America?" *Shakespeare Survey* 52 (1999): 88–98.

Howlett, Kathy M. *Framing Shakespeare on Film.* Athens: Ohio University Press, 2000.

Leitch, Thomas M. "The World According to Teenpix." *Literature/Film Quarterly* 20.1(1992): 43–47.

Marsden, Jean, ed. *The Appropriation of Shakespeare: Post-Renaissance Reconstructions of the Works and the Myths.* London: Harvester Wheatsheaf, 1991.

Mulvey, Laura. "Visual Pleasure in Narrative Cinema." *Feminisms: An Anthology of Literary Theory and Criticism.* Edited by Robyn R. Warhol and Diane Price Herndl. New Brunswick: Rutgers, 1997: 438–47.

O. Dir. Tim Blake Nelson. Lions Gate, 1998/2001. Videocassette.

Shakespeare, William. *The Taming of the Shrew.* In *Four Comedies.* Edited by David Bevington. New York: Bantam, 1988.

Taylor, Gary. *Reinventing Shakespeare: A Cultural History, from the Restoration to the Present.* New York: Weidenfeld & Nicolson, 1989.

William Shakespeare's Romeo + Juliet. Dir. Baz Luhrmann. Twentieth Century Fox: 1996. Videocassette.

Worthen, W.B. "Staging 'Shakespeare': Acting, authority, and the rhetoric of performance." In *Shakespeare, Theory, and Performance*. Edited by James Bulman. London: Routledge, 1996.

Notes

1. I must acknowledge my hesitancy to suggest these films constitute a unique film genre, despite the temptation to do so. Although I do believe the films I have chosen are connected through their respective similarities to and deviance from already-established film genres (the teen film, the romantic comedy, even perhaps the "Shakespeare film"), I wish to trace a pattern of experience here and not establish firm guidelines for a new genre. To show how, why, and to what end these films can be grouped together, I intend to focus on the audience's practice of *recognition* in watching these films instead of the way in which these films replicate certain generic standards.

2. I use the term "teenpic" as a variation on Thomas M. Leitch's coinage of "teenpix," the consequences of which he explores in *The World According to Teenpix* (1992). I adopt (and adapt) the term for its suggestion that the teenpic excludes all films not starring, concerned with, and marketed towards teenagers. I must acknowledge my own naïveté in assuming that the teen presence in these films goes beyond its target audience, but again, Leitch's term creates a world in which the teen experience saturates every facet of the film.

3. The tag line for *William Shakespeare's Romeo + Juliet*, featured on the movie poster and the back of the VHS video, was "The Greatest Love Story Ever Told."

4. I qualify my analysis here as reductive to acknowledge the real aim of my larger argument: to show that the group of movies defined here as Shakespeare teenpix are united by the methods of reinterpretation and not necessarily the larger implications of that reinterpretation. That is, the Shakespeare teenpix are common in how they participate in "Shakespeare," not in what they produce of "Shakespeare."

5. In *The Taming of the Shrew*, of course, Katherina cannot accept and thus bitterly defies the qualities of the "good wife." In *10 Things*, Kat's father is an obstetrician who justifies his strict dating rules with a paralyzing fear that his daughters will become pregnant. His insistence that they are at constant risk of the consequences of sexuality is so strong that at one point Dr. Stratford forbids Kat to consider attending college on the other side of the country and outside of his realm of vigilance.

6. *Romeo + Juliet* has been linked to youth violence as well, specifically in the case of 15-year-old Kip Kinkel, who opened fire on his classmates after killing both of his parents in May of 1998. A teacher at his Springfield, Oregon, high school noted that he had been listening to the soundtrack for *Romeo + Juliet* the morning he killed his parents and had seen the film in an English class. In an interview for *Frontline*, the teacher commented: "From the opening scene, they begin to see that it might be 400 years old, but it's their play. To begin with, here's these kids in a street fight. In its entirety, the movie presents such a wasteland. This director, he gives you an image. He gives you a message of 'Violence is necessary. That's the world of teens. That's what's out there for them. And in fact, they seek it.' He gives you a message that nowhere in the world can these—in society can these kids go for help" (*Frontline* transcript, episode 1809. Air date: January 18, 2000). Although *O* has never been criticized with the severity of implying a causal relationship to youth violence, the trend noted here of the assumed volatility of these Shakespeare teenpix deserves closer study.

7. Some of the more prominent examples of this theme include Danny Hoch's one-man show "Jails, Hospitals, and Hip-hop" and the work of rap phenom Eminem.

10

"An Aweful Rule": Safe Schools, Hard Canons, and Shakespeare's Loose Heirs

Melissa Jones

> Marry, peace it bodes, and love, and quiet life,
> An aweful rule, and right supremacy.
> And to be short, what not, that's sweet and happy.
> — *The Taming of The Shrew*, V.ii.108–110

On April 20th, 1999, Americans watched the evening news report on yet another school killing spree, this one even worse than the others, though by this time the script of events seemed depressingly familiar. Amid the halls of an apparently model public high school, the repeated harassment and bullying of students under the eyes of peers and teachers transformed pedagogical space into the setting for a violently real and unsettling revenge fantasy. In the tragic resolution of this story, Eric Harris (age 17) and Dylan Klebold (age 18) killed themselves after murdering 12 students and one teacher at Columbine High School (Littleton, Colorado). It was the sixteenth American school shooting in five years.

Into this *mise en scène* of teen violence, Gil Junger premiered his romantic comedy *10 Things I Hate About You* (1999), a loose teen adaptation of Shakespeare's *The Taming of the Shrew*. The film's final classroom scene ends on a much higher note than Columbine's, but it is one still sounded from a register of aggression, which Kat Stratford (Julia Stiles) rings out clearly when she renounces her shrewish feminist politics and announces in its place her dutiful affection for her boyfriend, Patrick Verona (Heath Ledger). Her renunciation, a sonnet launched in imperfect iambic pentameter, takes the form of a list of the "ten things" she "hates"

about the film's modern-day Petruchio. The list begins playfully chasten-
ing, "I hate it when you make me laugh, even worse when you make me
cry," and concludes more pathetically, "I hate it when you're not around,
and the fact that you didn't call. But mostly I hate the way I don't hate you
… not even close … not even a little bit … Not at all." By simultaneously
invoking as parent texts both Shakespeare's Sonnet 141 and Katherina
Minola's final disquisition on obedience, this catalogue of girly teen angst
transformed into self-effacement raises important questions about cultural transmission and specifically about Shakespeare's use in popular culture. But more urgently, it demands that we consider the politics of staging
such questions in a public high school and for a teen audience in the context of numerous startling and diverse incidents of school violence (including peer sexual harassment, intensified bullying, and rage killing). The
film's *Shrew* frame complicates this equation further since the parent comedy itself relies upon narratives of brutality and domination to restore
shaky social relations. Perhaps tragically indeed, the film seems to find in
updating *Shrew*'s scheme to protect patriarchal issues a unique way of
both addressing and diffusing the anxiety produced by scenes of escalat-
ing violence in our public schools, key sites of social and cultural indoctrination.

The ironic defiance that launches Kat's "10 Things" admittedly bears
a trace of its professed model's saucy remark, "In faith, I do not love thee
with mine eyes," and of her lament, "Thy proud heart's slave and vassal
wretch [am I] to be." But the film's cinematic chronicling of the heroine's
abject humiliation mobilizes much greater pathos than the sonnet's wry
tone permits; this crucial alteration suggests that Shakespeare's Sonnet 141
is invoked here only to assert some mild cultural capital alongside the film
and poem's titular allusions to *The Taming of the Shrew*. The film also borrows from Shakespeare an approximation of *Shrew*'s plot: a bullying playboy is "hired" to woo the shrew to make her more fetching sister eligible
under the father's dictates. Additional surface references to Shakespeare
include in-class citations of the Bard, textual medleys of Shakespearean
quotations, and even one character's impersonation of the playwright in
order to score with a foxy Bardolator at prom. This easy amalgamation of
literary gleanings seems to participate in the type of anti-intellectual
profiteering on Shakespeare that critics Linda Boose and Richard Burt have
dubbed "Shakespearorama."[1] And yet, in Kat's tearful confession we hear
so keen an echo of Katherina Minola's famous paean to wifely duty, which
admonishes all women ("froward and unable worms!") to realize "our
strength as weak, our weakness past compare," that any easy dismissal of
the relation between parent text and heir must be reconsidered (V.ii.170–174).

Born out of the depths of Kat's teen emotions and highlighted by the camera's blazonry of the girl's breakdown, the fidelity and submission of her sonnet affectively re-sounds the closing (and longest) speech of Shakespeare's Kate, revealing in this moment the film's profound ideological adoption of *Shrew's* legacy.[2] Indeed, Katherina's call to her fellow women to "place your hands below your husband's foot," and her subsequent demonstration of this act, "if he please, / My hand is ready, may it do him ease" (V.ii.174–78), cannot — to any contemporary observer who has ever been in high-school — seem much more self-effacing than latter-day Kat's classroom prostration. Kat recaptures perfectly (if figuratively) Kate's posture of humiliation when she confesses her own unendurable weakness and her tearful devotion to Patrick, a gesture so painful that she must in the end flee the room sobbing.

The film's faithful deployment of *Shrew's* ideological structure and its enshrinement of Shakespeare in staged canon debates establish a relationship with the Bard as an enduring "transcendental parent" that resonates curiously with current reactionary and elitist positions in U.S. politics and education, which seek just such a universal and stabilizing cultural figure to offset mounting anxieties about cultural transmission. In fact, although *10 Things* draws from *Shrew* a particularly salient ideological frame, it emerges as part of a larger phenomenon of conservative Shakespearean adaptations that place Hollywood at the very center of popular debates on education.[3] This trend seems to be responding to distressing evidence that schools themselves are unable to perform their putative social function: that is, to regulate students sexually and intellectually and to train them to claim the privilege of their social and cultural inheritance, or "our way of life," in Slavoj Zizek's terms. This "way of life" represents more than simply a set of practices: It is a constitutive system of belief that organizes a community's practices, an affective investment of "something more" in a nation's understanding of itself and, by extension, in an individual's understanding of her own place in the nation's social order. "Members of a community who partake in a given 'way of life,'" Zizek explains, "*believe in their Thing*, where this belief has a reflexive structure proper to the intersubjective space: 'I believe in the (national) Thing' equals 'I believe that others (members of my community) believe in the Thing'… The national Thing exists [only] as long as members of a community believe in it; it is literally an effect of this belief in itself" (*Tarrying* 201–202).

It is no coincidence that films like *10 Things* seem to be taking over schools' role as guardians of our way of life and champions of high culture at the very moment when institutional education is most deeply shaken. The fetishistic turn to high culture both in Hollywood and in wider discourse surrounding school crises seems to evince a keen need for reassurance that all's well with schools' symbolic authority and — more vitally — the cultural legacy they are charged with promoting and protecting (when daily news reports from the schools suggest the contrary).[4] What makes *10 Things I Hate About You*'s intervention into this cultural conversation especially enlightening — and frightening — is the way it vigorously re-inscribes *Shrew*'s sadistic power dynamics to restore a general sense of well-being. Shakespeare's notoriously misogynist text, of course, extols profit-seeking Petruchio's unabashed wedding and "taming" of wealthy Baptista's outspoken daughter, Katherina. Petruchio's brutal "pedagogy" instructs Kate in her proper social role by quelling her problematic resistance to her father's and her husband's rule: He successfully starves, exhausts, and badgers his bride (what he calls his "aweful rule, and right supremacy") into domestic harmony, or "what not, that's sweet and happy" (V.ii.109–110). What the play teaches (and teaches *about* teaching) is that social disruptors are sweetest when bullied into submission and silenced in a patriarchal embrace, a paternalistic trope eagerly consumed by moviegoers today and increasingly adopted by educationists as well.[5]

Perhaps the most blatant example of this conservative retrenchment is the Kansas Board of Education's 1999 (August 23) decision to reintroduce creationism into state curriculum, defying decades of evolutionary science in favor of a symbolically absolute God-the-Father. The Kansas decision represents creationism's first success since 1968, when the Supreme Court declared unconstitutional on First Amendment grounds any laws forbidding the teaching of evolution (Gould 59). Recent mass media debates over the canon of English literature also exhibit this paternalistic tendency, though more subtly and perhaps even more dangerously, for the ostensibly civilized rhetoric of this debate often conceals the gendered power dynamics at its core. That same year, for example, *Harper's Magazine* (September, 1999) featured an essay by novelist Francine Prose lodging a trenchant complaint against multicultural curricula and female writers, or "soft canons," in English classes.[6] The essay echoes some of the earliest arguments against ideological reading practices, but it also evinces an awareness of the importance of political critique that makes its denigration of "soft canon" writers more pointed and all the more savage. Prose professes her relief that in their present school system, her two sons have read "Shakespeare, Hawthorne, and Melville." "But," she laments, "they've also slogged repeatedly through the manipulative melodramas of Alice Walker and Maya Angelou," which she suggests are only on reading lists as a response to "the present vogue for teaching 'values' through literature

… [which has been] cleverly substituted for what we used to call English" (76, 78). Prose's critique aims to tame the canon by disciplining the shrews, scolds, and melodramatic bitches who have strayed from their literary fathers, only to defile 'our' canon. Even Oprah Winfrey, whose celebrated book list has in past years boasted such authors as Maya Angelou, Toni Morrison, and Anna Quindlen, declared that she was suspending her club in 2002 because, according to the Associated Press, "she could not find any worthy books" (E6). No worthy new books, that is. After a ten month hiatus, Winfrey has returned to recommending again — but this time, she is sticking to the classics. "I cannot imagine a world where the great works of literature are not read," she explains, and tells of her "hope [that] *The Oprah Winfrey Show* will make classic works of literature ['books of enduring usefulness'] accessible to every woman and man who reads" (*Oprah.com*).[7]

When Kat first steps into her Padua High classroom, *10 Things I Hate About You* enters this heated conversation on the canon. Her African-American English teacher, Mr. Morgan (Daryl "Chill" Mitchell), begins class by asking, "Okay, then, what did everyone think of *The Sun Also Rises?*" Kat quips to an enthusiastic classmate, "Hemingway? He was an abusive alcoholic misogynist who squandered half his life hanging around Picasso trying to nail his leftovers." The remark establishes an anti-canon (or "soft canon") position that takes on force when, turning her attention back to the teacher, Kat asks, "What about Sylvia Plath or Charlotte Brontë or Simone de Beauvoir?" With broad strokes, the exchange identifies Kat's position on canonicity and the rites of literary inclusion as well-informed. Against this backdrop of women artists whose work and biographies include figures of the despotic male ("Daddy," Rochester, Sartre), Kat proceeds to echo the rudiments of early feminist literary criticism ("I guess in this society being male and an asshole makes you worthy of our time") and complain of "the oppressive patriarchal values that dictate our education." At home later that afternoon, Kat even curls up in an armchair reading Plath — one of her eclectic counter-canon writers— as if to suggest that she is not simply advocating women authors on principle, but reading them because she enjoys their work.

Kat finds support for her canon critique when Morgan nuances her position, additionally noting how race and class also serve as factors of exclusion. "I want to thank you for your point of view," he tells her; "I know how difficult it must be for you to overcome all those years of upper-middle class suburban oppression. Must be tough. But the next time you storm the PTA crusading for better lunch meat or whatever it is you white girls complain about, ask 'em why they can't buy a book written by a black man." Kat's wit and erudition — especially in comparison to her class-mates — initially draw us to her politics; however, the teacher's sarcastic riposte — though confirming Kat's objection — also lets us know that her anti-canon enthusiasm is somewhat bound by her own limited perspec-tive. Following the trajectory of this dubious advocacy, the movie eventu-ally undercuts Kat's ideological critique of canonicity entirely by making Kat's politics appear symptomatic of a youthful fervor more derivative and combative than insightful. When, for instance, Kat explains to her fam-ily in elementary Marxist terms that teens go to parties to escape "their meaningless, consumer-driven lives," her notably shallow sister, Bianca, mimics Kat's obviously tired sloganeering by wagging her head and rolling her eyes. Her mockery suggests that such ideological criticism is pre-dictable, empty, and, quite frankly, boring. Bianca's ability to see beyond the strictures of her sister's crude social critique renders Kat's insights more silly than savvy. Kat's shrewishness toward her family and classmates is by this point integrally and dismissively linked to her leftist politics. Her feminism even comes to look more like a personality disorder than a viable political position when, unprovoked, she lashes out verbally at classmates in the school's halls, classrooms, and even parking lot.

Junger's correlation of outspoken women and "psychos" poignantly recalls Shakespeare's own depiction of Katherina Minola's violent fits at the play's start. "I did but tell her she mistook her frets, / And bow'd her hand to teach her fingering," Kate's beleagured music tutor informs Bap-tista, continuing, "When, with a most impatient devilish spirit, / 'Frets, call you these?' quoth she, 'I'll fume with them.' / And with that word she strook me on the head" (II.i.149–153). But where critics recuperate Kate's physical and verbal defiance as symbolic resistance to patriarchal gender mandates, Junger's adaptation undercuts the power of this representative economy by way of a reductio ad absurdem. Kat's narrow understanding of her own class and race privilege alongside her arrogant, self-proclaimed marginality undermines her political credibility, and her inexplicable ani-mus casts her representative status further into doubt. The film's (and Kat's own) ultimate discovery of the bankruptcy of her social critique thus quite easily collapses all the feminist and Marxist resistance she initially claims to stand for into the lone figure of one misguided kid. When Kate devolves into Kat, the "shrew" transforms from a metaphor into a metonym; women's resistance to patriarchal dominance is here reduced to a girl with a grudge, and Kat's symbolic authority is evacuated by her "per-sonality" — angry and disordered.

10 Things continues to advance its conservatism under a Shake-spearean banner in two later English classroom scenes, belying any initial advocacy of a more inclusive, critical canon. By the second class, Mr. Morgan is rapping Shakespeare's Sonnet 141, explaining to the class, "I know Shakespeare's a dead white guy, but he knows his shit, so we can overlook that." What Morgan means by "shit" he does not say, but according to the film's logic, that shit is how best to represent the subjugation of shrewish women. Indeed, in response to the request that students write their own versions of the sonnet, the once-belligerent Kat inquires passionately, "do you want this in iambic pentameter?" gushing, "I think it's a really good assignment." With this reversal of temperament, *10 Things* suggests that a Shakespeare-panacea can be prescribed for any academic abrasion to salve and soothe contending political positions. At Padua High, Shakespeare acts as a unifying sign of "our way of life," in whose name students can all overlook differences of race, class, and gender. The larger implication is clear as well: Postmodernist thought (textualism, deconstruction) and identity and ideological criticism (feminism, race-criticism, Marxism) produce classroom division; literary fathers heal them. The film thus gently lays the blame for any academic disorder outside patriarchy's province.

The particular allure of this (antifeminist) reinvestment in father figures can, I suspect, be traced to an anxiety about cultural transmission

Bianca (Larisa Oleynik) heads off on a long-promised date with Cameron (Joseph Gordon-Levitt), leaving Kat (Julia Stiles) behind to make amends with her father and pen her "10 Things" poem to Patrick.

that has been recently fueled by school violence. The targeted violence of young men takes direct aim at our "national Thing" when it reveals schools' loss of symbolic authority and — more deeply unsettling — an out of control culture of dominance among adolescents. Fourteen-year-old Michael Carneal, for example, opened fire on an early-morning prayer circle at Heath High School and killed three students, wounding five others (Paducah, Kentucky, 1997); Kipland F. Kinkel, similarly, sprayed Thurston High's cafeteria with bullets, leaving two dead and 22 wounded (Springfield, Oregon, 1998); and Westside Middle School's Andre Golden and Mitchell Johnson killed four students and one teacher in Jonesboro, Arkansas (Westside Middle School, 1998) out of rage, revenge, and a perverse masculine "self-fashioning." By 1999, the Columbine teens' murderous success seemed to pronounce spectacularly the failure of the Arnoldian[8] project to promote civility, national unity, and a general gentling of the human condition through education and a shared legacy of "high culture." And only a month later (May 24, 1999), the Supreme Court's decision on the *Davis v. Monroe County Board of Education* case testified to another sort of violent excess besetting schools— sexual harassment. The decision found that schools are liable (under Title IX)[9] for student-to-student sexual harassment, but only "'where they are *deliberately indifferent* to sexual harassment, of which they have actual knowledge, that is so severe, pervasive, and objectively offensive that it can be said to deprive the victims of access to ... educational opportunities'" (Kopels and Dupper 442, my emphasis). This decision follows closely upon the June 1998 Court ruling in *Gebser v. Lago Vista Independent School District*, which, likewise, narrowly defined the circumstances under which schools can be liable for sexual harassment — in this case, teacher-student harassment — as those in which school officials showed "deliberate indifference" (Thompson 99).

A wider perspective reveals that these two issues— uncontrolled student violence and sexual aggression — represent more than just isolated instances of problems within local educational systems. Rather, they are only the most recent, chilling evidence of a fundamental social reality. In an effort to draw out the etiology of school violence, Robert Morrell's survey of student aggression, "A Calm After the Storm? Beyond Schooling as Violence," adeptly traces the problem of violence and "violent hegemonic masculinities at school" back to a basic social inequity, gender inequity (41). Bullying and sexual harassment are examples of students' indoctrination into a social order that extols hypermasculinity, both symptoms of a culture-wide ethos of dominance. Government reports on "targeted school violence" like the *Final Report and Findings of the Safe School Initiative*

(2002) also link boys' explosive, premeditated violence to an increasingly virulent culture of bullying and harassment. Indeed, the report notes that "many attackers felt bullied, persecuted, or injured prior to the attack," and they "described being bullied in terms that suggested these experiences approached torment" (38). Despite this troubling observation, the report's final recommendations aim primarily to thwart the revenging victims of bullying—not the bullying itself; and the Supreme Court's ambivalent rulings on sexual harassment reveal an even greater degree of governmental reluctance to address violence in schools as a part of a system-wide problem. The general unwillingness to heed Morrell's monition that educationists shift emphasis from "violence as a rather amorphous phenomenon which afflicts schools—to the formulation of violence as a feature of gender relations and identities with which schools will have to deal" (41) bespeaks a deep cultural investment in preserving this system of gendered violence.

What is most shocking about these spectacular violent episodes for everyday citizens is perhaps not the unexpectedness of the violence but instead the traumatic recognition (or mis-recognition) that such violence is the sine qua non of "our way of life," predicated on a brutal patriarchalism. We begin to discern the real power relations that structure our institutions, traditions, and culture at these sites of excess. The anxious retrenchment of conservative ideology that we are seeing today in schools and in mass media is not, I suspect, an *actual* response to outside attacks from fringe group radicals—from teenage loners to feminists, multi-culturalists, and any other so-called liberals; rather, it is the desperate attempt to restore faith in that same violent "way of life," even as its very excesses threaten our belief in its authority.[10] Thus the convenient scapegoating of all things that are "not your father's Shakespeare" (pop-culture, loose canons, soft discipline), in conjunction with new militaristic responses to students (locker checks, mandatory uniforms, video surveillance), paternalistic curricular shifts, and renewed emphasis on "traditional values," tries very hard to locate the threat to kids, to schools, and to "us" externally.[11] *10 Things* even manages to get this sovereign remedy for social disturbance out where it matters most—amongst students themselves.[12] The film explores the joint imperatives of mediating "our" violence and hardening "our" canons in its usage of Shakespeare at an average suburban high school, one that is charged with potentially explosive sexual aggression and a familiar culture of peer bullying and intimidation. *Shrew*'s (and *10 Things*'s) distinctive brand of antifeminist pedagogy does not just perform the act of keeping women in line; more, its merry "taming" justifies the system of dominance in which the subjugation of women is supposedly necessary, for it is this symbolic order that masculinity's violent excesses jeopardize. More broadly, this lesson offers the exercise of patriarchal will as necessary guarantors of "our way of life."

Junger establishes Shakespeare's cultural authority mostly by way of classroom dialogue and public confessions of bardolatry, and his concluding revelation of the salutary effects of a Shakespearean education on shrews and African-Americanists alike finalizes this impetus. However, it is the film's explicitly sexualized scenes of bullying aggression that effectively mitigate the dangers of our brutal masculine "Thing" by suggesting that enduring gendered violence as a means to the patriarchal end is a grim but ultimately harmless necessity. In the first of these scenes of harassment, Junger sends the film's contemporary Lucentio, Cameron James (Joseph Gordon-Levitt), into danger in the office of the school's suggestively named guidance counselor, Ms. Perky. The camera begins by glancing at him fidgeting in his seat, nervously awaiting instructions on his first day of class. It then cuts to Perky, who looks up at Cameron over her school-marmish bifocals, gives him a terse smile, and says pointedly, "I'll be right with you." We then turn to a close-up of Perky's computer screen, where she has just typed, "his hand slid up her creamy white thighs. She could feel his huge member pulsing." She finishes typing the adverbial, "with desire," in a shot that frames the top part of the laptop screen against the blurred background of Cameron's exposed throat. When Perky's hands reach up to shut the laptop, she seems also to be reaching toward the boy's neck before ultimately lowering the computer screen and turning her full attention to him. The montage effect of shifting from Cameron, to counselor, to computer screen, and then back again to each of the characters puts the triad in dialogue, but importantly, they are never in the shot together. This compounding gesture seems to position Perky's computer screen — and the erotic scene from the cheap romance novel she is typing — as a sort of sexual intermediary between Perky and Cameron. Student and counselor do not talk, but the eroticized descriptions emblazoned by her on-screen text inflect the encounter between the two, intimating but never avowing the erotic potentiality lurking at the edges of their exchange.

The subsequent scene between the counselor and Patrick-Petruchio materializes this potentiality and then normalizes it, ultimately sublimating the sexual aggression back into Perky's text. When Patrick explains to Perky that he did not actually "expose himself to the lunch lady" (it was only "a bratwurst"), she uncrosses her legs, gets up from the desk upon which she is perched, and walks toward him with a swagger, eyeing him up and down. Focusing first on his genitals in a "two-shot" frame that encloses them both, she remarks, "aren't we the optimist," then looks him directly in the eyes before glancing back at his body. Viewers are initially invited to follow Perky's gaze and sexually objectify Patrick; our looking aligns with her institutional power, and we too are invited to imagine his "bratwurst." However, the camera quickly forces us to reject her point of view and identify instead with Patrick, as the closeup shot of him reveals his distasteful recognition of her come-on and pauses on his look of mingled pity and disgust. The teen and not the adult is in the position of power as the character obviously more in touch with appropriate social codes of behavior. Patrick's composure discourages viewers from imagining him as a victim and instead invites us to share in his mockery of this quirky woman whose sexuality can only be realized in her bad romance novel.

Thus just as we glimpse the real antagonism that structures the relationship between authority and its "students," and just as we see this power relationship played out in the form of sexualized aggression and dominance, the film submerges this flash of recognition. So although the counselor's treatment of Patrick Verona clearly approaches the limits of sexual harassment, his witty riposte and cool demeanor throughout the scene demonstrate that the behavior is all "in good fun." Patrick even gets in on the game when he responds to her sarcastic observation, "I see we're making our visits a weekly ritual," with his own suggestive grin and urbane remark, "only so we can have these moments together." After Patrick leaves the office unscathed and unflustered, our gaze is directed back to Perky's computer screen where we see the word "member" replaced with "bratwurst." With this, Junger's controlling camera submerges her fantasy of Patrick's penis into the text of her novel and out of the school room, effectively diverting the potential obscenity of the real into the figural in a fittingly degraded mode of feminine expression — the bodice-ripper romance.

The camera's focus in these scenes overtly controls our perception and our emotional response, severely limiting the range of oppositional readings available to us—or to the film's teen consumers. The effect of the switch from the classroom's interlocutory-style canon debates to the camera's affectively charged but tacit examination of power intimates a distinction between logic and emotion that in the end conscripts a viewer dually, both consciously and unconsciously. The unspoken relief we feel at the resolution of Junger's harassment scenes thus complements and even accentuates our knowing delight at Kat's academic reform. In fact, with this complementarity, Junger's adaptation enforces the original *Shrew's* indulgently misogynist resolution even more effectively than actual *Shrew* performances, which often find ways to resist the comedy's totalizing narrative by permitting viewers to gaze freely (and perhaps subversively) and by allowing actors to perform parts ironically (or just badly).[13]

When Kat enacts Perky's bodice-ripper fantasy later in the film by flashing her breasts to her soccer coach (enabling Patrick to sneak out of detention), she completes the transfer of responsibility for sexual harassment from the ideologically invested system onto the individual foibles of students and/or teachers. In effect, by according students equal sexual agency in negotiating harassment and by enlisting our emotional investment in this fantasy of equal power, 10 Things upholds the belief in the justice of our social hierarchy. Even bullies, whose masculinity is defined by social and sexual dominance and whose excesses have spurred the most public and most grisly challenges to our social order, can be recuperated into the "right supremacy" of the film's so-called benign patriarchal economy (or Petruchio's "what not, that's sweet and happy"). Early in the film, for example, a series of shot-reverse-shots establish Patrick, a fearsome loner, standing opposite mild-mannered Cameron; from Patrick's perspective, we watch Cameron attempt to make small-talk while, off-scene, we hear drilling. A closeup shot studies Cameron's face as his expression changes from nervous friendliness to shocked fear; we then follow his gaze downward to the suggestive hole Patrick has just power-drilled into the French for Daily Life textbook shielding Cameron's groin. Patrick's bully grin reveals his enjoyment of the milder boy's mock-sexual (and textual) violation. Over the course of the movie, however, this bullying is transformed, and Patrick metamorphoses into patriarchy's benevolent big brother/father figure. To the audience's relief and satisfaction, the hero-bully's dominance gets re-cognized into its proper social place; we realize that he needs to be tough to tame Kat and to mentor Cameron. In embracing the bounty of Patrick's paternalism, audiences must retroactively rewrite, forgetting even, the real menace of his early violence.

The movie similarly instructs us to forget the obscene masculinity encoded in the sexually predatory Joey's harassment of classmates; yes, he magic-markers a penis drawing onto an "A/V-nerd's" cheek; and yes, he extorts sex from younger girls in exchange for popularity; but this behavior is dissociated from patriarchal ideology in the end by virtue of Joey's very public unmanning (he gets punched out by a girl at the prom!). He was never a real man at all, we discover. This conservative, palliative intervention in the current debate on teen bullying and sexual harassment reflects the same impulse to reinvest belief in patriarchal mandates as does the movie's reification of Shakespeare as transcendental sign of our culture. Both can benignly countenance gendered violence and the blurring of power's abuses (teachers' and students') as further instances of traditional — even Shakespearean — "good fun."[14]

Cameron (Joseph Gordon-Levitt) and Bianca (Larisa Oleynik) slow dance at the prom underscoring the couple's mutual affection while also celebrating the two right jabs Bianca has just landed on Joey's (Andrew Keegan) nose.

Kat (Julia Stiles) and Patrick's (Heath Ledger) warlike courtship is temporarily refigured as a carefree paintball skirmish.

The strained gender relations that threatened patriarchal interests and gave rise to the persecution of gender-specific crimes such as "scolding," "whoring," and "witchcraft" in Shakespeare's England set the stage for his *Shrew*'s strategic antifeminism. As Lynda Boose notes, the period's anxious conflation of women's sexual, rhetorical, and religious crimes can be observed in the play's critique of Kate's assertiveness: her shrewish and aberrant rejection of men, we see, threatens the proper transmission of her father's commercial, genetic, and cultural legacy (via his daughters' marriages). Petruchio's taming thus has the dual effect of restoring Kate to her social place and of reestablishing the property relations that her misconduct has disrupted; her once unruly body now promises in marriage to reproduce Baptista's blood, fortune, and cultural doctrine. Here, the Father's symbolic authority can be found written—finally—in his daughter's forever-kneeling form.

10 Things I Hate About You, too, inscribes its paternalism on the bodies of its girls, and its concern for its daughters' verbal, sexual, and textual transgressions during a time of heightened cultural anxiety mirrors Shakespeare's own. But, importantly, *10 Things* makes this connection very

At Bogey Lowenstein's party, Joey's (Andrew Keegan) machismo and narcissistic posturing begin to bore Bianca (Larisa Oleynik).

explicit, rendering its boldly didactic moral lesson all the more inescapable for girls by working backward along *Shrew*'s associative chain of "unruliness" to play on the stigma of girls' sexual activity that remains—even today—relatively unchallenged. Where Shakespeare's Baptista is ostensibly concerned with his daughter's verbal slippages, the film's reincarnation, Dr. Stratford, an anxiety-fraught obstetrician, clearly identifies his daughters' potential sexual misprisions as his primary parental concern. Pithy quips like, "kissing is not what keeps me up to my elbows every day in placenta," locate his fears quite explicitly. And anecdotes such as, "I delivered a baby to a 15-year old girl today, and you know what she said to me? ... She said 'I should have listened to my father,'" pose his ideal resolution. In fact, in one grotesquely authoritative display, Stratford forces Bianca to wear a sign of his rule. While rehashing his directives on chastity, Stratford straps onto his daughter "the belly," a ponderous vest that simulates a pregnant woman's naked stomach and breasts. This strangely incestuous moment of physical subjugation dramatizes the gender violence that inheres in the film's multifaceted reassertion of father figures. And even though Kat seems to render such anxiety baseless because she views the "boys at school" as "unwashed cretins," she later reveals that her antisocial rejection of "normal" teen dating is the direct result of an earlier sexual misstep. In obvious defiance of her father's mandates, she confesses that she did "it," "just once, right after mom left. Everyone was doing it, ... So, I did it ... Afterwards I swore I would never do anything just because everyone else was, and I haven't." Neatly, then, *10 Things* links Kat's present-day loquacity, antisocial behavior, and feminist politics to a moment of sexual infidelity to her father—her own and her mother's, whose departure from the family under scandalous circumstances catalyzes her daughter's early transgression.

Kat's subsequent succumbing to Patrick's charms and resumption of normative heterosexual power relations in the final scenes also, it seems, witness her renunciation of shrewish antisociability and unfriendly feminist politics. She and Bianca now get along; she and dad reconcile; she and Patrick go to the senior prom. And in her embrace of Shakespeare, Kat simultaneously abandons her anti-canon rhetoric and publicly surrenders herself to "her man" or, rather, "men." The original Petruchio's approbation of Kate's final self-abnegating monologue is now famously recognized in his charge, "why there's a wench! Come on, and kiss me, Kate" (V.ii.179), which silences his wife literally and figuratively. In its closing scene, Gil Junger's *10 Things I Hate About You* exults in the brutal power relations revealed in this silencing for the very audience most at risk of subjugation—teens, and girls in particular. In so doing, Junger's adaptation not only reifies the anxious taming gesture of its parent text's paternalism; but, further, it validates and even celebrates the gendered violence that student "bodies" face daily. Reveling in the "sweet and happy" of its hero's "awful rule," *10 Things I Hate About You* concludes with Patrick playfully muzzling his own domesticated Kat. When she chastens, "and you can't just ...," he kisses her still moving lips silent. She tries again with "and another thing," and once more finds her mouth sealed in a kiss that endures while the aptly pathetic tune, "I want you to want me, I need you to need me," accompanies the camera's shift from a close-up of the couple, to an aerial perspective that situates them amid a parking lot full of cars and teens, to a final panoramic shot that ominously captures the surrounding landscape. We suddenly discover that the Cheap Trick tune we are hearing emanates from the school's prom band itself sitting atop the school, and this final perspective hints that we too are caught in the film's echoing "cheap trick" rendition.

Works Cited

Associated Press. "Oprah's Revived Book Club Will Stick to Classics." *Herald Times* 2 Mar. 2003, sec. E:6.

Boose, Lynda. "Scolding Brides and Bridling Scolds: Taming the Woman's Unruly Member." *Shakespeare Quarterly*, 42:2 (1991): 179–213.

Boose, Lynda E. and Richard Burt. "Totally Clueless? Shakespeare goes Hollywood in the 1990s." *Shakespeare the Movie*. Edited by Lynda E. Boose and Richard Burt. New York: Routledge, 1997. 8–22.

Charnes, Linda. "Dismember Me: Shakespeare, Paranoia, and the Logic of Mass Culture." *Shakespeare Quarterly*, 48.1 (1997): 1–16.

Demeter, Emily. "Civilizing Subordination: Domestic Violence and The Taming of the Shrew." *Shakespeare Quarterly*, 48.3 (1997): 273–94.

Hawkes, Terence. "Wittgenstein's Shakespeare." *"Bad" Shakespeare*. London: Associated University Presses, 1998. 56–60.

Henderson, Diana E. "A Shrew for the Times." In *Shakespeare the Movie*. Edited by Lynda E. Boose and Richard Burt. New York: Routledge, 1997. 148–168.

Hodgdon, Barbara. "Katherina Bound; or, Play(K)ating the Strictures of Everyday Life." *PMLA*, 107.3 (1992): 538–53.

Junger, Gil, dir. *10 Things I Hate About You.* 1999.

Kopels, Sandra and David Dupper. "School-Based Peer Sexual Harassment." *Child Welfare*,78.4 (1999): 435–461.

Lanier, Douglas M. "Shakescorp Noir." *Shakespeare Quarterly*, 53.2 (2002): 157–180.

Morrell, Robert. "A Calm After the Storm? Beyond Schooling as Violence." *Educational Review* 54.1 (2002): 37–46.

Naremore, James. "Film and the Reign of Adaptation." In *Film Adaptation*. Edited by James Naremore. New Brunswick: Rutgers University Press, 2000. 1–17.

"Oprah's Book Club is Coming Back!" *Oprah.Com*. 5 Mar. 2003. www.oprah.com/books/classics/books_classics_news.jhtml.

Prose, Francine. "I Know Why the Caged Bird Cannot Read: How American High School Students Learn to Loathe Literature." *Harpers Magazine*, 299.1792 (Sept 1999): 76–84.

Shakespeare, William. "The Taming of the Shrew." *The Riverside Shakespeare*. Boston: Houghton Mifflin Co., 1974.

Thompson Publishing Group. "Supreme Court Ruling Reinforces Need for Strong Anti-Harassment Policies, Training." *Educator's Guide to Controlling Sexual Harassment*, 6.10 (July 1999): 1.

United States Secret Service and United States Department of Education. *The Final Report and Findings of the Safe School Initiative: Implications for the Prevention of Attacks in the United States*. Washington, D.C., May 2002.

Zizek, Slavoj. *The Sublime Object of Ideology*. New York: Verso, 1989.

_____. *Tarrying with the Negative*. Durham: Duke University Press, 1993.

Notes

1. In "Totally Clueless? Shakespeare goes Hollywood in the 1990s," Boose and Burt look at the popularization and "devolution" of Shakespeare in response to youth culture market demands, where reference to the Bard more often than not serves the interests of "pop-culture/youth culture (for which we may also read masculine culture)," which they read as "a kind of Hollywood pandering to the anti-intellectual machismo of its adolescent buyer" (19).

2. Despite assorted forays in to the Bard's other works, such as *Macbeth* and "Sonnet 141," and a few ersatz Renaissance-sounding lines here and there, the movie's only direct quotation from *Shrew* comes in Carmen-Lucentio's exclamation upon seeing his Bianca, "I burn, I pine, I persish," in a Midwestern accent. And the movie's only specific references to *Shrew* are its titular allusion and a single description of Kat as "our shrew." All additional resemblance to the original text is structural—but so striking that the adaptation could stand as an example *par excellence* of a reformed and faithful "loose" heir.

3. For just a few, see: *Never Been Kissed* (dir. Kaja Gossnell, 1999), *Midsummer* (dir. James Kerwin, 1999), *Romeo and Juliet* (dir Colin Cox, 2000), *Get Over It* (dir. Tommy O'Haver, 2001), *O* (dir. Tim Blake Nelson, 2001), *Rave Macbeth* (dir. Klaus Knosel, 2001), and *Scotland, PA.* (dir. Billy Morissette, 2001). Douglas M. Lanier's recent "Shakescorp Noir" also examines what he refers to as an ambivalent, "counterdiscourse" movement in Shakespearean adaptation that emerges concurrent with mass-market popularization of Shakespeare. Some of his examples of "counterdiscourse" are *Titus* (dir. Julie Taymor, 1999), *Richard III* (dir. Richard Loncraine, 1995) and *The Postman* (dir Kevin Costner, 1997).

4. Linda Charnes's brilliant "Dismember Me: Shakespeare, Paranoia, and the Logic of Mass Culture," examines a similar phenomenon of the paternal metaphor's failure to guarantee the symbolic order in Shakespeare's *Hamlet,* where the Ghost's "enjoyment" of his sin renders him a "father who knows," or an "obscene father." Hamlet's dilemma, Charnes argues, is that of the noir detective, whose own "humiliated father" corrupts the symbolic authority of all that the paternal metaphor stands for—God, King, Father, Law—rendering his world one of noir paranoia.

5. For a useful survey of *The Taming of the Shrew*'s historical reception, see Diana Henderson's "A Shrew for the Times," which places my reading of *10 Things* along a continuum of *Shrew* adaptations in its observation that *Shrew* always reemerges (in performance and filmic adaptations) at times of high conservativism and in response to feminist social and political advances.

6. My metaphoric use of "soft canons" plays upon traditional signs of masculinity and femininity, but I also borrow it more immediately from Karen L. Kilcup's *Soft Canons: American Women Writers and the Masculine Tradition* (Iowa City: University of Iowa Press, 1999). Other important criticism of the English and American literary canon includes Paul Lauter's *Canons and Contexts* (New York: Oxford University Press, 1991); Barbara Herrnstein Smith's *Contingencies of Value: Alternative Perspectives for Critical Theory* (Cambridge:

Harvard University Press, 1988); and John Guillory's *Cultural Capital: The Problem of Literary Canon Formation* (Chicago: University of Chicago Press, 1993).

7. Although I focus on popular canon debates, academic studies of Shakespeare's cultural capital and "essential" quality are just as interested as Prose and Winfrey in sussing out the opposition between a text's ideological "uses" and its "enduring usefulness." Ideological critics like Terence Hawkes (*Meaning by Shakespeare*, New York: Routledge, 1992), for example, argue that Shakespeare's plays "are not transparent entities yielding immediate access to single, coherent, preordained meanings.... Like words themselves, in short, they have no essential meanings, only uses" (59). Whereas Harold Bloom (*Shakespeare: The Invention of the Human*, New York: Riverhead Books, 1998), whose legendary injunction against "the School of Resentment" garnered him lucrative profits in the popular market, argues in traditionalist fashion that Shakespeare's oeuvre transcends history.

8. By "Arnoldian," I am referring, of course, to Matthew Arnold's argument about the role of (high) culture in promoting civility in *Culture and Anarchy* (1869), which evolved as a response to industrialization and still enjoys tremendous influence in the structuring of educational systems today. In fact, as James Naremore observes, "the study of English literature in American universities owes its very existence to this [Arnoldian definition and defense of high culture]" (3).

9. Title IX of the Education Amendments of 1972 provides that "'No person in the United States shall, on the basis of sex, be excluded from participation in, be denied the benefits of, or be subjected to discrimination under any education program or activity receiving Federal financial assistance'" (Kopels and Dupper 438).

10. Zizek's observation that "Belief is an affair of obedience to the dead, uncomprehended letter" (*Sublime* 44) dramatizes that the power of this belief to structure a subject's social order depends on the letter's (Law, Father, God, symbolic big Other) absolute, disinterested, and *uncomprehended* authority.

11. Morrell is useful again here in his sharp observation that "[t]hese discourses produce an obsession with militaristic solutions because they conceive of violence in terms of we and they and an enemy. They also blind observers to what else is going on (and sometimes this is very positive). They prevent a recognition that violence is a symptom of social inequality and they turn us from what is most difficult—that none of us is free of violence" (45).

12. The film opened in the U.S. on March 31, 1999, and its obvious success (budget: $16mil; U.S.A. gross by 29 Aug. 99: $38.176mil.) testifies to its immense popularity with teen (and parent) audiences.

13. Arguments in favor of and against the play's negotiability abound. Diana Henderson's "A Shrew for All Times," for example, makes this very argument in favor of performative resistance; whereas Barbara Hogdon ("Katherina Bound; or, Play (K)ating the Strictures of Everyday Life") maintains that the play *always* structurally encodes male dominance: "whether in its Elizabethan guise as a tale of 'good husbandry' or in this recent thrust at historicized counterdiscourse, the play always represents Katherina bound" (551).

14. For an insightful study of the problems of reading Shakespeare's own "taming" as similar good fun, see Emily Demeter's "Civilizing Subordination: Domestic Violence and *The Taming of the Shrew*," which argues that a viewer's "pleasure" in the play comes at the cost of "indulging" the play's reliance on strategies of "civilized" domestic violence to effect its happy marriage.

11

Prospero's Pharmacy: Peter Greenaway and the Critics Play Shakespeare's Mimetic Game

Dan DeWeese

Shakespeare's Prospero seems incompetent. He is condescending and short with his daughter Miranda, despite the fact that she displays nothing but love and admiration for him. He has bungled his relationship with his adopted son Caliban to the point that the estranged beast dreams of murdering his foster father at the first opportunity. He maintains an awkwardly uneven association with his best and most potent ally, Ariel — a friend he seems to revel in demeaning by rehashing ad nauseam (Prospero claims it is a monthly ritual) the story of how he released Ariel from Sycorax's spell. And despite what appears to be obsessive overplanning of his plot, Prospero interrupts one of the few moments of delight he offers when he realizes that he has nearly forgotten to protect himself from advancing murderers.

Looming over these details, however, is the role incompetence might have played in the reason Prospero was exiled from Milan in the first place. The only narrative we get of what must have been a harrowing scene — a father and his young daughter surprised in the night, thrown into a small boat, and cast onto the dark ocean — comes to us through Prospero himself, in which he portrays himself as a victim of his brother Antonio's overweening greed and ambition. Yet Prospero's story includes troubling details. Intent only on his study of the "liberal arts," Prospero admits to a virtual abdication of his dukedom: "The government I cast upon my brother, / And to my estate grew stranger, being transported / And rapt

155

in secret studies" (I.ii.75–77), and later, "I, thus neglecting worldly ends, all dedicated / To closeness and the bettering of my mind..." (I.ii.89–90). A stranger to his estate, neglecting worldly ends, rapt in secret studies—these are not the traditional qualities of a noble and reliable duke, father, or narrative protagonist.

They are the necessary qualities, of course, of what Prospero really is: a magician. In "Plato's Pharmacy," Jacques Derrida makes an observation regarding the role of the magician. Examining Plato's use of the term *pharmakeus*, Derrida raises the subject of an interesting synonym:

> The word in question is *pharmakos* (wizard, magician, poisoner), a synonym of *pharmakeus* (which Plato uses), but with the unique feature of having been overdetermined, overlaid by Greek culture with another function....
>
> The character of the *pharmakos* has been compared to a scapegoat. The evil and the outside, the expulsion of the evil, its exclusion out of the body (and out) of the city — these are the two major senses of the character and of the ritual [130].

Derrida goes on to cite further details regarding the ritual whereby a *pharmakos* was exiled from the city (suffering blows to the genitals and being burned alive were possibilities), but the general idea is sufficient: considered a source of poison, the *pharmakos* was a likely candidate for violent expulsion from his society.

From the perspective of narrative facility, it would have been far better for Shakespeare to earn the audience's sympathy for his protagonist by writing Prospero as a noble and hardworking duke, overthrown by immoral bandits rotten to the core. Instead, however, Shakespeare muddies the waters of his protagonist's history; making him a magician indicates that at least by the end of his career, Shakespeare understood the implications of the *pharmakon* structure. While Derrida's essay offers details regarding the recommended method for expelling the local *pharmakos*, *The Tempest* examines what life a *pharmakos* might expect to lead after being expelled from the city. Prospero is a magician who has apparently avoided the low blows and been spared the flames; in some ways, then, he is like a Jesus who slipped out the back of the garden of Gethsemane, or a Socrates who chose not to take the hemlock.

Prospero's complexity has been a perpetual problem for readers. Harold Bloom, a man who prides himself on being a traditional and supposedly clear-eyed reader, seems mystified by the choice. "Why does Shakespeare make Prospero so cold?" he asks. "The play's ethos does not seem to demand it, and the audience can be baffled by a protagonist so clearly in the right and yet essentially antipathetic" (669). Seemingly, it does not occur to Bloom that perhaps his understanding of the play's ethos is in need of revision, and neither does he explore the possibility that an audience that finds Prospero antipathetic is anything but baffled — that, in fact, finding Prospero antipathetic might indicate an accurate understanding of Shakespeare's intention. The *pharmakon* structure plays itself out in a social milieu just as easily as it does in a psychological one, and an audience of theorists is not required for the phenomenon to be comprehensible. It seems reasonable to assume that an audience shown a magician who has shirked his political duties might find Prospero's exile appropriate: rather than attending his responsibilities to his dukedom and his daughter, Prospero, it seems, was turning himself into a wizard. He had it coming, really.

Though René Girard analyzes the play's mimetic structures, he comes to the same conclusion. Citing the same lines in which Prospero admits neglecting his estate, Girard points out that "[i]f Prospero had deliberately plotted to turn a potential into an actual rival, he could not have gone

Ferdinand (Mark Rylance), Prospero (John Gielgud), and Miranda (Isabella Pasco) in Peter Greenaway's *Prospero's Books*. Though he presents himself as the careful manager of his daughter's marriage, Prospero's manipulations are born of a desire for revenge.

about it more adroitly than he did.... Prospero perversely incited this brotherly desire for his own ducal being.... No sooner had he lost it, however, than he furiously desired it back" (349). Girard later asks (mostly rhetorically) why, if Prospero was as popular a duke as he claimed to be, his subjects did not defend him from Antonio's abduction plot. But Prospero could not have loaded the dice any more powerfully against himself: not only did he entice his brother's betrayal, but he did so while studying magic, thereby inheriting a persona (the *pharmakos*) that his subjects would agree needed to be exiled. Girard's mimetic principles predict Antonio's betrayal of Prospero; the support Antonio's plot received from others is a result of Prospero's role in Derrida's *pharmakon* equation. Both Girard's and Derrida's analyses identify Prospero as a likely sacrificial victim; they simply arrive at the sacrificial destination from different directions. *The Tempest* we are describing, then—borne of Derrida's *pharmakon*, operating along Girard's mimetic lines—is entirely different from *The Tempest* Bloom and perhaps most audiences read, in which Prospero is "so clearly in the right." Our Prospero is neither clearly in the right nor clearly in the wrong. As a magician or wizard, he can be neither. It is difficult to know what to make of Prospero because, in many ways, it seems that *The Tempest* is about Prospero's inability to know what to make of himself.

Or is it that Prospero is uncertain regarding how best to go about *unmaking* himself? He ends the play, after all, by abjuring his "rough magic," promising to bury his staff and drown his (singular) book (V.i.50–57). Shakespeare, it seems, chooses a not insignificant challenge for himself in *The Tempest*: he attempts to center a play on a character who, rather than being developed or created, actually desires the opposite: to become less and less a character—to be unmade. But this is where we stumble upon another problem with the character of Prospero. If Prospero is an ambivalent *pharmakos* possessed of no absolute value or essence, then what good does it do for him to drown his book? In other words, how can Prospero hope to unmake himself, when the role he plays is that of a character barely present in the first place? Though Bloom strangely and hyperbolically claims of Prospero that "the unholy powers of the magus surpass anything we could have expected" (a statement that begs the questions: Where? When?), he ends in roughly the same arena of doubt regarding Prospero's promise to abjure his magic, saying, "We are listening not to a poet-playwright but to an uncanny magician whose art has become so internalized that it cannot be abandoned, even though he insists it will be" (683).

Enter Peter Greenaway, bearing *Prospero's Books*. If there is a director suited to "the ethos" (to use Bloom's term) of late Shakespeare, it is probably Greenaway. Shakespeare, after all, was not averse to a good, self-referential joke ("Pyramus and Thisbe" comes to mind), and neither did he shrink from calling attention to the constructed nature of his plays: there are the oft-mentioned plays within plays, actors playing characters who, in turn, act as other characters, clowns who comment on the characters and the plot, and so forth. But it is the Shakespeare of the romances (*The Winter's Tale*, for one, but even more so *The Tempest*), in which traditional notions of genre are subverted or transcended, who provides material particularly apt to the interests of Greenaway, a filmmaker who has said, "I don't think the cinema is a particularly good narrative medium. My interest, I suppose, would concentrate on other notions that the film represents. If you want to be passionately attached to narrative, then be a writer, not a filmmaker" (177).

The Shakespeare who wrote *The Tempest* might have felt similarly about narrative. We have already discussed his seeming lack of concern with establishing a sympathetic, goal-oriented protagonist, and as no significant obstacles to Prospero's control are ever presented, the play is decidedly lacking in significant conflict or suspense. There are various ways of trying to express the play's narrative anomie — Bloom labels it "virtually plotless" (666), Stephen Greenblatt introduces it as "a kind of echo chamber of Shakespearean motifs" (3047), Girard claims that "The entire play is *within the play*" (343), but regardless of the terminology, it is clear that Greenaway places himself firmly in this line. His film opens with a text crawl against a dark background, including the following:

> Prospero, once the Duke of Milan, now reigns over a faraway island, living there with his only daughter, Miranda.... One evening, Prospero imagines creating a storm powerful enough to bring his old enemies to his island. He begins to write a play about this tempest, speaking aloud the lines of each of his characters....

By depicting Prospero himself as the writer of *The Tempest*, Greenaway reverses Bloom's claim that we are not listening to a poet-playwright. Greenaway's Prospero has so internalized his knowledge and his very conception of the world, that *The Tempest* takes place only in his head. One cannot help but wonder if Greenaway read and agreed with Girard on the nature of the tempest in *The Tempest*:

> It is *une tempête sous un crâne*, as Victor Hugo would say — Prospero's own, a work of (im)pure imagination, the very play we are watching. The tempest has only one effect; it brings all the enemies of Prospero under

his power, in the one place where all his wishes are immediately fulfilled, his island, the nonexistent world of literary creation [350].

Although the idea that the tempest occurs only in Prospero's imagination may seem a small detail, it radically reconceives the play. While Shakespeare's *Tempest* originally appears to depict the process whereby a *pharmakos* reintegrates himself into society, Greenaway suggests that once a magician is expelled, there is no going back. Greenaway's Prospero spends more time in his own head than he does on his island, and the part-revenge, part-reintegration story that he calls *The Tempest* is clearly the mere fantasy of an impotent sorcerer whose magic is no longer relevant.

Not content merely to indulge the Prospero-as-Shakespeare reading of *The Tempest*, Greenaway forces a third persona into the conflation, saying,

> To explain the strategies, which I would like to think are legitimate, is to first of all consider the possibility that since this is Shakespeare's last play, it is in some sense Shakespeare's farewell to the theater — and this might well be Gielgud's last grand performance. So this may represent his farewell to magic, farewell to theater, farewell to illusion. So using that as a central idea, there was my wish to find a way of uniting the figures of Prospero and Gielgud and Shakespeare. From that, everything else follows... [149]

It is typical of Greenaway to (over)load his characters in this way; the difficulty one has with suspending disbelief in his films (with forgetting for more than a few minutes that one is watching a film directed by Peter Greenaway about some characters and events that are fictional constructs, created only in the service of symbolic or narrative expediency) is intentional. "I want to regard my public as infinitely intelligent, as understanding notions of the suspension of disbelief, and as realizing all the time that this is not a slice of life, this is openly a film" (salon.com). We will let the validity of Greenaway's notions regarding the relation of intelligence to suspension of disbelief pass without comment and simply recognize that staging *The Tempest* in Prospero's head (and having Gielgud do the voice of every character) is only the first, and most obvious, of the ways in which Greenaway makes blatant the constructed nature of the entertainment he creates. His camera tends to remain on one plane, pointed in one direction, occasionally tracking slowly to the side, roughly the point of view of someone floating gracefully toward the aisle from a good seat in the middle of the third or fourth row. The primary actors keep mostly to the same plane, moving left and right in front of the camera, but rarely

John Gielgud as Prospero, considering how best to write the next scene in Peter Greenaway's *Prospero's Books*. Greenaway said he wished "to find a way of uniting the figures of Prospero, Gielgud, and Shakespeare."

forward or backward, almost as if they are butterflies pressed between glass or slides ready for examination under a microscope.

Formally trained as a painter, Greenaway is also obsessed with the concept of the frame. In *Prospero's Books*, he bombards the viewer with frames within frames, images within and/or superimposed over other images, compositions that recall famous paintings or myths, and so forth. Unconcerned with the traditional primacy of narrative, Greenaway constructs *Prospero's Books* as a series of moving paintings—a kind of illuminated text. Working on a massive set, his compositions are intricate and gorgeous, often revealing an impressive spatial depth. Greenaway's images routinely possess more layers than those created by perhaps any other living director. One could go through the entire film watching only the deep background and find more than enough visual material to keep the eye busy; even in shadows that appear to be a hundred yards from the camera, there are often barely-visible figures lurking. Far from reminding one of other "art house" directors who use low budgets as an excuse for creating only the simplest images, Greenaway's fantastically complex choreographies put one more in mind of the grandiose cinematic gestures of someone like Busby Berkeley, who worked on similarly immense sets, solving what must have been similar problems regarding the careful use of whole troupes of dancers and actors.

The layering and choreography would be a kind of cold virtuosity if the subject matter did not demand them, but with *The Tempest*, Greenaway is in possession of material that allows him to indulge his talents to the fullest. Greenblatt calls the play "an echo chamber"; when Gielgud intones the play's first word —*Boatswain!*— it is echoed multiple times by different, modulating voices, a process that continues until the voices are echoing entire lines, as if Prospero is somehow giving birth to the voices, teaching them to speak (an idea that nicely anticipates Caliban's famous lament regarding his feelings about having been taught language by Prospero). There are physical echoes, as well: when Prospero lights a candle, for instance, hundreds of other candles in the room alight into a spontaneous, sympathetic blaze; there is not one, but multiple ginger-haired Ariels, ranging in age from toddler to adult (at one point, three of them assume a tableau that mimes one of Raphael's cherub paintings); and Greenaway takes literally Shakespeare's suggestion (mouthed by Caliban) that the island is populated with countless voices and spirits.[1] Almost every frame of the film is filled with extras in various states of dress; the tracking shot that comprises the opening credits sequence alone includes so many historical and literary tableaux that anyone interested in fully unpacking the sequence might want to set aside a few months for research. It is difficult to read Shakespeare's Prospero as anything other than profoundly isolated; Greenaway's Prospero, on the other hand, appears to share his accommodations with the population of a small (though mute) city.

The most obvious change Greenaway has made is in his title. When an interviewer alluded to Prospero's pledge to destroy his book at the end of *The Tempest*,[2] Greenaway responded, "I have a great antipathy to that ending and would take up a quarrel with Shakespeare, if I could be so bold.... You must remember the last two [books]—a collection of Shakespeare's plays and *The Tempest*—are preserved" (141). If there is a shortcoming in Greenaway's vision, it stems from this sentiment. Shakespeare's *Tempest* is about a man walking away from his book; Greenaway's *Tempest*, however, is structured around a kind of pervasive bibliophilia;[3] by preserving the Shakespeare volumes, Greenaway validates the very fetish Shakespeare sought to destroy. Greenaway, then, creates a film text whose views are exactly antithetical to those apparently held by Shakespeare, or at least the Shakespeare who wrote *The Tempest*.

Greenaway is far from alone in stubbornly refusing to relinquish his fetishization of the book. Borges, in a lecture entitled "The Enigma of Shakespeare," claimed "a book of genius is a book that can be read in a slightly or very different way by each generation…. We can read Shakespeare's work, but we do not know how it will be read in a century" (473). It is interesting to note that Borges uses the phrase "Shakespeare's work" as representative of "a book of genius." Like Greenaway, Borges thinks of Shakespeare not so much as a man, but as a book — specifically, the book that Greenaway has Caliban rescue from destruction at the end of *Prospero's Books*, the book of collected plays and poems, the book that Borges and Greenaway and anyone with sufficient funds can purchase and take home and hold in their hands while turning the pages; in the same lecture, Borges also claimed that "Shakespeare had the power to multiply himself marvelously; to think of Shakespeare is to think of a crowd" (470). But what is the crowd Borges thinks of, if not all of the characters from all of Shakespeare's plays, tromping through Borges' fertile mind?

It is that very image — Shakespeare's characters released from the bounds of their dramas, Othello rubbing elbows with MacBeth, Romeo attempting desperately to seduce Hermia, Beatrice and Benedick chatting with Petruchio and Kate, and so forth — that brings us back to *The Tempest* and *Prospero's Books*. Because Shakespeare, as is well known, had no book, his plays were only published posthumously. It is not Shakespeare who shares an island with mysterious voices and not Shakespeare whom Greenaway depicts striding through rooms filled to overflowing with other humans (or at least beings with human forms); these are scenes inhabited by Prospero. Because so little is known about Shakespeare the human, it is almost as if he exists as an empty vessel that his readers have a desperate need to fill, usually to overflowing. They want to substitute Prospero for Shakespeare; to substitute their favorite copy of *The Complete Shakespeare* for Shakespeare; to substitute Shakespeare's other characters for Shakespeare; anything, it seems, will do, as long as the emptiness is filled. Borges sees Shakespeare in a book, but also finds the bard in every one of the characters, who are found, of course, in the book, though they were not originally, as Shakespeare did not publish. Greenaway sees Shakespeare in Prospero, and Shakespeare in Gielgud, and Prospero in Gielgud. Prospero, of course, is a character in a book, so he sees both Shakespeare and Prospero in the very book that he depicts Prospero-as-Shakespeare as writing.

This is mimetic hysteria. Girard helps:

> Is this tempest taking place solely in Prospero's imagination, as we first suggested, or in the real world, as we are now suggesting? The genius of this play is that both answers are true simultaneously. Given the Shakespearean postulate of mimetic circularity, Prospero's imagination can be

everything and nothing at the same time, or almost nothing, only a slight exaggeration here and there. A great writer's invention does not have to coincide with the real world for the two to be fundamentally the same [351].

This is the most crucial point to be made regarding *The Tempest*. Unfortunately, it is a point that is utterly overlooked by every other critic, writer, reader, and director who has interpreted the play, all of whom rush so eagerly into the drama's circular mimetic game that they thoroughly lose track of the difference between an author, a character and a reader by the time they finish the first act. "A great writer's invention does not have to coincide with the real world for the two to be fundamentally the same." Girard has located the mimetic fallacy within the dispute over the equation of Prospero to Shakespeare: specifically, it is the assumption that the play somehow needs to intersect with the real world, with the "real Shakespeare." The character of Prospero need not be a mimetic representation of Shakespeare anymore than the character of Miranda need be a mimetic representation of Shakespeare's daughter. The tempest, the island, Prospero and Miranda, Ariel and Caliban, all of the other voices and spirits and characters inhabit an imagined reality all their own and need not answer to some presumed literary rule that every piece of literature should, at some level, be reducible to fairly straightforward biographical allegory.

In fact, once a closer look is taken at the usual reading of Prospero-as-Shakespeare, other flaws become readily apparent. First and most obvious is the oft-repeated claim that *The Tempest* is notable not only because it is Shakespeare's last play, but also because he knew as he was writing it that it would be his last play. There is no evidence to support this assumption, and there are two entire plays—*All Is True* and *The Two Noble Kinsmen*—that seem to controvert it.[4] The play's epilogue, too, is often read as a farewell to the theater, yet nothing Prospero says in the epilogue is inconsistent with the action of the play or otherwise implies a break in character, outside of the fact that Prospero addresses the audience directly, which is not itself unique, as the same direct address appears at the close of other Shakespearean plays. And perhaps most tellingly, despite the fact that Prospero pledges to break his staff and drown his book, the play does not dramatize those acts. The reading of Prospero-as-Shakespeare, then, requires the reader to read Prospero as a probable liar. Shakespeare, after all, continued to add to his "book" when he collaborated with Fletcher on *All Is True* and *The Two Noble Kinsmen*.

To see the degree to which *The Tempest*'s self-reflexive game sucks in those who involve themselves, one need only return to Greenaway's self-congratulatory statement about his ability to cast Gielgud in the Prospero role: "...since this is Shakespeare's last play, it is in some sense Shakespeare's farewell to the theater — and this might well be Gielgud's last grand performance. So this may represent his farewell to magic, farewell to theater, farewell to illusion" (149). We have already noted that Shakespeare continued to practice his magic, if a lesser version, after *The Tempest*. Gielgud, too, failed to satisfy the terms of Greenaway's implied contract, stubbornly continuing to appear in films almost every year until his death in 2000. Even Greenaway himself refused to overthrow his charms when it came to *The Tempest*. In an interview with *American Film*, he said, "There's a project I'd like very much to do, called *Prospero's Creatures*, about what happened before the beginning. Sort of a prelude to *The Tempest*. And I've also written a play called *Miranda*, about what happens afterwards on the ship on the way home" (128). So not only was Greenaway unable to keep from making more books about *The Tempest*, but Prospero appears in them. Despite Greenaway's excitement about lining up the farewells, neither *The Tempest* nor *Prospero's Books* was a farewell to anyone, whether living, dead, or fictional.

The strategy at work in Shakespeare's *Tempest* remains superior to its challengers. Rather than revealing or reinventing Shakespeare, the interpreters of *The Tempest* are, time and again, simply pulled into the play's, sacrificial game, becoming a part of the play. Shakespeare dangles Prospero in front of them in the same way Prospero dangles his dukedom in front of his brother Antonio. Antonio took the bait and so do Shakespeare's interpreters, deciding that Prospero is Shakespeare, that finally we have the man; finally he is writing about himself. Because he lunges so enthusiastically for the bait, Greenaway cannot help but blink when it comes time for the sacrifice. He refuses to allow the books to be destroyed, inventing the preposterous "solution" in which Caliban rescues the volumes from the water, one of the most specious moments in the film.[5] Strangely, Greenaway recognizes the fraudulence of the book-drowning gesture, but misinterprets it, saying, "There's one thing I would take issue with Shakespeare on: in the end he destroys his books, which I find very painful indeed. We can't unknowledge ourselves, we can't turn away knowledge once we've got it" (131). The fact that "we can't unknowledge ourselves," of course, is the very reason it is safe for Prospero to destroy his books: their loss will not reduce his powers one whit. For this same reason, it is safe for Shakespeare to sacrifice Prospero, to strip him of his powers and make him wave goodbye: Shakespeare knows full well that he is not his characters, and if he invites his audience to pin him down within the confines of a single persona, it is with the full knowledge that he can extricate himself from the role, safely slipping out the literary back door at any moment, and write again later.

There is something undeniably sinister about this game. Perhaps *The Tempest*, rather than being a comedy or a romance, is really a cousin of a darker literary genre: the taunting letters practicing serial killers often send to the police. In both cases the authors flaunt their position of control: both the killer and the playwright claim the power to kill at will, whenever and wherever they see fit. They simultaneously want and do not want to be caught: they want to be caught in order to receive credit for their crimes and assume the position of celebrity they feel they deserve; they do not want to be caught so that they can kill again, extending the game and adding to its complexity. The two desires operate simultaneously, and this is how Shakespeare uses his Prospero: "this is me," he teases, and then just as suddenly, "this is not me."[6] Prospero is Shakespeare's dummy, a corpse he animates in order to lead us off track. When he is done with it, he dumps it at the audience's feet, and they applaud.

Shakespeare misleads his audience so completely that not one of the critics explores the fullest implications of the game Prospero, and Shakespeare through him, is playing. A man who has been stranded on an island for a long time, Prospero has clearly been refining his powers, awaiting his opportunity for revenge. Prospero holds everyone in such sway, in fact, that he reveals his darkest potentials directly, but not one of the other characters questions him. "This thing of darkness I / Acknowledge mine" (V.i.278–279), he says of Caliban, admitting responsibility for a would-be rapist and murderer, the result of Prospero's own careful education. It is a telling moment, this acknowledgment of ownership, almost as if Shakespeare is at pains to remind us that Prospero has two children; the beautiful and virtuous Miranda must coexist with her monstrous, murderous sibling.

Perhaps for that reason the end of *The Tempest* is so unsettling. The popular reading of the play's conclusion is a sentimental one, in which Prospero (almost inexplicably) chooses to forgive his enemies, and then Shakespeare supposedly steps forward and bids his audience a fond adieu. But could not this be yet another bit of smoke and mirrors from the ambivalent *pharmakos*? Is it not implied that the next step in the narrative consists of Prospero on a boat, headed back to Milan? Is it possible that Prospero addresses the audience directly not to say goodbye, but to include them in his potent hypnosis? Bloom observes, "We are listening not to a poet-playwright but to an uncanny magician whose art has become so internalized that it cannot be abandoned." Greenaway rejoins: 'We can't unknowledge ourselves.' By promising to drown the book, to destroy the *pharmakeus*, Prospero seeks to earn passage to Milan and reentry into society. But does a *pharmakos* who destroys his *pharmakeus* really cease to be a danger to society? Does the magic come from the magician or from the wand? What is more dangerous, the poisoner or the poison?

Shakespeare wrote again after *The Tempest*, and we have established the likelihood that Prospero would have no problem continuing to use magic, should he choose to do so. Perhaps it is a cynical point, but had Prospero murdered his enemies right there on the island, he would have no means to return Milan. The last lines of the Epilogue, after all, allude to crime: "As you from crimes would pardoned be, / Let your indulgence set me free" (19–20). If both Derrida's *pharmakon* structure and Girard's mimetic structure point toward the need for a sacrificial victim and if we can agree that Prospero's supposed destruction of his book, even were it dramatized, would not be a true sacrifice, then where in the game that is *The Tempest* is the sacrificial victim? Prospero ends the play smiling at the audience. There is an axiom regarding identifying the sacrificial victim in a game: it begins, "If you can't spot the sucker..." One can only assume that it will be smooth sailing back to Milan.

Works Cited

Bloom, Harold. *Shakespeare: The Invention of the Human*. New York: Riverhead Books, 1998. 662–684.

Borges, Jorge Luis. "The Enigma of Shakespeare." In *Selected Non-Fictions*. Edited by Eliot Weinberger. New York: Viking, 1999. 463–473.

Derrida, Jacques. "Plato's Pharmacy." In *Dissemination*. Translated by Barbara Johnson. Chicago: University of Chicago, 1983. 63–171.

Girard, René. *A Theater of Envy: William Shakespeare*. New York: Oxford, 1991.

Greenaway, Peter. *Interviews*. Edited by Vernon and Marguerite Gras. Mississippi: University Press of Mississippi, 2000.

Greenblatt, Stephen. "The Tempest." In *The Norton Shakespeare*. Edited by Stephen Greenblatt. New York: Norton, 1997. 3047–3054.

Hawthorne, Christopher. "Flesh and Ink." *Salon.com*. (6 June 1997): n.p. Internet. 21 Apr. 2003.

Prospero's Books. Dir. Peter Greenaway. Miramax, 1991.

Shakespeare, William. *The Tempest*. In *The Norton Shakespeare*. Edited by Stephen Greenblatt. New York: Norton, 1997.

Notes

1. III.ii.130–135: "Be not afeard. The isle is full of noises, / Sounds, and sweet airs, that give delight and hurt not. / Sometimes a thousand twangling instruments / Will hum about mine ears, and sometime voices / That if I then had waked after long sleep / will make me sleep again..."

2. V.i.56–57: "And deeper than did ever plummet sound / I'll drown my book."

3. Despite the fact that the film is entitled *Prospero's Books*, I am not, in this essay, going to discuss the books Greenaway invents and depicts, primarily because they do not seem to me to be used to illuminate and/or alter Shakespeare's text in any way. The images, and

the way they are dropped into the film, are definitely interesting from a technical stand-point, the subjects of the books are certainly creative, and the voice-over artist who describes the books' contents possesses exactly the right kind of sonorous voice, but ... they just seem forced to me. I think Greenaway's fetishization of books and what they represent has a lot to bear (negatively) on his interpretation of *The Tempest*, but I think an examination of what he does at the end of the film with the book of plays and the book of *The Tempest* is sufficient to make those points.

4. The desire for an admired person's career to conform to a perfect, mythic narrative is, of course, just as pervasive as those careers' persistent refusal to do so. One need look no further than the lamentations that arise every time a former title-holding prizefighter un-retires in order to fight again, or the pained way in which fans follow an aging athlete's late-career seasons spent with some lesser team. Professional sports mythmakers do their best to ignore these embarrassingly mortal seasons in much the same way we prefer to pretend that Shakespeare perhaps did no more than copy-edit *All Is True* and *The Two Noble Kins-men*.

5. Greenaway's entire handling of the Caliban character strikes me as decidedly odd. Played by the dancer Michael Clark, Greenaway's Caliban is a lithe, androgynous, bendable fellow with dramatic eye makeup—hardly intimidating or monstrous. Like his depiction of the books themselves, Greenaway's conception of Caliban seems forced. I cannot help but won-der if part of the problem stems from the fact that, as a person who has decided to inter-pret *The Tempest* by structuring it around Prospero's books, Greenaway himself best occupies the Caliban role. He, after all, is the person so impressed by Prospero's books that he names his film after them, in much the same way Caliban obsesses over the potential powers held within Prospero's books. Both Caliban and Greenaway worship, in their own way, at the foot of Prospero and his library.

6. Greenaway's film, of course, dramatizes only the first half of the equation. It is, in its way, a film of only half of the *The Tempest*.

12

Shakespeare Film and Television Derivatives: A Bibliography

José Ramón Díaz Fernández

This chapter covers both film and television derivatives of Shakespeare and is restricted to those that have been the object of one or several critical studies. For a fuller catalogue, the reader should consult the filmographies listed in Section A. The bibliography is intended to be as comprehensive as possible, but certain types of entries have been omitted: abstracts, dissertations, and works containing very brief references. Reviews are not usually included if they do not specifically deal with the use of Shakespeare in the film. Reprints have not been included, either, unless they constitute a revised or expanded version of the original work.

This bibliography only includes English-language references, and the entries are classified according to five different categories: Section A provides a list of bibliographies and filmographies; Section B includes general studies, historical overviews, and essays on the use of the offshoots in the classroom; Section C lists derivatives based on a single play by Shakespeare whereas Section D presents those related to several of his works. The final section deals with the derivatives featuring Shakespeare as a character. Entries in Section C are arranged play-by-play and then chronologically if there are several offshoots of one specific play. In Sections D and E, however, films are always listed according to their release date. If an item in the bibliography covers more than one adaptation, the complete bibliographic reference will be given the first time it appears and, in order to avoid repetition, a system of cross-references has been added at the end of each film subsection to locate any other articles or books on it. Full citation for essay collections will be provided the first time the volume is mentioned, and an abbreviated version will be given for each article in the collection in its relevant subsection together with a cross-reference that will help to locate the complete reference. Where necessary, annotations are included to explain the contents of a volume or to offer information about the derivative(s) under discussion. These abbreviations have been used throughout for the following journal titles:

CS	*Creative Screenwriting*
LFQ	*Literature/Film Quarterly*
MSAN	*Marlowe Society of America Newsletter*
PS	*Post Script: Essays in Film and the Humanities*
SB	*Shakespeare Bulletin*
SClass	*Shakespeare and the Classroom*
SFNL	*Shakespeare on Film Newsletter*
SN	*Shakespeare Newsletter*
SQ	*Shakespeare Quarterly*
SY	*Shakespeare Yearbook*

The present bibliography could not have been compiled without the generous help of several individuals and institutions, and the following pages constitute a fitting acknowledgement to the constant support and encouragement I have received. I would like to thank H.R. Coursen, Miguel Angel González, Diana Harris, James L. Harner, A.J. Hoenselaars, Graham Holderness, Courtney Lehmann, Desirée López, Sofía Muñoz-Valdivieso, Laurie E. Osborne, Kenneth S. Rothwell, Mariangela Tempera and Juan J. Zaro for sending me photocopies of their publications or providing some of the information below. Once again, Gracia Navas deserves my most sincere thanks for her impeccable work at the Interlibrary Loan Service Section in my university. I should also like to thank the institutions I visited in my search for references: the Library of Congress, the British Library, the Folger Shakespeare Library, the Shakespeare Institute, the British Film Institute, and the University of London Library. Finally, I would like to thank the Spanish Ministry of Education and Culture for funding the research that led to the writing of the present article.

A. Bibliographies and Filmographies

A1. Eckert, C.W. *Focus on Shakespearean Films.* Englewood Cliffs: Prentice-Hall, 1972. 165–78. [Filmography.]
A2. Grant, C., ed. *As You Like It: Audio-Visual Shakespeare.* London: British Universities Film and Video Council, 1992.
A3. Holderness, G., and C. McCullough, comps. "Shakespeare on the Screen: A

Selective Filmography." *Shakespeare Survey* 39 (1987): 13–37. Reprinted in *Shakespeare and the Moving Image: The Plays on Film and Television*. Edited by A. Davies and S. Wells. Cambridge: Cambridge University Press, 1994. 18–49.

A4. McKernan, L., and O. Terris, eds. *Walking Shadows: Shakespeare in the National Film and Television Archive*. London: British Film Institute, 1994.

A5. McMurtry, J. *Shakespeare Films in the Classroom: A Descriptive Guide*. Hamden: Archon Books, 1994. 235–44. [Annotated filmography.]

A6. Parker, B.M. *The Folger Shakespeare Filmography: A Directory of Feature Films Based on the Works of William Shakespeare*. Washington: Folger Shakespeare Library, 1979.

A7. Rothwell, K.S. "An Annotated and Chronological Screenography: Major *Hamlet* Adaptations and Derivatives." In *Approaches to Teaching Shakespeare's* Hamlet. Edited by B.W. Kliman. New York: MLA, 2001. 14–27.

A8. _____, and A.H. Melzer. *Shakespeare on Screen: An International Filmography and Videography*. New York: Neal-Schuman, 1990. [A revised, updated edition by K.S. Rothwell and J.R. Díaz Fernández is currently in progress.]

A9. Sammons, E. *Shakespeare: A Hundred Years on Film*. London: Shepheard-Walwyn, 2000.

B. General Studies

B1. Ardolino, F. "'A Hit, a Very Palpable Hit': The Use of *Hamlet* in Sport Films." *SClass* 9.1–2 (2001): 48–51.

B2. Ball, R.B. *Shakespeare on Silent Film: A Strange Eventful History*. London: George Allen and Unwin, 1968.

B3. Béchervaise, N.E., ed. *Shakespeare on Celluloid*. Rozelle: St. Clair, 1999. Reprinted as *Teaching Shakespeare on Screen: "The Film's the Thing."* Vancouver: Pacific Educational, 2001.

B4. Boose, L.E., and R. Burt. *Shakespeare, the Movie: Popularizing the Plays on Film, TV, and Video*. London: Routledge, 1997. 8–22.

B5. Brode, D. *Shakespeare in the Movies: From the Silent Era to Shakespeare in Love*. New York: Oxford University Press, 2000. Reprinted, with a new epilogue on films released in 1999–2000, as *Shakespeare in the Movies: From the Silent Era to Today*. New York: Berkley Boulevard Books, 2001. [Most chapters include a section discussing the most important derivatives.]

B6. Burt, R. "The Love That Dare Not Speak Shakespeare's Name: New Shakesqueer Cinema." In *Shakespeare, the Movie: Popularizing the Plays on Film, TV, and Video*. Edited by L.E. Boose and R. Burt. London: Routledge, 1997. 240–68. Reprinted in *Unspeakable ShaXXXspeares: Queer Theory and American Kiddie Culture*. New York: St. Martin's, 1998. 29–75.

B7. _____. *Shakespeare after Mass Media*. New York: Palgrave, 2002. 1–32.

B8. Cabat, J. "Beyond *West Side Story*: The Problem of Shakespearean Modernizations on Film." *Shakespeare* 3.2 (1999): 19–20.

B9. Haun, H. "Touch up Your Shakespeare, or How Hollywood Has Used, Bruised, or Otherwise Abused the Bard." *Films in Review* 33 (1982): 522–30.

B10. Howard, T. "Shakespeare's Cinematic Offshoots." *The Cambridge Companion to Shakespeare on Film*. Edited by R. Jackson. Cambridge: Cambridge University Press, 2000. 295–313.

B11. Klossner, M. "Offshoots for Children." *SFNL* 16.1 (1991): 9.

B12. McKernan, L. "The Real Thing at Last." In *Walking Shadows: Shakespeare in the National Film and Television Archive.* Edited by L. McKernan and O. Terris. London: BFI, 1994. 1–25.

B13. "Offbeat Shakespeare." *SFNL* 16.1 (1991): 9.

B14. Rothwell, K.S. *A History of Shakespeare on Screen: A Century of Film and Television.* Cambridge: Cambridge University Press, 1999. [Chapters 8 and 9 deal with many of the derivatives listed below. A revised, expanded edition including a new chapter on the films released after Branagh's *Hamlet* (1996) will appear in late 2003 or early 2004.]

B15. Welsh, J.M. "Seduced by Shakespeare, Transfixed by Spectacle." In *Shakespeare into Film.* Edited by J.M. Welsh, R. Vela, J.C. Tibbetts, et al. New York: Checkmark, 2002. xxiii–xxxi.

B16. Willson, R.F., Jr. "Bardic Bricolage: Tracing the Playtext in Hollywood Offshoots." *SClass* 2.1 (1994): 37–38.

B17. _____. "Bankable Genres: Shakespeare in Hollywood." *SN* 45.1 (224) (1995): 19.

C. Derivatives: Individual Plays

Antony and Cleopatra

1. *Bugsy*. Dir. Barry Levinson. USA, 1991.

C1. Eggert, K. "Age Cannot Wither Him: Warren Beatty's Bugsy as Hollywood Cleopatra." In *Shakespeare, the Movie* (B6). 198–214.

As You Like It

1. *Never Been Kissed*. Dir. Raja Gosnell. USA, 1999.

C2. Burt, R. *Unspeakable ShaXXXspeares: Queer Theory and American Kiddie Culture.* New York: St. Martin's, 1999. xi–xxvi. [Preface to the paperback edition.]

C3. _____. "T(e)en Things I Hate about Girlene Shakesploitation Flicks in the Late 1990s, or, Not-So-Fast Times at Shakespeare High." In *Spectacular Shakespeare: Critical Theory and Popular Cinema.* Edited by C. Lehmann and L.S. Starks. Madison: Fairleigh Dickinson University Press, 2002. 205–32. [Also discusses *Jawbreaker* (dir. Darren Stein; USA, 1999).]

Hamlet

1. *Playmates*. Dir. David Butler. USA, 1941.

C4. Lanier, D. "The Idea of a John Barrymore." *Colby Quarterly* 37 (2001): 31–53.

C5. _____. *Shakespeare and Modern Popular Culture.* Oxford: Oxford University Press, 2002. 50–81.

C6. Morrison, M.A. *John Barrymore, Shakespearean Actor.* Cambridge: Cambridge University Press, 1997. 261–96.

2. To Be or Not to Be. Dir. Ernst Lubitsch. USA, 1942.

C7. Ardolino, F. "The Defense of Acting in *To Be or Not to Be.*" *MSAN* 15.2 (1995): 2–3.

C8. Barnes, P. *To Be or Not to Be.* London: British Film Institute, 2002.

C9. Insdorf, A. "'To Be or Not to Be.'" *American Film* 5.2 (1979): 80–81, 85.

C10. Jones, N. "*Hamlet* in Warsaw: The Antic Disposition of Ernst Lubitsch." *EnterText* 1.2 (2001): 264–88. http://www.brunel.ac.uk/faculty/arts/Enter-Text/hamlet/jones.pdf.

C11. Tibbetts, J.C. "Backstage with the Bard: Or, Building a Better Mousetrap." *LFQ* 29 (2001): 147–64. Reprinted in *Shakespeare into Film* (B15). 207–26.

C12. Willson, R.F., Jr. *Shakespeare in Hollywood, 1929–1956.* Madison: Fairleigh Dickinson University Press, 2000. 74–84.

3. A Diary for Timothy. Dir. Humphrey Jennings. Great Britain, 1946.

C13. Coursen, H.R. *Watching Shakespeare on Television.* Rutherford: Fairleigh Dickinson University Press, 1993. 57–69.

C14. Hodgkinson, A.W., and R.E. Sheratsky. *Humphrey Jennings: More than a Maker of Films.* Hanover: University Press of New England, 1982. 155–61.

4. My Darling Clementine. Dir. John Ford. USA, 1946.

C15. Christensen, P.H. "'Shakespeare in Tombstone': Hamlet's Undiscovered Country." *SY* 8 (1997): 280–89.

C16. Simmon, S. "Concerning the Weary Legs of Wyatt Earp: The Classic Western According to Shakespeare." *LFQ* 24 (1996): 114–27.

C17. Willson, R.F., Jr. *Shakespeare in Hollywood, 1929–1956* (C12). 109–15.

5. The Bad Sleep Well. Dir. Akira Kurosawa. Japan, 1960.

C18. Ashizu, K. "Kurosawa's *Hamlet?*" *Shakespeare Studies* (Japan) 33 (1995): 71–99.

C19. Buhler, S.M. *Shakespeare in the Cinema: Ocular Proof.* Albany: State University of New York Press, 2002. 157–78.

C20. Hapgood, R. "Kurosawa's Shakespeare Films: *Throne of Blood, The Bad Sleep Well,* and *Ran.*" In *Shakespeare and the Moving Image* (A3). 234–49.

C21. Mellen, J. *The Waves at Genji's Door: Japan through Its Cinema.* New York: Pantheon Books, 1976. 405–07.

C22. Perret, M.D. "Kurosawa's *Hamlet*: Samurai in Business Dress." *SFNL* 15.1 (1990): 6.

C23. Phillips, S.J. "Rotten States: Shakespeare's *Hamlet* and Kurosawa's *The Bad Sleep Well.*" *SY* 8 (1997): 153–62.

C24. Prince, S. *The Warrior's Camera: The Cinema of Akira Kurosawa.* Princeton: Princeton University Press, 1991. 175–88.

C25. Richie, D. *The Films of Akira Kurosawa.* 3rd ed. Berkeley: University of California Press, 1996. 140–46.

C26. Rothwell, K. S. "Akira Kurosawa and the Shakespearean Vision: *The Bad Sleep Well* as a 'Mirror up to Nature.'" *Shakespeare Worldwide* 14/15 (1995): 169–85.

6. Ophélia. Dir. Claude Chabrol. France, 1962.

C27. Kliman, B.W. "Chabrol's *Ophélia*: Mirror for *Hamlet.*" *SFNL* 3.1 (1978): 1, 8.

C28. Newman, K. "Chabrol's *Ophélia*." *SFNL* 6.2 (1982): 1, 9. Reprinted as "Ghostwriting: *Hamlet* and Claude Chabrol's *Ophélia*." In *The Scope of Words: In Honor of Albert S. Cook*. Edited by P. Baker, S.W. Goodwin and G. Handwerk. New York: Peter Lang, 1991. 167–77.
See also: Buhler (C19).

7. *Enter Hamlet*. Dir. Fred Mogubgub. USA, 1965 (?).

C29. Kliman, B.W. "*Enter Hamlet*: A Demythologizing Approach to *Hamlet*." *SFNL* 15.1 (1990): 2, 12.

8. *Gilligan's Island:* "The Producer." Dir. Ida Lupino and George M. Cahan. USA, 1966.

C30. Burt, R. *Unspeakable ShaXXXspeares* (B6). 159–201.

9. *Nini 'Tirabuscio*. Dir. Marcello Fondato. Italy, 1970.

C31. Tempera, M. "To Laugh or Not to Laugh: Italian Parodies of *Hamlet*." *Enter-Text* 1.2 (2001): 289–301. http://www.brunel.ac.uk/faculty/arts/Enter-Text/hamlet/tempera.pdf.

10. *Intikam Melegi Kadin Hamlet / Angel of Vengeance: The Female Hamlet*. Dir. Metin Erksan. Turkey, 1977.

C32. Seidl, M. "*Hamlet*, the Sponge and Hamlet, the Angel of Vengeance: About a Turkish Version of *Hamlet*." *SY* 13 (2002): 401–18.

11. *Hamlet Act*. Dir. Robert Nelson. USA, 1982.

C33. Birringer, J.H. "Rehearsing the Mousetrap: Robert Nelson's *Hamlet Act*." *SFNL* 9.1 (1984): 1, 8.

C34. Gallop, J. "Beyond the Mirror." *Wide Angle* 7.1–2 (1985): 59–61.

C35. Swan, J. "*Hamlet* and the Technology of the Mind's Eye." *Seventh International Conference on Literature and Psychology*. Lisbon: Instituto de Psicologia Aplicada, 1991. 87–102.

12. *To Be or Not to Be*. Dir. Alan Johnson. USA, 1983.

C36. Willson, R.F., Jr. "*To Be or Not to Be* Once More." *SFNL* 8.2 (1984): 1, 3, 7.

13. *Withnail and I*. Dir. Bruce Robinson. Great Britain, 1986.

C37. Lawson, C. "'Melancholy Clowns': The Cult of *Hamlet* in *Withnail and I* and *In the Bleak Midwinter*." *SB* 15.4 (1997): 33–34.

14. *Hamlet Goes Business*. Dir. Aki Kaurismäki. Finland, 1987).

C38. Breight, C.C. "Smirnoff's Shakespeare: Aki Kaurismäki's *Hamlet Goes Business* and Other Socialist Comedies of the Suomi (aka Finnish) State." *Shakespeare and Renaissance Association of West Virginia: Selected Papers* 24 (2001): 56–63.

15. *When Hamlet Came to Mizoram*. Dir. Pankaj Butalia. India, 1989.

C39. Baker, D. "Ophelia's Travels." In *Gender and Culture in Literature and Film East and West: Issues of Perception and Interpretation: Selected Conference Papers*. Edited by N. Masavisut, G. Simson and L.E. Smith. Honolulu: University of Hawaii Press, 1994. 3–8.

C40. Chopra, V. "*When Hamlet Came to Mizoram*: A Film on *Hamlet*." *Hamlet Studies* 17.1–2 (1995): 119–21.

C41. Loomba, A. "*Hamlet* in Mizoram." In *Cross-Cultural Performances: Differences in Women's Re-Visions of Shakespeare*. Edited by M. Novy. Urbana: University of Illinois Press, 1993. 227–50.

16. *Highlander II: The Quickening*. Dir. Russell Mulcahy. USA, 1990.

C42. Dionne, C. "Shakespeare in Popular Culture: Gender and High-Brow Culture in America." *Genre* 28 (1995): 385–412.

17. *Rosencrantz and Guildenstern Are Dead*. Dir. Tom Stoppard. Great Britain, 1991.

C43. Abbotson, S.C.W. "Stoppard's (Re)Vision of *Rosencrantz and Guildenstern*: A Lesson in Moral Responsibility." *English Studies* 79 (1998): 171–83.

C44. Coursen, H.R. "En busca de Ricardo III: The Film and the Globe." *SClass* 6.2 (1998): 72–79.

C45. _____. "The Recent Shakespeare Films." *SB* 17.1 (1999): 38–41. Reprinted in *Shakespeare and His Contemporaries in Performance*. Edited by E.J. Esche. Aldershot: Ashgate, 2000. 23–33.

C46. _____. "Stoppard's *Rosencrantz and Guildenstern Are Dead*: The Film." In *Shakespeare: Text and Theater: Essays in Honor of Jay L. Halio*. Edited by L. Potter and A.F. Kinney. Newark: University of Delaware Press, 1999. 183–93.

C47. Hotchkiss, L.M. "The Cinematic Appropriation of Theater: Introjection and Incorporation in *Rosencrantz and Guildenstern Are Dead*." *Quarterly Review of Film and Video* 17 (2000): 161–86.

C48. Sheidley, W.E. "The Play(s) within the Film: Tom Stoppard's *Rosencrantz & Guildenstern Are Dead*." In *Screen Shakespeare*. Edited by M. Skovmand. Aarhus: Aarhus University Press, 1994. 99–112.

C49. Stoppard, T. Rosencrantz and Guildenstern Are Dead: *The Film*. London: Faber, 1991.

C50. Wheeler, E. "Light It Up and Move It Around: *Rosencrantz and Guildenstern Are Dead*." *SFNL* 16.1 (1991): 5.

18. *L.A. Story*. Dir. Mick Jackson. USA, 1991.

C51. Buhler, S.M. "Antic Dispositions: Shakespeare and Steve Martin's *L.A. Story*." *SY* 8 (1997): 212–29.

C52. Castaldo, A. "A Text of Shreds and Patches: Shakespeare and Popular Culture." *Shakespeare and Renaissance Association of West Virginia: Selected Papers* 20 (1997): 59–71.

C53. Charnes, L. "Dismember Me: Shakespeare, Paranoia, and the Logic of Mass Culture." *SQ* 48 (1997): 1–16.
See also: Coursen (C13).

19. *Last Action Hero*. Dir. John McTiernan. USA, 1993.

C54. Burt, R. *Unspeakable ShaXXXspeares* (B6). 127-58. [Also discusses *Skyscraper* (dir. Raymond Martino; USA, 1995) and *The Postman* (dir. Kevin Costner; USA, 1997).]

C55. Castaldo, A. "To Thine Own Reading Be True: Shakespeare and Authority in Contemporary Movies." *Schuylkill* 2.2 (1999): 62–73. http://www.temple.edu/gradmag/summer99/castald.htm.

C56. Coursen, H.R. "'That Would Be Scanned.'" *SClass* 2.1 (1994): 30–31. Reprinted in *Teaching Shakespeare with Film and Television: A Guide*. Westport: Greenwood, 1997. 61–68.

C57. Deitchman, E.A. "From the Cinema to the Classroom: Hollywood Teaches *Hamlet.*" *Spectacular Shakespeare* (C3). Edited by C. Lehmann and L.S. Starks. 172–86.

C58. Mallin, E.S. "'You Kilt My Foddah': or Arnold, Prince of Denmark." *SQ* 50 (1999): 127–51.

20. *Prince of Jutland / Royal Deceit*. Dir. Gabriel Axel. Denmark, 1994.

C59. Kahan, J. "Royal Deceit." *SB* 19.1 (2001): 43.

21. *In the Bleak Midwinter / A Midwinter's Tale*. Dir. Kenneth Branagh. Great Britain, 1995.

C60. Bucker, P. "The 'Hope' Hamlet: Kenneth Branagh's Comic Use of Shakespeare's Tragedy in *A Midwinter's Tale.*" *SY* 8 (1997): 290–305.

C61. Buhler, S.M. "Double Takes: Branagh Gets to *Hamlet.*" *PS* 17.1 (1997): 43–52. Reprinted in *Shakespeare in the Cinema: Ocular Proof*. Albany: State University of New York Press, 2002. 95–123.

C62. Coursen, H.R. "*A Midwinter's Tale.*" *SB* 14.3 (1996): 38. Reprinted in *Teaching Shakespeare with Film and Television: A Guide*. Westport: Greenwood, 1997. 133–36.

C63. Howlett, K.M. "Playing on the Rim of the Frame: Kenneth Branagh's *A Midwinter's Tale.*" *Upstart Crow* 19 (1999): 110–28. Reprinted in *Framing Shakespeare on Film*. Athens: Ohio University Press, 2000. 178–200.

C64. Lanier, D. "'Art thou base, common and popular?': The Cultural Politics of Kenneth Branagh's *Hamlet.*" *Spectacular Shakespeare* (C3). 149–71. [Also discusses *A Midwinter's Tale* (154–58).]

C65. Lehmann, C. "Shakespeare the Savior or Phantom Menace?: Kenneth Branagh's *A Midwinter's Tale* and the Critique of Cynical Reason." *Colby Quarterly* 37 (2001): 54–77.

C66. Smith, E. "'Either for tragedy, comedy': Attitudes to *Hamlet* in Kenneth Branagh's *In the Bleak Midwinter* and *Hamlet.*" *Shakespeare, Film, Fin de Siècle*. Edited by M. T. Burnett and R. Wray. Houndmills: Macmillan, 2000. 137–46.

C67. Starks, L.S. "An Interview with Michael Maloney." *PS* 17.1 (1997): 79–87.

C68. Wray, R., and M.T. Burnett. "From the Horse's Mouth: Branagh on the Bard." *Shakespeare, Film, Fin de Siècle* (C66). 165–78.

See also: Tibbetts (C11), Lawson (C37), Coursen (C45).

22. *Hamlet: For the Love of Ophelia, Parts One and Two*. Dir. Luca Damiano. Italy, 1996.

C69. Burt, R. *Unspeakable ShaXXXspeares* (B6). 77–125. [Also discusses *Taming of the Screw* (dir. Jim Powers; USA, 1997).]

Henry IV, Parts I and II

1. *My Own Private Idaho.* Dir. Gus Van Sant. USA, 1991.

C70. Arroyo, J. "Death, Desire and Identity: The Political Unconscious of 'New Queer Cinema.'" In *Activating Theory: Lesbian, Gay, Bisexual Politics.* Edited by J. Bristow and A.R. Wilson. London: Lawrence & Wishart, 1993. 70–96.

C71. Arthur, P., and N.C. Liebler. "Kings of the Road: *My Own Private Idaho* and the Traversal of Welles, Shakespeare, and Liminality." *PS* 17.2 (1998): 26–38.

C72. Bergbusch, M. "Additional Dialogue: William Shakespeare, Queer Allegory, and *My Own Private Idaho.*" In *Shakespeare without Class: Misappropriations of Cultural Capital.* Edited by D. Hedrick and B. Reynolds. New York: Palgrave, 2000. 209–25.

C73. Breight, C. "Elizabethan World Pictures." In *Shakespeare and National Culture.* Edited by J. Joughlin. Manchester: Manchester University Press, 1997. 295–325.

C74. Buhler, S.M. "'Who Calls Me Villain?': Blank Verse and the Black Hat." *Extrapolation* 36 (1995): 18–27.

C75. Burt, R. "Baroque Down: The Trauma of Censorship in Psychoanalysis and Queer Film Re-Visions of Shakespeare and Marlowe." In *Shakespeare in the New Europe.* Edited by M. Hattaway, B. Sokolova and D. Roper. Sheffield: Sheffield Academic, 1994. 328–50.

C76. Charnes, L. "We Were Never Early Modern." *Philosophical Shakespeares.* Edited by J.J. Joughin. London: Routledge, 2000. 51–67.

C77. Chedgzoy, K. *Shakespeare's Queer Children: Sexual Politics and Contemporary Culture.* Manchester: Manchester University Press, 1995. 36–43.

C78. Davis, H.H. "'Shakespeare, he's in the alley': *My Own Private Idaho* and Shakespeare in the Streets." *LFQ* 29 (2001): 116–21.

C79. Goldberg, J. "Hal's Desire, Shakespeare's Idaho." In *Henry IV, Parts One and Two.* Edited by N. Wood. Buckingham: Open University Press, 1995. 35–64.

C80. Howlett, K.M. *Framing Shakespeare on Film.* Athens: Ohio University Press, 2000. 149–77. Reprinted in *The Reel Shakespeare: Alternative Cinema and Theory.* Edited by L.S. Starks and C. Lehmann. Madison: Fairleigh Dickinson University Press, 2002. 165–88.

C81. Román, D. "Shakespeare Out in Portland: Gus Van Sant's *My Own Private Idaho,* Homoneurotics, and Boy Actors." In *Eroticism and Containment: Notes from the Flood Plain.* Edited by C. Siegel and A. Kibbey. New York: New York University Press, 1994. 311–33.

C82. Willson, R.F., Jr. "Hal and Poins Visit Portland." *SN* 41.4 (211) (1991): 51.

C83. _____. "Recontextualizing Shakespeare on Film: *My Own Private Idaho, Men of Respect, Prospero's Books.*" *SB* 10.3 (1992): 34–37.

C84. Wiseman, S. "The Family Tree Motel: Subliming Shakespeare in *My Own Private Idaho.*" *Shakespeare, the Movie* (B6). 225–39.

Henry V

1. *Bedknobs and Broomsticks.* Dir. Robert Stevenson. USA, 1971.

C85. Hopkins, L. "*Bedknobs and Broomsticks*: Disney's *Henry V.*" *SB* 16.1 (1998): 46–47.

2. *Independence Day*. Dir. Roland Emmerich. USA, 1996.

C86. Friedman, M.D. *"Independence Day*: The American *Henry V* and the Myth of David." *LFQ* 28 (2000): 140–48.
See also: Burt (C54).

Julius Caesar

1. *The Cosby Show:* "Shakespeare." Dir. Jay Sandrich. USA, 1987.

C87. Burt, R. "Slammin' Shakespeare in Acc(id)ents Yet Unknown: Liveness, Cinem(edi)a, and Racial Dis-integration." *SQ* 53 (2002): 201–26. [Also discusses *True Identity* (dir. Charles Lane; USA, 1991) and *Get Over It* (dir. Tommy O'Haver; USA, 2001).]
See also: Lanier (C5).

King Lear

1. *Broken Lance*. Dir. Edward Dmytryk. USA, 1954.

C88. Conrad, P. *To Be Continued: Four Stories and Their Survival*. Oxford: Clarendon, 1995. 127–31.
C89. Kliman, B.W. *"Broken Lance* Is Not *Lear.*" *SFNL* 2.1 (1977): 3.
C90. Pendleton, T.A. "The Return of *The Broken Lance.*" *SFNL* 3.1 (1978): 3.
C91. Willson, R.F., Jr. *Shakespeare in Hollywood, 1929–1956* (C12). 115–22.

2. *Harry and Tonto*. Dir. Paul Mazursky. USA, 1974.

C92. Schoenbaum, S. "Looking for Shakespeare." *Shakespeare's Craft: Eight Lectures*. Edited by P.H. Highfill. Carbondale: Southern Illinois University Press for George Washington University, 1982. 156–77.

3. *King Real and the Hoodlums*. Dir. John Fox. Great Britain, 1983.

C93. Bennett, S. *Performing Nostalgia: Shifting Shakespeare and the Contemporary Past*. London: Routledge, 1996. 57–63.
C94. Kershaw, B. "King Real's King Lear: Radical Shakespeare for the Nuclear Age." *Critical Survey* 3 (1991): 249–59.

4. *The Dresser*. Dir. Peter Yates. Great Britain, 1983.

C95. Greenberg, H.R. *"The Dresser*: Played to Death." *Psychoanalytic Review* 72 (1985): 347–52.
C96. Meyer-Dinkgräfe, D. "From Theatre to Film: Ronald Harwood's *The Dresser.*" *SB* 8.3 (1990): 37–38.
See also: Burt (C30).

5. *King Lear*. Dir. Jean-Luc Godard. USA and Switzerland, 1987.

C97. Bennett, S. *Performing Nostalgia* (C93). 63–69.
C98. _____. "Godard and Lear: Trashing the Can(n)on." *Theatre Survey* 39 (1998): 7–19.
C99. Diniz, T.F.N. "Godard: A Contemporary *King Lear.*" In *Foreign Accents: Brazilian Readings of Shakespeare*. Edited by A.C. Resende. Newark: University of Delaware Press, 2002. 198–206.
C100. Donaldson, P.S. *Shakespearean Films/Shakespearean Directors*. Boston: Unwin Hyman, 1990. 189–225.

C101. Holland, P. "Two-Dimensional Shakespeare: *King Lear* on Film." *Shakespeare and the Moving Image* (A3). 50–68.

C102. Impastato, D. "Godard's *Lear* ... Why Is It So Bad?" *SB* 12.3 (1994): 38–41.

C103. Murray, T. "The Crisis of Cinema in the Age of New World Memory: The Baroque Performance of *King Lear*." In *The Cinema Alone: Essays on the Work of Jean-Luc Godard 1985–2000*. Edited by M. Temple and J.S. Williams. Amsterdam: Amsterdam University Press, 2000. 159–78.

C104. Robinson, M. "Resurrected Images: Godard's *King Lear*." *Performing Arts Journal* 11.1 (31) (1988): 20–25.

C105. Rosenbaum, J. *Placing Movies: The Practice of Film Criticism*. Berkeley: University of California Press, 1995. 184–89.

C106. Rothwell, K.S. "Godard *Lear*: The Critical Moment." *SFNL* 12.2 (1988): 5.

C107. _____. "In Search of Nothing: Mapping *King Lear*." In *Shakespeare, the Movie* (B6). 135–47.

C108. Walworth, A. "Cinema *Hysterica Passio*: Voice and Gaze in Jean-Luc Godard's *King Lear*." In *The Reel Shakespeare* (C80). 59–94.
See also: Buhler (C19).

6. *A Thousand Acres*. Dir. Jocelyn Moorhouse. USA, 1997.

C109. Ezell, P. "*A Thousand Acres*: *King Lear* for the Heartland." *CS* 5.2 (1998): 16–19.

7. *The King Is Alive*. Dir. Kristian Levring. Denmark, 2001.

C110. Chumo, P.N. "*The King Is Alive*." *CS* 8.4 (2001): 20–22.

C111. Nochimson, M.P. "*The King Is Alive*." *Film Quarterly* 55.2 (2001–2002): 48–54.
See also: Tibbets (C11).

8. *King of Texas*. Dir. Uli Edel. USA, 2002.

C112. Coursen, H.R. "*King of Texas*." *SB* 20.3 (2002): 40–41.

Macbeth

1. *Joe Macbeth*. Dir. Ken Hughes. Great Britain, 1955.

C113. Willson, R.F., Jr. *Shakespeare in Hollywood, 1929–1956* (C12). 94–101.

2. *The Siberian Lady Macbeth*. Dir. Andrzej Wajda. Yugoslavia, 1961.

C114. Ray, S. Macbeth *on Celluloid: The Mirror and the Image*. Translated by P. Dattagupta. Calcutta: CinEd, 1997. [Also discusses *Seemabaddha* (dir. Satyajit Ray; India, 1971).]

3. *Columbo*: "Dagger of the Mind." Dir. Richard Quine. USA, 1973.

C115. Jaster, M.R. "The Earnest Equivocator: Columbo Undoes Macbeth." *Journal of American Culture* 22.4 (1999): 51–55.

4. *Macbeth Horror Suite*. Dir. Carmelo Bene. Italy, 1996.

C116. Tempera, M. "*Macbeth* Revisited: Verdi, Testori, Bene." *SY* 10 (1999): 70–84.

5. *Scotland, Pa*. Dir. Billy Morrissette. USA, 2002.

C117. Rippy, M. *Chronicle of Higher Education* (19 Apr. 2002): B16.

C118. Willson, R. F., Jr. "*Scotland, Pa*." *SB* 20.3 (2002): 41–42.

The Merchant of Venice

1. *Gentleman's Agreement*. Dir. Elia Kazan. USA, 1946.

C119. Willson, R.F., Jr. "Shylock in Hollywood: *Gentleman's Agreement*." *SFNL* 13.2 (1989): 1, 8.

2. *Starship Troopers*. Dir. Paul Verhoeven. USA, 1997.

C120. Mallin, E.S. "Jewish Invader and the Soul of State: *The Merchant of Venice* and Science Fiction Movies." In *Shakespeare and Modernity: Early Modern to Millennium*. Edited by H. Grady. London: Routledge, 2000. 142–67. [Also discusses the film *Independence Day*.]

A Midsummer Night's Dream

1. *Gregory's Girl*. Dir. Bill Forsyth. Great Britain, 1980.

C121. Fabb, N. "Dreaming Shakespeare: Locating *Gregory's Girl*." *Critical Quarterly* 29 (1987): 100–07.

2. *A Midsummer Night's Sex Comedy*. Dir. Woody Allen. USA, 1982.

C122. Forsyth, N. "Shakespeare and Méliès: Magic, Dream and the Supernatural." *Études Anglaises* 55 (2002): 167–80.

C123. Shelburne, S. "The Filmic Tradition of *A Midsummer Night's Dream*: Reinhardt, Bergman, Hall, and Allen." In *Screen Shakespeare* (C48). 13–24.

3. *A Midsummer Night's Dream*. Dir. Celestino Coronado. Spain and Great Britain, 1984.

C124. Rothwell, K.S. "Shakespeare on Film All Over the World." *SFNL* 10.2 (1986): 5.
See also: Forsyth (C122).

Othello

1. *Desdemona*. Dir. August Blom. Denmark, 1911.

C125. Hodgdon, B. "Kiss Me Deadly; or, the Des/Demonized Spectacle." In *Othello: New Perspectives*. Edited by V.M. Vaughan and K. Cartwright. Rutherford: Fairleigh Dickinson University Press, 1991. 214–55. [Also discusses *All Night Long* (dir. Basil Dearden; Great Britain, 1962).]

2. *Les Enfants du paradis*. Dir. Marcel Carné. France, 1945.

C126. Carné, M., and J. Prévert. *Children of Paradise: A Film by Marcel Carné*. Translated by D. Brooke. New York: Simon and Schuster, 1988.

C127. Ganim, R. "Prévert Reads Shakespeare: Lacenaire as Iago in *Les enfants du paradis*." *Comparative Literature Studies* 38 (2001): 46–67.

C128. Potter, L. *Othello*. Manchester: Manchester University Press, 2002. 135–56.
See also: Tibbetts (C11).

3. *A Double Life*. Dir. George Cukor. USA, 1947.

C129. Ardolino, F. "Metadramatic Murder in *A Double Life*." *MSAN* 14.2 (1994): 3–4.

C130. Potter, L. "Unhaply, for I Am White: Questions of Identity and Identification When Othello Goes to the Movies." *TLS: The Times Literary Supplement* 5 March 1999: 18–19.

C131. Rippy, M.H. "All Our *Othellos*: Black Monsters and White Masks on the American Screen." *Spectacular Shakespeare* (C3). 25–46. [Examines Cukor's film and the 1983 "Homicidal Ham" episode of the TV series *Cheers*.]

C132. Willson, R.F., Jr. *Shakespeare in Hollywood, 1929–1956* (C12). 84–93. **See also:** Lanier (C5), Tibbetts (C11), Hodgdon (C125), Potter (C128).

4. *Jubal*. Dir. Delmer Daves. USA, 1956.

C133. Willson, R.F., Jr. *Shakespeare in Hollywood, 1929–1956* (C12). 122–29.

5. *O*. Dir. Tim Blake Nelson. USA, 2001.

C134. Coursen, H.R. "*O*." *SClass* 9.1–2 (2001): 52–55.

C135. Mounkhall, S. *Shakespeare* 5.3 (2001): 14–16.

C136. Welsh, J. "Classic Demolition: Why Shakespeare Is Not Exactly 'Our Contemporary,' or, 'Dude, Where's My Hankie?'" *LFQ* 30 (2002): 223–27.

6. *Othello*. Dir. Geoffrey Sax. Script by Andrew Davies. Great Britain, 2001.

C137. Coursen, H.R. "The PBS *Othello*: A Review Essay." *SB* 20.1 (2002): 38–39.

C138. Hopkins, L. "*Othello*. Adapted for Television by Andrew Davies." *Early Modern Literary Studies* 8.1 (2002): 11.1–4 http://purl.oclc/org/emls/08-1/othellorev.htm. **See also:** Welsh (C136).

Richard III

1. *Show of Shows*. Dir. John G. Adolfi. USA, 1929.

C139. Ball, R.B. "The Beginnings of Shakespeare Sound Films." *SN* 23.5 (127) (1973): 48.

C140. Freedman, B. "Critical Junctures in Shakespeare Screen History." *The Cambridge Companion to Shakespeare on Film* (B10). 47–71. **See also:** Morrison (C6), Tibbetts (C11).

2. *Tower of London*. Dir. Rowland V. Lee. USA, 1939.

C141. Forse, J.H. "Staging (on Film) *Richard III* to Reflect the Present." *Popular Culture Review* 12.1 (2001): 33–39.

C142. Pendleton, T.A. "What [?] Price [?] Shakespeare [?]" *LFQ* 29 (2001): 135–46. [Also discusses *Tower of London* (dir. Roger Corman; USA, 1962).]

3. *The Goodbye Girl*. Dir. Herbert Ross. USA, 1977.

C143. Willson, R.F., Jr. "Shakespeare in *The Goodbye Girl*." *SFNL* 2.2 (1978): 1, 3–4. **See also:** Burt (B6), Dionne (C42).

4. *Black Adder, Part I*: "The Foretelling." Dir. Martin Shardlow. Great Britain, 1983.

C144. Lanier, D. *Shakespeare and Modern Popular Culture*. Oxford: Oxford University Press, 2002. 82–109. **See also:** Forse (C141).

5. *Looking for Richard*. Dir. Al Pacino. USA, 1996.

C145. Bartels, E.C. "Shakespeare to the People." *Performing Arts Journal* 19.1 (1997): 58–60.

C146. Buhler, S.M. *Shakespeare in the Cinema: Ocular Proof*. Albany: State University of New York Press, 2002. 33–49. [Also discusses *Master Will Shakespeare* (dir. Jacques Tourneur; USA, 1936).]

C147. Coursen, H.R. "*Looking for Richard*." *SClass* 5.1 (1997): 17–20. Reprinted in *Shakespeare: The Two Traditions*. Madison: Fairleigh Dickinson University Press, 1999. 137–61. Also reprinted in *The Cambridge Companion to Shakespeare on Film* (B10). 99–116.

C148. Crowdus, G. "Words, Words, Words: Recent Shakespearean Films." *Cineaste* 23.4 (1998) : 13–19.

C149. Fedderson, K., and J.M. Richardson. "Looking for Richard in *Looking for Richard*: Al Pacino Appropriates the Bard and Flogs Him back to the Brits." *Postmodern Culture* 8.2 (1998). http://jefferson.village.virginia.edu/pmc/text-only/issue.198/8.2.r_fedderson-richardson.

C150. _____. "Praising and Burying the Bard: Epideictic Dilemmas in Recent Adaptations of Shakespeare." In *Relocating Praise: Literary Modalities and Rhetorical Contexts*. Edited by A.G. den Otter. Ontario: Canadian Scholars' Press, 2000. 119–27.

C151. Ford, J.R. "Pursuing the Story: Piecing out Conventions in Loncraine's *Richard III*, Luhrmann's *Romeo & Juliet*, and Pacino's *Looking for Richard*." *SClass* 6.1 (1998): 62–69.

C152. Hodgdon, B. "Replicating Richard: Body Doubles, Body Politics." *Theatre Journal* 50 (1998): 207–25.

C153. Lanier, D. "Now: The Presence of History in *Looking for Richard*." *PS* 17.2 (1998): 39–55.

C154. Lawson, C. "The Don Who Would Be King: *Looking for Richard* (USA, 1996), but Finding Al." *SClass* 8.1 (2000): 44–48.

C155. Linton, D. "You Can Call Me Al: Looking at *Looking for Richard*." *Upstart Crow* 18 (1998): 67–83.

C156. Lyons, D. "Lights, Camera, Shakespeare." *Commentary* 103.2 (1997): 57–60.

C157. O'Brien, G. "The Ghost at the Feast." *New York Review of Books* 6 Feb. 1997: 11–16.

C158. Salamon, L.B. "*Looking for Richard* in History: Postmodern Villainy in *Richard III* and *Scarface*." *Journal of Popular Film and Television* 28.2 (2000): 54–63.

C159. Sinyard, N. "Shakespeare Meets *The Godfather*: The Postmodern Populism of Al Pacino's *Looking for Richard*." In *Shakespeare, Film, Fin de Siècle* (C66). 58–72.

C160. Tolaydo, M. "*Looking for Richard*—An Interview with Producer Michael Hadge." *Shakespeare* 1.1 (1996): 2.

C161. Varnell, M.A. "*Looking for Richard*." *SB* 15.1 (1997): 35–36.

See also: Tibbetts (C11), Coursen (C44 and C45), Castaldo (C55).

Romeo and Juliet

1. *Romeo y Julieta*. Dir. Miguel M. Delgado. Mexico, 1943.

C162. Pilcher, J.M. *Cantinflas and the Chaos of Mexican Modernity*. Wilmington: Scholarly Resources, 2001. 83–92.

C163. Vela, R. "Shakespeare, Hollywood, and Mexico: The Cantinflas *Romeo y Julieta.*" *LFQ* 30 (2002): 231–37.

2. *West Side Story.* Dir. Robert Wise and Jerome Robbins. USA, 1961.

C164. Conrad, P. *To Be Continued: Four Stories and Their Survival.* Oxford: Clarendon, 1995. 89–93.

C165. Hapgood, R. "*West Side Story* and the Modern Appeal of *Romeo and Juliet.*" *Deutsche Shakespeare-Gesellschaft West: Jahrbuch 1972:* 99–112.

C166. Holderness, G. *Visual Shakespeare: Essays in Film and Television.* Hatfield: University of Hertfordshire Press, 2002. 151–82.

C167. Joyce, J.J. "Music and Meaning in Four Versions of the Romeo and Juliet Story." *Cithara: Essays in the Judaeo-Christian Tradition* 39.2 (2000): 3–14.

C168. Kimbrough, R.A. "Teaching Musical and Balletic Adaptations of *Romeo and Juliet*; or, Romeo and Juliet, Thou Art Translated!" In *Approaches to Teaching Shakespeare's* Romeo and Juliet. Edited by M. Hunt. New York: MLA, 2000. 186–90.

3. *Le voyage à Venise / Carnival in Venice.* Dir. Jean-Daniel Cadinot. France, 1986.

C169. Burt, R. "No Holes Bard: Homonormativity and the Gay and Lesbian Romance with *Romeo and Juliet.*" In *Shakespeare without Class* (C72). 153–86. [Also discusses *Romeo and Julian* (dir. Sam Abdul; USA, 1993).]

4. *Tromeo and Juliet.* Dir. Lloyd Kaufman. USA, 1997.

C170. Armstrong, P. *Shakespeare in Psychoanalysis.* London: Routledge, 2001. 181–224.

C171. Burt, R. *Unspeakable ShaXXXspeares* (B6). 104–05, 229–31.

C172. Hedrick, D., and B. Reynolds. *Shakespeare without Class* (C72). 3–47.

C173. Kaufman, L., and J. Gunn. *All I Need to Know about Filmmaking I Learned from* The Toxic Avenger. New York: Berkley Boulevard Books, 1998. 285–313.

C174. Kidnie, M.J. "'The Way the World Is Now': Love in the Troma Zone." *Shakespeare, Film, Fin de Siècle* (C66). 102–20.

The Taming of the Shrew

1. *Kiss Me Kate.* Dir. George Sydney. USA, 1953.

C175. Christensen, A.C. "Petruchio's House in Postwar Suburbia: Reinventing the Domestic Woman (Again)." *PS* 17.1 (1997): 28–42.

C176. Coursen, H.R. *Shakespearean Performance as Interpretation.* Newark: University of Delaware Press, 1992. 49–73.

C177. Hodgdon, B. "Katherina Bound; or, Play(K)ating the Strictures of Everyday Life." *PMLA* 107 (1992): 538–53. Reprinted in *The Shakespeare Trade: Performances and Appropriations.* Philadelphia: University of Pennsylvania Press, 1998. 1–38.

C178. Lawson-Peebles, R. *Approaches to the American Musical.* Exeter: University of Exeter Press, 1996. 89–108.

See also: Burt (C30), Dionne (C42).

2. *Kiss Me, Petruchio*. Dir. Wilford Leach (stage) and Christopher Dixon. USA, 1981.

C179. Geimer, R. "Shakespeare Live—on Videotape." In *Shakespeare and the Triple Play: From Study to Stage to Classroom*. Edited by S. Homan. Lewisburg: Bucknell University Press, 1988. 201–06.

C180. Henderson, D.E. "A Shrew for the Times." *Shakespeare, the Movie* (B6). 148–68.

See also: Coursen (C176).

3. *Moonlighting*: "Atomic Shakespeare." Dir. Will MacKenzie. USA, 1986.

C181. Oruch, J. "Shakespeare for the Millions: 'Kiss Me, Petruchio.'" *SFNL* 11.2 (1987): 7.

C182. Radner, H. "Quality Television and Feminine Narcissism: The Shrew and the Covergirl." *Genders* 8 (1990): 110–28. Reprinted in *Shopping Around: Feminine Culture and the Pursuit of Pleasure*. New York: Routledge, 1995. 1–13.

See also: Coursen (C176), Hodgdon (C177), Henderson (C180).

4. *10 Things I Hate About You*. Dir. Gil Junger. USA, 1999.

C183. Coursen, H.R. "Let me count the ways." *SClass* 7.2 (1999): 57–58.

See also: Burt (C2, C3 and C87).

The Tempest

1. *Yellow Sky*. Dir. William Wellman. USA, 1948.

C184. Kennedy, H. "Prospero's Flicks." *Film Comment* 28.1 (1992): 45–49.

2. *Forbidden Planet*. Dir. Fred McLeod Wilcox. USA, 1956.

C185. Buchanan, J. "*Forbidden Planet* and the Retrospective Attribution of Intentions." In *Retrovisions: Reinventing the Past in Film and Fiction*. Edited by D. Cartmell, I.Q. Hunter and I. Whelehan. London: Pluto, 2001. 148–62.

C186. Cavecchi, M., and N. Vallorani. "Prospero's Offshoots: From the Library to the Screen." *SB* 15.4 (1997): 35–37.

C187. Coursen, H.R. "Using Film and Television to Teach *The Winter's Tale* and *The Tempest*." In *Approaches to Teaching Shakespeare's* The Tempest *and Other Late Romances*. Edited by M. Hunt. New York: MLA, 1992. 117–24. Part reprinted in *Teaching Shakespeare with Film and Television: A Guide*. Westport: Greenwood, 1997. 27–41.

C188. Jolly, J. "The Bellephoron Myth and *Forbidden Planet*." *Extrapolation* 27 (1986): 84–90.

C189. Knighten, M. "The Triple Paternity of *Forbidden Planet*." *SB* 12.3 (1994): 36–37.

C190. Lerer, S. "*Forbidden Planet* and the Terrors of Philology." *Raritan* 19.3 (2000): 73–86.

C191. Martín, S. "Classic Shakespeare for All: *Forbidden Planet* and *Prospero's Books*, Two Screen Adaptations of *The Tempest*." In *Classics in Film and Fiction*. Edited by D. Cartmell, I. Q. Hunter, H. Kaye and I. Whelehan. London: Pluto, 2000. 34–53.

C192. Miller, A. "'In this last tempest': Modernising Shakespeare's *Tempest* on Film." *Sydney Studies in English* 23 (1997–98): 24–40.

C193. Morse, R. "Monsters, Magicians, Movies: *The Tempest* and the Final Frontier." *Shakespeare Survey* 53 (2000): 164–74.

C194. Trushell, J. "Return of *Forbidden Planet?*" *Foundation: The Review of Science Fiction* 64 (1995): 82–89.

C195. Vaughan, A.T., and V.M. Vaughan. *Caliban: A Cultural History.* Cambridge: Cambridge University Press, 1991. 199–214.

C196. Vaughan, V.M., and A.T. Vaughan. *Critical Essays on Shakespeare's* The Tempest. New York: G.K. Hall, 1998. 1–14.

C197. Willson, R.F., Jr. *Shakespeare in Hollywood, 1929–1956* (C12). 101–09.

C198. Youngs, T. "Cruising against the Id: The Transformation of Caliban in *Forbidden Planet.*" In *Constellation Caliban: Figurations of a Character.* Edited by N. Lie and T. D'haen. Amsterdam: Rodopi, 1997. 211–29.
   See also: Lanier (C144), Kennedy (C184).

3. *Tempest*. Dir. Paul Mazursky. USA, 1982.

C199. Bruster, D. "The Postmodern Theatre of Paul Mazursky's *Tempest.*" *Shakespeare, Film, Fin de Siècle* (C66). 26–39.

C200. Coppedge, W.R. "Mazursky's *Tempest*: Something Rich, Something Strange." *LFQ* 21 (1993): 18–24.

C201. Knapp, P.A. "Reinhabiting Prospero's Island: Cassavetes' *Tempest.*" In *Transformations: From Literature to Film.* Edited by D. Radcliff-Umstead. Kent: Kent State University, 1987. 46–54.

C202. Taylor, G. *Paul Mazursky's* Tempest. New York: New York Zoetrope, 1982.

C203. Viera, M. "An Interview with Leon Capetanos." *CS* 2.1 (1995): 34–38.

C204. Yogev, M. "'Music for nothing': Shakespeare's and Mazursky's *Tempests.*" *JTD: Journal of Theatre and Drama* 5–6 (1999–2000): 81–100.
   See also: Kennedy (C184), Cavecchi and Vallorani (C186), Coursen (C187), Miller (C192), Vaughan and Vaughan (C195 and C196).

4. *The (Southern) Tempest*. Dir. Jack Bender. USA, 1998.

C205. Coursen, H.R. "Three Recent Shakespeare Productions on Television." *SB* 17.4 (1999): 33–35.

C206. Hoenselaars, A.J. "Gone with the Wind." *Folio* 8.1 (2001): 46–48.

Twelfth Night

1. *Twelfth Night*. Dir. Ron Wertheim. USA, 1972.

C207. Coursen, H.R. "Cinderella's *Twelfth Night.*" *MSAN* 10.1 (1990): 5–6.

C208. Osborne, L.E. *The Trick of Singularity:* Twelfth Night *and the Performance Editions.* Iowa City: University of Iowa Press, 1996. 105–36.
   See also: Burt (B6 and C69).

D. Other Derivatives

1. *Shakespeare Wallah*. Dir. James Ivory. India, 1965.

D1. Bhatia, N. "Imperialistic Representations and Spectatorial Reception in *Shakespeare Wallah.*" *Modern Drama* 45 (2002): 61–75.

D2.   Chaudhry, L., and S. Khattak. "Images of White Women and Indian Nationalism: Ambivalent Representations in *Shakespeare Wallah* and *Junoon*." In *Gender and Culture in Literature and Film East and West: Issues of Perception and Interpretation: Selected Conference Papers*. Edited by N. Masavisut, G. Simson and L.E. Smith. Honolulu: University of Hawaii Press, 1994. 19–25.

D3.   Long, R.E. *The Films of Merchant Ivory*. London: Viking, 1991. 46–52.

D4.   Pym, J. *The Wandering Company: Twenty-One Years of Merchant-Ivory Films*. London: British Film Institute, 1983. 36–40.

D5.   Rothwell, K.S. "*Shakespeare Wallah*." *SFNL* 12.1 (1987): 10.

D6.   Wayne, V. "*Shakespeare Wallah* and Colonial Specularity." In *Translations/Transformations: Gender and Culture in Film and Literature East and West*. Edited by V. Wayne and C. Moore. Honolulu: University of Hawaii Press, 1993. 34–41. Reprinted in *Shakespeare, the Movie* (B6). 95–102.
     See also: Tibbetts (C11).

2. *Theatre of Blood*. Dir. Douglas Hickox. Great Britain, 1973.

D7.   Ardolino, F. "Metadramatic Grand Guignol in *Theater of Blood*." *SFNL* 15.2 (1991): 9.

D8.   Cartmell, D. *Interpreting Shakespeare on Screen*. Houndmills: Macmillan, 2000. 1–20.
     See also: Tibbetts (C11), Pendleton (C142).

3. *So Fine*. Dir. Andrew Bergman. USA, 1981.

D9.   Burt, R. *Unspeakable ShaXXXspeares* (B6). 29–75. [Also discusses *In and Out* (dir. Frank Oz; USA, 1997).]
     See also: Burt (C87).

4. *Porky's II*. Dir. Bob Clark. USA, 1983.

D10.   Hedrick, D.K. "Teen Shakespeare: Modern Commercial Culture and Collectivity in *Porky's II*." *Litteraria Pragensia* 6.12 (1996): 76–89.
     See also: Burt (B6).

5. *Dead Poets Society*. Dir. Peter Weir. USA, 1989.

D11.   Ardolino, F. "The Use of Shakespeare in *Dead Poets Society*." *MSAN* 14.1 (1994): 7.
     See also: Burt (B6), Castaldo (C55).

6. *The Lion King*. Dir. Roger Allers and Rob Minkoff. USA, 1994.

D12.   Finkelstein, R. "Disney Cites Shakespeare: The Limits of Appropriation." In *Shakespeare and Appropriation*. Edited by C. Desmet and R. Sawyer. London: Routledge, 1999. 179–96.

D13.   Gavin, R. "*The Lion King* and *Hamlet*: A Homecoming for the Exiled Child." *English Journal* 85.3 (1996): 55–57.

D14.   Stenberg, D. "The Circle of Life and the Chain of Being: Shakespearean Motifs in *The Lion King*." *SB* 14.2 (1996): 36–37.

7. *Renaissance Man*. Dir. Penny Marshall. USA, 1994.

D15.   Burt, R. *Unspeakable ShaXXXspeares* (B6). 203–38.
     See also: Lanier (C5), Castaldo (C55), Deitchman (C57), Burt (C87).

8. *Free Enterprise.* Dir. Robert Meyer Burnett. USA, 1999.

D16. Lanier, D. *Shakespeare and Modern Popular Culture.* Oxford: Oxford University Press, 2002. 1–20.
See also: Burt (B7).

9. *Monty Python's Flying Circus.* TV series. Great Britain, 1969–74.

D17. Larsen, D. *Monty Python, Shakespeare and English Renaissance Drama.* Jefferson and London: McFarland, 2003.

10. *Star Trek.* TV and film series. USA.

D18. Cantor, P.A. "Shakespeare in the Original Klingon: *Star Trek* and the End of History." *Perspectives on Political Science* 29 (2000): 158–66.

D19. Dionne, C. "The Shatnerification of Shakespeare: *Star Trek* and the Commonplace Tradition." In *Shakespeare after Mass Media.* Edited by R. Burt. New York: Palgrave, 2002. 173–91.

D20. Dutta, M.B. "'Very bad poetry, Captain': Shakespeare in *Star Trek.*" *Extrapolation* 36 (1995): 38–45.

D21. Hegarty, E. "Some Suspect of Ill: Shakespeare's *Sonnets* and *The Perfect Mate.*" *Extrapolation* 36 (1995): 55–64.

D22. Hines, S.C. "What's Academic about *Trek.*" *Extrapolation* 36 (1995): 5–9.

D23. Holderness, G.A. "Illogical, Captain!" *Oxford Quarterly* 1–2 (1997): 43–46.

D24. Houlahan, M. "Cosmic Hamlets?: Contesting Shakespeare in Federation Space." *Extrapolation* 36 (1995): 28–37.

D25. Kreitzer, L. "The Cultural Veneer of *Star Trek.*" *Journal of Popular Culture* 30.2 (1996): 1–28.

D26. Pendergast, J.S. "A Nation of Hamlets: Shakespeare and Cultural Politics." *Extrapolation* 36 (1995): 10–17.

D27. Reinheimer, D. "Ontological and Ethical Allusion: Shakespeare in *The Next Generation.*" *Extrapolation* 36 (1995): 46–54.
See also: Burt (B7), Castaldo (C52), Burt (C54), Buhler (C74), Morse (C193), Lanier (D16).

E. Shakespeare as a Character in the Derivatives

1. *Old Bill through the Ages.* Dir. Thomas Bentley. Great Britain, 1924.

E1. Pearson, R.E. "Shakespeare's Country: The National Poet, English Identity and British Silent Cinema." In *Young and Innocent? The Cinema in Britain 1896–1930.* Edited by A. Higson. Exeter: University of Exeter Press, 2002. 176–90.

2. *The Immortal Gentleman.* Dir. Bernard Smith. Great Britain, 1935.

E2. Kingsley-Smith, J.E. "Shakespearean Authorship in Popular British Cinema." *LFQ* 30 (2002): 158–65. [Also discusses *Time Flies* (dir. Walter Forde; Great Britain, 1944).]

3. *The Twilight Zone: The Bard.* Dir. David Butler. USA, 1963.

E3. Lanier, D. *Shakespeare and Modern Popular Culture.* Oxford: Oxford University Press, 2002. 110–42.

4. *Will Shakespeare.* Dir. Peter Wood, Mark Cullingham and Robert Knights. Great Britain, 1978.

E4. Ardolino, F. "Marlowe in *Will Shakespeare* and *Shakespeare in Love.*" *MSAN* 19.2 (1999): 2–4.

5. *Shakespeare in Love.* Dir. John Madden. USA, 1998.

E5. Buhler, S.M. *Shakespeare in the Cinema: Ocular Proof.* Albany: State University of New York Press, 2002. 179–93.

E6. Burt, R. "*Shakespeare in Love* and the End of the Shakespearean: Academic and Mass Culture Constructions of Literary Authorship." *Shakespeare, Film, Fin de Siècle* (C66). 203–31.

E7. Combs, R. "Shakespeare: Words, Words, Words." *Film Comment* 35.3 (1999): 32–35.

E8. Coursen, H.R. "*Shakespeare in Love.*" *SClass* 7.1 (1999): 31–34. Reprinted in *Shakespeare in Space: Recent Shakespeare Productions on Screen.* New York: Peter Lang, 2002. 71–93.

E9. Daileader, C.R. "Nude Shakespeare in Film and Nineties Popular Feminism." In *Shakespeare and Sexuality.* Edited by C.M.S. Alexander and S. Wells. Cambridge: Cambridge University Press, 2001. 183–200.

E10. Fedderson, K., and J.M. Richardson. "'Love Like There Has Never Been in a Play': *Shakespeare in Love* as Bardspawn." *West Virginia University Philological Papers* 47 (2001): 145–49.

E11. Goodwin, N. "*Shakespeare in Love.*" *Shakespeare* 3.1 (1999): 6–9.

E12. Greenblatt, S. "About That Romantic Sonnet." *New York Times* 6 Feb. 1999: A29.

E13. Iyengar, S. "Shakespeare in HeteroLove." *LFQ* 29 (2001): 122–27.

E14. Keevak, M. *Sexual Shakespeare: Forgery, Authorship, Portraiture.* Detroit: Wayne State University Press, 2001. 115–23.

E15. Klett, E. "*Shakespeare in Love* and the End(s) of History." *Retrovisions* (C185). 25–40.

E16. Lan, Y.L. "Returning to Naples: Seeing the End in Shakespeare Film Adaptation." *LFQ* 29 (2001): 128–34.

E17. Lehmann, C. "*Shakespeare in Love*: Romancing the Author, Mastering the Body." *Spectacular Shakespeare* (C3). 125–45. Reprinted in *Shakespeare Remains: Theater to Film, Early Modern to Postmodern.* Ithaca: Cornell University Press, 2002. 213–33.

E18. McAdam, I. "Fiction and Projection: The Construction of Early Modern Sexuality in *Elizabeth* and *Shakespeare in Love.*" *Pacific Coast Philology* 35 (2000): 49–60.

E19. Nichols, M.P. "A Defense of Popular Culture." *Academic Questions* 13 (1999–2000): 73–78.

E20. Pidduck, J. "*Elizabeth* and *Shakespeare in Love*: Screening the Elizabethans." In *Film/Literature/Heritage: A* Sight and Sound *Reader.* Edited by G. Vincendeau. London: British Film Institute, 2001. 130–35.

E21. Pigeon, R. "'No Man's Elizabeth': The Virgin Queen in Recent Films." *Retrovisions* (C242). 8–24.

E22. Quealy, G. "Hollywood's the Thing: Public's Elizabethan Consciousness Piqued by New Films." *Shakespeare Oxford Newsletter* 34.4 (1999): 4–5.

E23. Rothwell, K.S. *Cineaste* 24.2–3 (1999): 78–80.

E24. Varnell, M. *"Shakespeare in Love."* *SB* 17.3 (1999): 40–41.

E25. Werner, S. *Shakespeare and Feminist Performance: Ideology on Stage.* London: Routledge, 2001. 1–20.

See also: Tibbetts (C11), Burt (C169), Armstrong (C170), Hedrick and Reynolds (C172), Kingsley-Smith (E2), Lanier (E3), Ardolino (E4).

Contributors

Ariane M. Balizet is a doctoral candidate at the University of Minnesota, Twin Cities. Part of her current work on the myth of the Jewish male menstruation in Shakespeare's *Merchant of Venice* was presented recently at an Institute for Feminist Theory and Research international conference in Liverpool, England.

Andrew Barnaby is an associate professor of English at the University of Vermont. He has published essays on Machiavelli, Bacon, Shakespeare, Milton, and Marvell and is coauthor of *The Literate Experience: The Work of Knowing in Seventeenth-Century Writing*. He is currently working on a book tentatively titled *Confronting Morality: Narrative Trauma, and the Search for an Ending*.

Eric C. Brown is assistant professor of English at the University of Maine at Farmington. He has published previously on Trevor Nunn's *Twelfth Night*, and his essays on Shakespeare have appeared in *Shakespeare Quarterly*, *Shakespeare Survey*, and *Texas Studies in Literature and Language*. His current research interests include cinematic adaptations of Milton.

Dan DeWeese teaches in the writing department at Portland State University in Portland, Oregon. His fiction has appeared in *Missouri Review, New England Review*, and *Northwest Review*.

José Ramón Díaz Fernández is associate professor of English at the University of Malaga (Spain). He has published articles on Shakespeare, Kyd, F.R. Leavis, contemporary British fiction, and English literature in film. In 1999, he coordinated the "Shakespeare on Screen" centenary conference, and in 2000 he was invited to join the international committee of correspondents for *The World Shakespeare Bibliography* as the specialist on Shakespeare on screen. He cochaired (with Peter S. Donaldson) the "Shakespeare on Film" seminar at the Seventh World Shakespeare Congress in 2001, and he has also chaired seminars on the same subject in Helsinki and Strasbourg. He is currently editing a collection of essays on film and television adaptations of Shakespeare plays.

Patrick Finn is assistant professor of English at St. Mary's College, Calgary. His research and teaching focus on late medieval and Renaissance literature, textual and media studies, and bibliography and information technology. He is currently working on a collection of essays entitled *Shakespeare and Information Technology*, is creating an electronic, critical edition of *Hamlet Q1*, and is coauthoring a book with Samuel A. Chambers entitled *The Culture of Politics, the Politics of Culture*.

Melissa J. Jones is completing her Ph.D. in English at Indiana University, Bloomington. Her dissertation looks at the development of an early modern pornographic imagination in Tudor-Stuart England.

Parmita Kapadia received her Ph.D. from University of Massachusetts, Amherst, and she is currently assistant professor at North Kentucky University. She specializes in Shakespeare and post-colonial India. She has published and presented on the appropriation of English language by Bombay theater, the use of Indian theater techniques (jatra folk theater) in Shakespeare productions, and the teaching of postcolonial literature. Professor Kapadia is currently working on a project that explores the application of Asian color symbolism to Shakespeare's plays.

James R. Keller is professor of English and director of the Honors College at Mississippi University for Women. He is the author of three previous books: *Princes, Soldiers, and Rogues: The Politic Malcontent of Renaissance Drama* (Peter Lang); *Anne Rice and Sexual Politics* (McFarland); and *Queer (Un)Friendly Film and Television* (McFarland). He is the author of over 40 articles and chapters on topics including film, early modern drama and poetry, modern drama, cultural studies, and African American literature.

Aaron Kelly is Leverhulme Postdoctoral Fellow in Scottish and Irish Literature at the University of Edinburgh. He is author of these forthcoming monographs: *Irvine Welsh* (Manchester University Press) and *The Thriller and Northern Ireland Since 1969* (Ashgate); is coeditor with Alan Gillis of *Critical Ireland* (Four Courts); and is also coeditor, with Nicholas Allen, of *Cities of Belfast* (Four Courts).

Jody Malcolm received her M.A. in English from the University of West Florida in 1994 and is now a full-time faculty member there, teaching composition and literature. Her primary interests are intertextuality and myth. Her article "*The Tain* Re-Visioned and *The Crying Game*" was published in *Folklore Forum* (winter 1999).

David Salter is a lecturer in English literature at the University of Edinburgh. His principal research interests lie in the culture of the later Middle Ages and the early modern period, particularly romance and saints' lives. He is the author of *Holy and Noble Beasts: Encounters with Animals in Medieval Literature* (Cambridge: D.S. Brewer, 2001), and he is currently working on a cultural history of the Franciscan Order.

Leslie Stratyner is a professor of English at Mississippi University for Women, where she teaches courses on medieval and Anglo-Saxon literatures, oral formulaic theory, epic and myth. Dr. Stratyner has published and given papers on subjects as varied as Elvis, the medieval romance, *The Odyssey*, *The Dream of the Rood*, and *Star Trek*. She lives in Columbus, Mississippi, with her husband and daughter.

Ayanna Thompson is currently an assistant professor of English Literature at the University of New Mexico, where she teaches courses on early modern literature and culture. She has published articles on Shakespeare, Dryden, Ravenscroft, and Tennyson. Recently, she completed a book length manuscript that analyzes the intersections of race and torture on the Early Modern stage.

R.S. White taught at the University of Newcastle on Tyne from 1974 to 1988 and is now professor of English, communications, and cultural studies at the University of Western Australia. He has published books on Shakespeare and on Keats and Hazlitt. He published *Natural Law in English Renaissance Literature* and has recently completed a sequel, *Natural Rights in Romanticism of the 1790s.* He has taught "Shakespeare on Film" for many years. He is a fellow of the Australian Humanities Academy.

Index